Reframing Institutional Logics

How are we to characterise the context in which organisations operate? The notion that organisational activity is shaped by institutional logics has been influential, but it presents a number of problems. The criteria by which institutions are identified, the conflation of institutions with organisations, the enduring nature of those institutions and an exaggerated focus on change are all concerns that existing perspectives do not tackle adequately. This book uses the resources of historical work to suggest new ways of looking at institutional logics. It builds on the work of Roger Friedland who has conceived of institutional logics being animated by adherence to a core substance that is immanent in practices. Development of this idea in the context of organisation theory is supported by ideas drawn from the work of the social theorist Margaret Archer and the broader resources of the philosophical tradition of critical realism. Institutions are seen to emerge over time from the embodied relations of humans to each other and to the natural world on which they depend for material existence. Once emergent, institutions develop their own logics and endure to form the context in which agents are involuntarily placed and that conditions their activity. The approach adopted offers resources to 'bring society back in' to the study of organisations.

The book will appeal to graduate students who are engaging with institutional theory in their research. It will also be of interest to scholars of institutional theory, of the history of organisations and those seeking to apply ideas from critical realism to their research.

Alistair Mutch is Professor of Information and Learning at Nottingham Trent University. He has published widely on organisation theory and history. Educated at secondary level in both England and Scotland, he obtained a joint honours LLB in jurisprudence and history from the University of Dundee in 1976. Exposure to the distinctive educational, religious and legal traditions of Scotland, which has continued to influence his later work, was followed by the study of history at the University of Manchester, from where he obtained both an MA and a PhD, the latter being for a study of the nineteenth century rural history of Lancashire. Following ten years' experience as an accountant with British Telecom, he joined NTU in 1990, where he has worked ever since. His *Religion and National Identity: Governing the Church of Scotland in the Eighteenth Century* (Edinburgh, 2015) brought a novel and innovative approach to the study of religious governance practices, one that has implications for the study of the relationship between religion and economic activity.

Routledge Studies in Management, Organizations and Society

This series presents innovative work grounded in new realities, addressing issues crucial to an understanding of the contemporary world. This is the world of organised societies, where boundaries between formal and informal, public and private, local and global organizations have been displaced or have vanished, along with other nineteenth century dichotomies and oppositions. Management, apart from becoming a specialized profession for a growing number of people, is an everyday activity for most members of modern societies.

Similarly, at the level of enquiry, culture and technology, and literature and economics, can no longer be conceived as isolated intellectual fields; conventional canons and established mainstreams are contested. **Management, Organizations and Society** addresses these contemporary dynamics of transformation in a manner that transcends disciplinary boundaries, with books that will appeal to researchers, student and practitioners alike.

Recent titles in this series include

Business and Peace-Building
The Role of Natural Resources Companies
Carol Janson Bond

Organizational Research Methods
Storytelling In Action
David M. Boje

Reframing Institutional Logics
History, Substance and Practices
Alistair Mutch

For more information about this series, please visit: https://www.routledge.com

Reframing Institutional Logics

History, Substance and Practices

Alistair Mutch

Routledge
Taylor & Francis Group

NEW YORK AND LONDON

First published 2019
by Routledge
711 Third Avenue, New York, NY 10017

and by Routledge
2 Park Square, Milton Park, Abingdon, Oxon, OX14 4RN

*Routledge is an imprint of the Taylor & Francis Group,
an informa business*

Library of Congress Cataloging-in-Publication Data
Names: Mutch, Alistair, 1954– author.
Title: Reframing institutional logics : history, substance and
practices / Alistair Mutch.
Description: New York, NY : Routledge, 2019. |
Series: Routledge studies in management, organizations
and society | Includes bibliographical references and index.
Identifiers: LCCN 2018034614
Subjects: LCSH: Organizational sociology. | Social institutions.
Classification: LCC HM786 .M87 2019 | DDC 302.3/5—dc23
LC record available at https://lccn.loc.gov/2018034614

ISBN: 978-1-138-56911-9 (hbk)
ISBN: 978-1-138-48235-7 (pbk)
ISBN: 978-1-351-05815-5 (ebk)

Typeset in Sabon
by codeMantra

For Kath, with love

Contents

List of Figures

List of Tables

Acknowledgements

My first engagement with institutionalist theory in organisation studies was hardly propitious. After attending a discussion group on the topic at the annual colloquium of the European Group for Organisation Studies (EGOS – of which more below), I came away with the feeling that it was not for me. The failure, in my eyes, to be clear about what an institution was and the focus on agency and change seemed to jar with the framings I had brought with me from both social theory and history, especially as shaped by the traditions of the British Marxist historians and the proponents of critical realism. However, further reading exposed me to the work of Roger Friedland and Robert Alford whose 1991 essay posed ideas that seemed to me both out of kilter with the mainstream of institutional theory and likely to be more productive. I was then privileged to speak on the same panel as Roger at an event in Cardiff University, and I have enjoyed conversations with him in a variety of locations, conversations that were always challenging, interesting and thought provoking. Our interactions have been hugely helpful to me but, of course, he bears no responsibility for the direction I have taken.

This book represents an effort to align some of the ideas I have taken from his work with not only ideas in organisation theory but also, crucially, with the framework provided by the inspiring work of Margaret Archer. Again, I have been privileged to work on joint projects with Maggie and to engage in conversations that have helped me develop the ideas presented here. My understanding of her work and the broader critical realist tradition have been helped, in particular, by the series of seminars organised under the auspices of the Economic and Social Research Council in the UK. Here I thank those involved, especially Tony Lawson, Paul Edwards, Steve Vincent and Joe O'Mahoney. The latter works with a group of colleagues at Cardiff University whom I consider as friends as well as influential interlocutors: Rick Delbridge, Mike Reed and Tim Edwards. Collective and collegial endeavour has been vital to the development of my ideas, even if my writing tends to be a solitary affair. In particular, discussions at the standing working group on organisation history at EGOS over many years have been vital to the development of the ideas presented here. All of the participants played their part, but I want to thank in particular those who have organised the meetings and related events: Stephanie Decker, Mick Rowlinson, Dan Wadwhani, Lars Engwall, Behlul Usikiden and Mathias Kipping.

Conversations over the years have also helped with specific parts of the book, often seeding ideas. For example, the explanations of the mysteries of Canadian sports by Bill Foster and Roy Suddaby have influenced the attention paid here to the distinction between clubs and franchises in organised sports (and the discussions about progressive rock were also welcome!). Elke Weik helped me to think about the role of feelings in the acceptance of logics. My work and conversations with Alan McKinlay on Scottish diaries and accountability helped in my development of the wider ideas presented here. Hugh Willmott not only was a helpful, if challenging, editor for a journal article that first collected together and crystallised some of the ideas presented here, but also has been encouraging and supportive at various stages of my career. I am grateful to Duarte Pitta Ferraz for facilitating my exposition of some of these ideas at Nova Business School in Lisbon, Portugal, as well as for his friendship.

I have been lucky to work for nearly thirty years at a university that, at the time of writing this, was the UK's 'University of the Year'. Nottingham Trent University is a teaching-led organisation, but one that values research as informing that teaching. Being research informed rather than research intensive (to use current jargon) has meant that I have been uniquely free to pursue an odd combination of historical research and work in organisation theory (not to mention information systems and pedagogy). Having the freedom to follow what seem like disconnected strands of inquiry but that (in my mind at least) prove to be connected and to have shaped this book has owed a great deal to the support of many colleagues. If I thank here Martin Reynolds, Tony Watson, Melanie Currie, Baback Yazdani and Edward Peck, in rough chronological order of influence, this is not to downplay the contribution of others. I also wish to acknowledge the excellent service provided by colleagues in our library, who have had to put up with my grumbling when they provide me with an ebook rather than the physical copy I would still prefer. The access to materials they supply is second to none and has enabled my work over the years. That work has in many cases involved work in a range of archives and libraries too numerous to mention here, but I thank all those I have acknowledged in the literature that supports this book.

I was prompted to write this book by David Varley from Routledge, who then moved on to greater things – but thanks for the prompt! I also thank Terry Clague for his support over the years and the support staff at Routledge for their help.

It is surprising how conversations about the intricacies of the music of Jethro Tull with Greg Walker have infiltrated their way into considerations of organisation theory as well as being enjoyable in their own right. I have also enjoyed and benefitted from conversations about the writing process with John Orley. Over the years my family have often been mystified (even more than my colleagues) about the range of topics that I have got involved in, but they have let me get on with it as well as providing welcome grounding. My uncle, the Reverend Malcolm Peach, introduced me to the fascinations of history and church architecture, as well as helping to shape, along with my mother, Gwen Mutch, and late father, Sandy Mutch, my engagement with the study of religious practice that is so prominent in this book. All this work would not have been possible without the support that Kath has given, support that is reflected, I hope, in the dedication. It has also made possible Adrienne, Andrew and Ella, as well as Bronwyn and Isla, who will have to make their futures within the constraints of the logics that history has given them – may they be happy and successful in so doing.

Introduction
What's in a Word?

Introduction

Institutional theory has, in the years since the early 1990s, become a significant approach to the study of organisations. Its great value is in providing an alternative to decontextualised accounts that rest on assumptions of 'rational' action on the part of organisations and individuals. Rather than viewing the context in which organisations operate as an objective given, institutionalism, in its several guises, draws our attention to the ways in which the demands of the context shape organisational responses. A concern with legitimacy, for example, might mean that organisations adopt practices that do not appear 'objectively' to be a response to the fulfilment of their purpose. Indeed, that very purpose can be shaped by the meaning systems in which the organisation operates at any particular time and place. These insights, to be developed further in what follows, have spawned a considerable body of work. We have learned much, for example, about the importance of professionalism as a source of practices and norms for action. There are many rich and detailed accounts of the ways in which practices are adopted, translated or resisted. And yet doubts persist about some of the core commitments of the approach.

There has been much debate about the status of agency in institutional theory, with the concern that it is better at explaining patterns of practice adoption than why the practices were selected in the first place. It downplays, that is, the choices and debates, struggles and conflicts, that lie behind the surface of organisations. To correct such perceived weaknesses has been the ambition of approaches such as institutional entrepreneurship and institutional work. The focus here has been on the capacities and work engaged in by actors striving to bring about change. While producing rich accounts of situated action that get beyond superficial appearances, the danger is a focus on heroic individuals with the risk of smuggling the rational actor of contingency theory back in. An alternative approach, and the one that informs this book, is the institutional logics approach.

First broached in an essay in 1991 by Roger Friedland and Robert Alford, this approach sought, in the words of their title, to 'bring society back in' (Friedland and Alford, 1991). It posited that society as being comprised of a number of institutional orders, each possessing its own distinctive logic. Such logics not only provided resources on which actors could draw but could also form relations of contradiction or complementarity that might provide the motor for change. This approach was taken up, initially as a minor note within institutional theory, by Patricia Thornton and others. It has gradually gained purchase in organizational analysis, cemented by the publication of a significant overview text in 2012 (Thornton, Occasio and Lounsbury, 2012). The interpretation of institutional logics presented there has been subject to critique, not least by Friedland himself (Friedland, 2012). His own development of the idea has taken a different direction, one that argues for the religious core of any institution (Friedland, 2009, 2014). This notion has had a significant impact on this book. In particular, it prompts questions about the taken-for-granted status of a number of the candidates for institutional status. Part of the agenda for this book is an exploration of how we derive those meaning systems that attract the label of 'institution'.

It is here that we run up against the ambiguity and complexity of language. After all 'institution' is a term readily used in everyday speech. Just as with many other terms, this is not a problem in context, where our understanding of the background conditions allows us to disambiguate meaning. But in formal analysis we need to exercise a little more care, so it is worth considering the range of meanings available to us. In everyday parlance, individuals, organisations and practices can all be referred to as institutions. For example, it is very common for organisations of higher education such as universities to be referred to as institutions. Indeed some, such as research institutes, have derivatives of the word in their title. The use of the label of institution to refer to organisations can be further qualified by the adjective 'total'. Viewed in this way, organisations such as the asylums studied by Erving Goffman (1991), are seen as controlling all aspects of inmates' lives, thoughts as much as actions. Individuals, too, can be labelled as institutions, where the sense is that they have become, as it were, 'part of the furniture', a central part of organisational life. Likewise, practices can be regarded as so natural that they are simply the obvious response to a situation. What is common to such usage is a sense of enduring taken-for-grantedness. However, this goes beyond mere habit or routine. There is a sense of value and meaning attached to the various phenomena. All of these usages have their merit for our discussion, but the danger is that we lose that focus on 'bringing society back in'. This is the merit of the logics perspective, but an examination of how the term is frequently used indicates that more often than not we are talking about firm- or field-level logics. By contrast, this book develops a perspective that stresses institutional logics as durable societal phenomena.

A further concern with the development of the institutional logics perspective in the organisational theory literature is that there is a persistent stress on agency, on the capacity of actors to select aspects of logics and blend them. By conceptualising logics as modular in construction, Thornton, Occasio and Lounsbury (2012) draw in turn on the influential work of Anne Swidler (1986) of culture as comprising a 'toolkit' of items that can be selected and deployed by knowledgeable actors. The problem here is the downplaying of the enduring nature of the institutions that comprise society. The conflation of practices, which can be relatively easy to select and modify, with more enduring aspects of social structure means that we also do not have any sense of the criteria by which we determine what is an institution. Rather, an institution is any practice that has become taken-for-granted. The process, that is, becomes the focus of attention, rather than the enduring outcome of that process. A focus on institutionalisation, as opposed to institutions, is a common link between the 'old' institutionalism associated with the work of Philip Selznick and the 'new' institutionalism of the 1990s. As Selznick argued 'Institutionalization is a process' (Selznick, 1957: 16). Further '"to institutionalize" is to infuse with value beyond the technical requirements of the task at hand' (Selznick, 1957: 17). For Selznick such a process could apply to any practice, but his key focus is on the transformation of organisations from technical solutions to problems to institutions infused with value. While this focus on value, as opposed to legitimacy and mimicry, is what distinguishes the 'old' from the 'new' institutionalism, it is the focus on process that endures, as will be explored in subsequent chapters (Selznick, 1996). By contrast with this focus on process, I argue that institutions develop historically, emerging from human interventions with each other and their environment to answer persistent and perennial problems of humans as social beings. In order to do this, I take history far more seriously than many existing accounts. To illustrate some of the benefits of a historical approach, let me consider in some detail an exemplary work of history that has themes very relevant to the nature of institutional logics, but one that has been mysteriously overlooked in the organisational literature.

Economy and Culture

In his book *The Fabrication of Labor*, Richard Biernacki (1995) presents a compelling case for taking mundane practices of labour seriously. He uses comparative historical examination to argue that practices are not just represented by culture, but that their specifications are given by culture, indeed, that practices embody particular concepts, in his case of the nature of labour itself. These practices then can be drawn upon as the taken-for-granted instantiation of these concepts and turned into theoretical discourse. Biernacki's evidence and discussion of detailed practices is persuasive, but his situating of the constellation of practices that he examines, and the wider concepts that they produce and reproduce, raises some concerns, specifically about the nature and status of culture in the broader sense, beyond the bounds of economically productive activity.

The comparative historical evidence that Biernacki uses is drawn from the woollen textile industries of England and Germany in the late nineteenth century. Both industries were at a similar stage of technological development, both competed in the same markets with similar products and both had broadly similar ownership structures. Given due allowance for the inevitable idiosyncrasies of historical development, these factors make for a fair comparison. The evidence used is drawn from a wide range of sources such as piece rate lists and mill plans but rests heavily on newspaper reports. These are used to extract the 'silent practices' that in turn embodied concepts of labour: labour as embedded in products in the case of Britain, labour as abstract labour power in the case of Germany. In both cases, argues Biernacki (1995: 3), '[e]ach country's intellectual representatives brought the implicit theory embedded in the quotidian practices of manufacture into the explicit theory of political economy.'

In the textile mills of Yorkshire, weavers were paid based on the length and density of the woven cloth that they produced. They could be fined retrospectively when the products came to market and were found to be faulty. Weavers could tend a number of looms and were paid by the loom number. When they sought a position, weavers 'asked if the employer had "any looms to let"' (Biernacki, 1995: 83). Mills were designed in such a fashion that they presented a fortress-like face to the world, with an entrance closely monitored. Workers could be excluded if they were a fraction late, but once in the mill had relative freedom of movement. The overlookers who had charge of a set of looms had both technical and supervisory functions, but in Yorkshire they styled themselves as 'loom tuners' emphasizing their technical function. They were frequently paid in a ratio to the earnings of the weavers whose looms they oversaw. 'Even where British overlookers hired weavers themselves,' notes Biernacki, 'this could be seen as a technical function, a means of equipping looms with weavers, not weavers with looms' (Biernacki, 1995: 173). The whole constellation of practices, ones shared by weavers and owners alike, suggested a concept of the value of labour as embedded in finished products and workers as independent contractors.

By contrast, examination of a similar range of practices in Germany indicates a patterned variance. Piece rates were determined not only by length but also by every 1,000 times the shuttle passed across the fabric, determined by pick clocks attached to the looms and seen by employers as a direct means of measuring labour input. Fines were made for infraction of rules that were posted inside the factory and exacted on the spot.

Money so raised was put into factory welfare funds, thus making it clear that they were for disciplinary infractions, not market failure. Weavers were paid as individuals and sought 'a position' when they looked for work. They faced none of the controls on entry that the Yorkshire weavers were faced with, but the cellular design of German mills restricted their movement and rendered them liable to closer monitoring. Once in the mill, they were subject to tightly specified sets of rules. While overlookers supervised a similar number of looms in Germany as in Yorkshire and carried out similar technical tasks, it was their supervisory duties that were emphasised. They were regarded by owners as part of the fixed costs of the mill and accounted for and paid accordingly. The sum of all these practices, argues Biernacki, was that they embodied a concept of labour as labour power. 'German owners and workers,' he concludes, 'viewed employment as the timed appropriation of workers' labor power and disposition over workers' labor activity. In contrast, British owners and workers saw employment as the appropriation of workers' materialized labor via its products' (Biernacki, 1995: 12).

Differences in the concepts of labour enacted in routine practices also shaped the patterns of struggle over the distribution of value and authority relations at work. In England, weavers' complaints 'emphasized the overlookers' personal failings rather than their exercise of the authority that inhered in their office' (Biernacki, 1995: 185). There appeared to be a more egalitarian relationship between weaver and overlooker, often characterised by teasing of overlookers by weavers. In Germany, overlookers were prepared to take legal action over what was perceived as a lack of respect for their position by those they supervised. In Yorkshire, overlookers formed their own trade unions and took strike action in sympathy with weavers. By contrast, German overlookers were clearly part of the authority structure together with foremen and were treated as professional staff. In England, strikes were dominated by questions of pay. They sought, for example, compensation for lost time in an adjustment of piece rates, whereas German weavers made it a specific demand. 'The German workers,' says Biernacki, 'did not attribute lost time to the prejudices of overlookers but addressed it as a basic problem in the employment relation' (Biernacki, 1995: 364). German workers were prepared to take action over workplace conditions and over specific aspects of the working day. Again, this suggests differing conceptions of both labour and the employment contract. In England, 'The system put employers in the role of merchants who resold finished products at a guaranteed margin rather than that of entrepreneurs who sought a profit by combining labor power with other resources' (Biernacki, 1995: 87). Such a conception had implications for political action and intellectual theorisation alike. In England, it led to an emphasis on taking control of the means of distribution, using the imaginary of the economy as a set of independent producers. Such a conception, argues Biernacki, informed the work of Adam Smith and his focus on exchange. By contrast, in Germany the lived experience of factory practices emphasised the exploitation at the point of production of abstract labour power and so shaped both the formulation and the reception of Marx's ideas.

Bringing mundane practices out of the shadows of historical inquiry brings out their importance in the shaping of lived experience. 'The definition of labor as a commodity,' suggests Biernacki,

> was recreated day in, day out by a cluster of micro-procedures that did not require the producers to lend their attention to the meaning of labor in order to preserve its shape. The concept was received through experience rather than instruction; it was lived before it was turned to account.
>
> (Biernacki, 1995: 434)

Practices are therefore not just technical functions but also cultural signifiers. They cannot be simply 'read off' intellectual discourse. As he puts it '[a]dherence to an ideal did not descend downward from contemplative knowledge of the general but percolated upward from practical knowledge of the concrete' (Biernacki, 1995: 203). The focus on signifying practices as a counterweight to a focus on linguistic representations has been developed by other historians such as William Sewell (2005). Biernacki suggests that the concepts of labour as a commodity revealed by the examination of practices in woollen textiles might be found in other aspects of productive activity of the two countries, although he is cautious about over-generalisation. In Britain, for example, he outlines remuneration practices in mining and iron-making to 'indicate that the intervention of culture led not to uniformity but to isomorphisms in practice across different sectors of the British economy' (Biernacki, 1995: 87). Clearly, as he suggests, there is a need for further work to excavate the detail of practices following the template that he supplies. However, he also suggests reasons why the differing concepts of labour might have arisen, for which he turns to a diachronic account to supplement the synchronic investigation of practices. In the case of England, he points to the unintended emergence of a free market in products following the events of the seventeenth century. At the same time, however, he points to the continuing state regulation of the returns due to labour that persisted until the mid-eighteenth century. It was this combination that led, he argues, to the imaginary that pervades the work of British political economists and finds its apogee in the work of Adam Smith. The model here is one of independent producers, often modelled on access to subsistence through possession of agricultural resources, who sell their products freely on the open market. By contrast, he argues, Germany saw not the slow emergence of a free market in products but the simultaneous freeing of both labour and merchandise from restrictions in the Prussian decrees of 1810. In this process, the urban guilds, as representatives of independent artisan producers, retained some control but in a fashion that marginalised their role in economic development. The imaginary of independent producers exchanging their labour as embedded in the products they exchanged was therefore not available. What was available was the example of unfree agricultural labour that, suggests Biernacki, 'allowed feudal agricultural labor in Germany to supply a vivid template for the appropriation of labor in the factory during the transition to liberal commercialism' (Biernacki, 1995: 299). The conjunction of the transition to free labour, the marginalisation of the independent producer and the template of feudal labour dues led to a conception focused on the extraction of labour power at the point of production and, in turn, to the shaping of the ideas embodied in the work of Marx.

Biernacki turns to the examples of France and Italy to flesh out his model of the historical development of ideas about the value of labour as a commodity that then formed the basis of the cultural shaping of workplace practices. It is in this broader schema that some doubts arise, not about the forces he discusses but about the restriction of the discussion to economic practices. The question of the wider impact of culture is thus raised. There is a tension here between a careful discussion of culture as shaping and embodied in practices and culture as a rather vague and amorphous body of ideas standing somewhat apart from the productive economy. It would appear that this domain of 'culture' is the domain of ideas alone, without domains outside of the economy also being structured by material practices. One indication of this neglect comes in Biernacki's discussion of Weber's work. Writing of the *Protestant Ethic* thesis he contends that the

> rise of this-worldly asceticism may have given its adherents a novel appreciation of the ultimate significance of their actions, but it did not as a matter of course lead them to build new institutional structures. In Weber's depiction, entrepreneurs who ran the putting-out system for the weaving trade and whose conduct was motivated by the Calvinist world view did not have to reshape the organization of their enterprises.
>
> (Biernacki, 1995: 32)

But what, we might argue, of the 'institutional structures' that such adherents built to put their beliefs into action in the religious domain? Biernacki himself actually hints at some of the answer when he repeats a famous misquotation of Pascal (drawing on Althusser):

> the signifying processes incorporated into the concrete procedures of work configured the concepts to which workers would have ready access for verbal analyses of the employment relation. Through their

experience of the symbolic instrumentalities of production, such as the piece-rate scales, workers acquired their understanding of labor as a commodity and their expectations for its use in the same way that Pascal allegedly would have advised them to acquire religious conviction: "Kneel down, move your lips in prayer, and you will believe".

(Biernacki, 1995: 383)

In other words, (ignoring the misinterpretation of Pascal), belief can emerge from practice. Weber himself, although his prime focus was never on mundane practice, provides some hints in his rather neglected work on religious sects (Mutch, 2009). He draws attention to the organisational practices that were necessary to put religious belief into practice, such as the provision of certificates testifying to the status of those transferring from one congregation to another. Philip Gorski (2003), in his work on the roots of the disciplinary revolution in Europe, also points to the need to examine the concrete practices of discipline that emerged, he argued, from the Reformed Protestantism of the Netherlands and Prussia. In the latter case, he argues that the particular form of authoritarian discipline that characterised Prussia cannot be understood without examining the religious practices that shaped it.

We can provide a further concrete example that actually supports Biernacki's examination of the dependence of Adam Smith on the fiction of the independent producer. Smith, of course, was a Scot, shaped by Scottish Presbyterianism. While his own religious convictions were not strong, being at best a Deist, his respect for the social role of the Scottish clergy was strong. ('There is scarce perhaps to be found anywhere in Europe a more learned, decent, independent, and respectable set of men, than the greater part of the Presbyterian clergy of Holland, Geneva, Switzerland, and Scotland' (Smith, 1999: 810)). The practices of the Church of Scotland in selecting ministers provide support for the focus on individual producers and can be illustrated by the events in one parish. (The following account is based on the detailed examination in Mutch (2015)) In 1740, two candidates for the vacant position of the minister of the parish of Kells in south-west Scotland were presented to the congregation for approval. Two hundred people assembled in the parish church on a miserable wet day, but the congregation was split down the middle, leading to extensive debates over which candidate had been approved. Much turned in these debates on the status of those who had cast their vote, this being restricted to those who held property in the parish and male heads of household. In determining the latter, what was excluded was any who were regarded as 'menial servants'. So, for example, objections were raised against the widower John Moffat in Liggot, who lived on his own. The objection was countered that he was still a head 'till he turn a menial servant'. James Grierson, it was argued, was a servant to William Rorison and so not entitled to a vote. To this objection, it was countered that he 'hath a Tack [tenancy] from Mr Rorison and a Familie of Servants in Garroch to whom he pays wages and gives Maintenance and Mr Rorison Dyets [eats] with him when he is there.' John Donaldson's claim was contested on the grounds of his age, but 'if the hiring and Maintaining Servants and by his own personal Industry Supporting an Aged Mother will not Entitle John Donaldson to be the head of a Familie the Respondent does not know what will'. John Millar could not have a vote, it was contended, because he was a journeyman with Samuel Bowman and so not an independent producer (although it turned out that he had not subscribed his name to the call anyway). The outcome of these objections is not important in the current context: the fact that they were made is what matters. And what mattered was the status of independent head of household, something that formed a background assumption for Smith.

In the case of the impact of the material practices associated with the Presbyterian form of religion, there is support for Biernacki's focus on the fiction of the independent producer. But there are hints, too, in his evidence of other material practices. One of those is the construction of factory codes, their ratification by local police forces and the willingness and ability of German workers to take legal action. Biernacki (1995: 162) discusses in some detail the case of 'Herr K', a department head in a silk mill who took legal action when part of his sphere of supervision was hived off into a separate department. Biernacki uses this case to suggest that it turned on the demand that all of a worker's labour power ought to be put to productive use, but what seems more significant is the availability of recourse to the law. In other cases, 'German overlookers also charged their underlings in court with having affronted them' (Biernacki, 1995: 191). Biernacki is anxious to see these actions as arising from the practical activities of production, rather than from wider cultural practices, but that can be countered by work in comparative law. In examining the criminal law relating to insult and the preservation of personal honour in Germany, James Whitman points out that

> The criminal law of insult purports to protect the 'personal honour' of all Germans, not just of minorities and it belongs to a lively, and sometimes comical, everyday culture in which insulted Germans are convinced that they have been victims of a criminal offence. The ideas of 'respect' and 'personal honour' that inform the current law and culture of insult are, in turn, deeply rooted in German society and in German social history. In particular, the law of insult, as it exists today, has aristocratic sources. Germans involved in insult litigation display a kind of touchy sense of their own 'honour' that is very much reminiscent of the old aristocratic duellists' world of the eighteenth and nineteenth centuries.
>
> (Whitman, 2013: 332)

In other words, supervisors in Germany were drawing on broader cultural norms that provided the opportunity for legal action in a way that was not open to their English equivalents. There does seem to be at least a case here for a contrast between the common law that obtained in England and the codification of the law in Germany. Biernacki points to the way in which the work of the English jurist Blackstone 'treated the relation between the employer and the laborer as one based not on contract but on status' (Biernacki, 1995: 229). In such a conceptualisation, failure to perform duties could be framed as a matter of criminal misbehaviour, rather than as a breach of civil contract. But what is significant is also that Blackstone was working on the basis of gathering together decisions reached through cases adjudicated on in a common law system, one that depended on those cases being brought to court. By contrast, in both Prussia and France civil law systems rested on the codification of laws based on principles, the prime example that Biernacki cites being the Code Napoleon. It is the logic that adheres in the practice of drawing up such codes that appears to be missing in his consideration.

It is missing because of his conceptualisation of the impact of culture outside the workplace in terms of discursive formulations. In his approach, he is anxious to avoid the conceptualisation of culture as a response to economic conditions as most famously exemplified in the work of the British labour historian E.P. Thompson (1968). Thompson's approach to culture is seen to cast it as the subjective response to the experience of productive practices, whereas Biernacki wants to see culture as a system of ideas that has a role in forming those productive practices. However, he is anxious to counter the advocates of the 'linguistic turn', who see culture as an autonomous force. So, he argues 'By this reasoning, the discursive resources deployed in civic politics, religion, family networks, or other contexts may also intervene firsthand in workers' (and employers') understanding of life at the point of production' (Biernacki, 1995: 432). Culture, outside the workplace, is not seen here as involving material practices, such as religious rituals, but is solely limited to discourse. So

> Ideas incarnated in a constellation of manufacturing techniques can be reproduced with less variance than ideas whose transmission depends principally upon discursive formulations. [...] The specification of labor [in signifying practices] escaped those vagaries of constant reinterpretation and reappropriation to which verbal formulations are subject. Verbal formulations draw upon language's modulation of register, its interminable ability to inflect and ironize statements. These communicative resources discourage the stable transmission of concepts. Although the concepts of labor could be put into words for political and theoretic excursus, there was no need of words for their social reproduction. They survived through the arrangement of industrial practices and through the relative univocality of their

material operation. Unlike the leading myths and narratives deployed in the realms of civic politics and religion, the manufacturing practices did not derive their power from their ability to act as a reservoir of multiple and potentially inconsistent meanings.

(Biernacki, 1995: 434)

The alternative is one that sees society not as a division between economy and culture, but one that sees society as a set of domains, of which the economy is one, each of which operates according to its own logic, each instantiated in material practices and symbolic constructions. This leads the way open for not just abstract ideas, but concrete practices, to act as to-hand, taken-for-granted templates for action.

Ironically, such a conceptualisation is supported by E.P. Thompson's later work. In his exploration of the infamous 'Black Acts' of eighteenth century England, legislation that sought, though judicial terror, to defend the property rights of landowners as they applied to the hunting of game, he argued that seeing the law as a simple mirror of class interests was flawed. In opposition to the traditional Marxist formulation of culture as a superstructure built on an economic base, Thompson insisted

> The law may also be seen as ideology, or as particular rules and sanctions which stand in a definite and active relationship (often a field of conflict) to social norms; and, finally, it may be seen simply in terms of its own logic, rules and procedures – that is, simply as law. And it is not possible to conceive of any complex society without law.
>
> (Thompson, 1977: 260)

Recognising this had important implications for the way in which society operated, for if the law had 'its own characteristics, its own independent history and logic of evolution' then it could not act as a simple mirror of class interests (Thompson, 1977: 262). This had important implications for the ways in which actors behaved. They 'will, on occasion,' argued Thompson, 'act not according to their own interests but according to the expectations and values attached to a certain role. The role of juror carried (and still carries) such an inheritance of expectations' (Thompson, 1977: 189). All these points will carry weight in our later discussions, but they show how historical work can deepen our understanding of how we might 'bring society back in' to our study of organisations.

Margaret Archer and Roger Friedland

My argument draws in particular on two authors whose work has profoundly shaped my approach, Margaret Archer and Roger Friedland. Archer is a sociologist whose has drawn on the resources of critical realism to develop an approach to the study of social life that insists on the relationship between agency and structure (Archer, 1995). It is an approach that I have argued elsewhere is historical in nature due to its focus on emergence (Mutch, 2014). Indeed, Archer's early work on the formation of educational systems covers a period of several hundred years in examining the impact of political structures on educational innovations (Archer, 1979). Her work aims to provide what she terms a 'social ontology'. It is work that has developed over a series of books to present a rich and complex argument about social structure and agential reflexivity. In terms of social ontology, however, there are two preliminary points to make. One is that her work has increasingly focused on the nature of agential reflexivity, perhaps to the neglect of the social conditions that shape such reflexivity. It is fair to acknowledge that her work has to be read as a complete corpus, in which the earlier focus on explicating the status of structure and culture has to always be borne in mind. However, it does often seem that there is much scope for further exploring the constitution of society. The second is that she is little concerned with organisations. Her work operates at the level of societies, often operating at a rather grand scale. This can mean, as I will argue later, a neglect of practices. However, in returning to her earlier work, informed by debates in institutional theory, we can pick up some hints about the constitution of that society as a set of related institutional orders. Part of the contribution of the book, that is, is to suggest how this aspect of social ontology, of the nature of human society, might be conceptualised.

In that endeavour, I have been strongly influenced by the work of Friedland, as noted above. As a sociologist of religion, his work has been rather more influential in the domain of organisation theory than in his home discipline. That makes him a profoundly interesting thinker to work with, but it does raise a certain amount of frustration. His profoundly suggestive coupling of practices and substances in forming institutional logics gives us a broad indication of how to approach the formation of logics, but not of how we might establish a list of logics (Friedland, 2014). As we will see, one key aspect of the work of Thornton, Occasio and Lounsbury (2012) is the provision of such a list: they have argued for family, community, religion, state, market, profession and corporation. As I will argue later, the grounds for selecting these candidates is not clear. I seek to provide such criteria, criteria that result in an alternative set of institutions: religion, play, knowledge, law, military, politics, economy, family and medicine. I seek, that is, to make Friedland's arguments rather more concrete. That might be a chimerical activity, but it is one that I feel necessary to embark on to help with the understanding of organisational life.

In order to do this, I step back from the extensive literature exploring aspects of institutional life to seek some conceptual clarity. I refer to many examples from the organisational literature in order to provide an overview of debates, but it is not my aim to provide a comprehensive account. There are other sources that do an admirable job of this, such as the *Handbook of Organizational Institutionalism* (Greenwood et al, 2008). Rather, I draw on material, such as the work by Biernacki that I have already explored, that lies rather outside the traditional bounds of institutional approaches. Of course, I run the risk here of covering a wide range of material in superficial fashion, no doubt to the annoyance of specialists in the areas I touch upon. I cannot, in the compass of this book, cover all the complexities of the domains I consider. In my defence, however, my aim is to point to the contours of social life, with a view to challenging existing perspectives and opening up new ways of looking at the logics that give meaning to social life, providing an opening to the arts and humanities and a richer picture of organisational life.

In so doing, I draw extensively on my own work, which has been particularly concerned with the nature of religious practices. This gives a particular cast to the book, one which is strongly shaped, I realise, by the influence of Scotland. In part, this is autobiographical in character. My own situation as the child of a Scottish father and English mother, who has lived and been educated on both sides of the border, has made me sensitive to the differences between two of the countries that occupy one small island. The inevitable comparison between the different practices to be found in two countries that ostensibly have much in common has led me to explore the distinctive religious practices associated with divergent religious polities. My detailed study of Scotland in this regard has led me to further institutional differences in the law and education that have shaped the argument that is developed in this book (Mutch, 2015, 2018). However, the process of developing this argument has also brought home to me how much Scottish intellectual traditions have shaped our understanding of modern social life. 'The Scots are institutionalists', writes Christopher Berry (2013: 207) in his *The Idea of Commercial Society in the Scottish Enlightenment*. Scottish thinkers such as Adam Ferguson shaped the origins of modern social theory and had influence on theorists such as Karl Marx. 'Their hope,' writes Berry (2013: 204), 'emanates from their insight that social institutions are the locus of societal differences, and their social scientific account of social or moral causation made them aware that behaviour and values are largely a product of institutions'. That the Scottish Enlightenment thinkers explored their particular problematics owed much to their social situation in a country where there was a stark contrast between the decaying remnants of one set of social practices, such as the clan system, in the Highlands check by jowl with the rapid economic and social changes of the Lowlands. In turn, Scotland as a whole was a junior partner in the enterprise that was Britain, where the distinctive Scottish legal, religious and educational traditions stood in stark contrast to the more powerful English partner. It was this combination of social location that gave the Scots such distinctive experiences and fostered their interest in the comparative method, something that I also essay in what follows. In this regard, it is necessary to say that, as well as leaning heavily on the Scottish experience for examples, I also draw most of my examples from Europe and North America. This raises the spectre of ethnocentricity, the projection of concepts derived from one part of the world onto very different societies, thus distorting the nature of those societies. I discuss the nature of abstraction, universalism and essentialism in a later chapter, but I recognise here the limits that my sources pose to my discussion. In part, these limits are a product of both the availability of, and my familiarity with, the literature. In particular, it remains the case that much of the discussion in the existing literature on the candidate institutional logics that I explore has been concerned either with belief as articulated in formal statements or with the development of organisational forms. There is often relatively little on the sort of social practices that Biernacki explores in such splendid detail, especially for areas of the world outside of the Western intellectual tradition. Perhaps this will spur other scholars on to explore such practices, which may in turn modify the arguments I present here. However, that is for the future.

Overview

The book opens with an outline of the philosophical tradition of critical realism. Its concepts of stratification and emergence offer conceptual resources to underpin the discussion that follows. The application of the ideas of critical realism to social theory is developed through a detailed examination of the work of Margaret Archer. Her morphogenetic framework is outlined as providing the core resources for rest of the book. In particular, I focus on three elements of her work: the standing of institutions, the notion of situational logics and the importance of history. The last point is of particular importance as the book as a whole lays great stress on the need to take history seriously not just as a quarry of examples but as a source of conceptual clarity on issues such as multiple temporalities.

Having provided some working conceptual tools, I review the development of some key concepts in institutional theory. Having introduced the early development of the ideas, I consider the critique of the lack of attention to agency and the bodies of work that this provoked. The problems with both institutional entrepreneurship and institutional work are outlined, leading to discussion of the variety of ways that institutions have been conceptualised in relevant disciplines. The stress in economics of institutions operating 'above' organisations is thought to be useful, but not the assumption that institutions are just a response to market deficiencies. This is particularly the case with the varieties of capitalism stream of work. The comparative business systems perspective offers more value, but culture still only achieves marginal status. However, the emphasis on comparative work and the need for abstraction is valuable. Another approach that is considered is that known as the sociology of conventions. Its emphasis on the sources of justification directs our attention to the power of rhetoric, but the sources it uses and its conceptualisation of justification limits its scope. So we turn to the development of the institutional logics approach by Thornton, Occasio and Lounsbury (2012). Their criteria for selecting the logics they consider are found to be unclear and based on induction from the organisational literature. Coupled with a superficial use of history, this means that they tend, in Friedland's words, to 'economize logics'.

Friedland, outside the boundaries of organisation theory, has developed what he terms a religious perspective on institutions. Logics are, he argues, a combination of substance and practices. The earlier discussion of critical realism is used to suggest that the view of logics as immanent in practices is consistent with, and potentially productive for, a morphogenetic approach. That such a combination raises questions for some of Archer's formulations is a theme that runs through the book and shows how adjustments have to be made to social theories to apply them to organisational analysis. Chapter 3 then follows this discussion by exploring what the critical realist tradition says about the nature of personhood, for this underpins the attempt here to view institutions as emergent from embodied relations with other humans and the natural world. Institutions, on this view, emerge from the limited capacities of human beings that lead to collective solutions to problems of existence. In this chapter, I also consider how history helps us in providing examples of how human beings have tackled the perennial problems they face. In particular, I pay some attention to the difficulties of examining practices historically, drawing on work in cultural and social history. The first three chapters thus provide general conceptual orientation and resources that are elaborated and applied in the rest of the book.

The next three chapters are concerned with elaboration of the core terms taken from Friedland: substance, practice and logic. It is in the chapter on substance that I propose a number of candidate institutions as comprising the social ontology of societies in different and historically specific constellations. It is also where I tackle the nature of abstraction and the difficulties of establishing criteria that emerge from what we understand about the human condition but pay due attention to historical specificity. I provide a brief outline of the candidate institutions as a means of framing the discussion that follows in the next two chapters. In Chapter 5, I examine the nature of practices, distinguishing these from the attention paid to practice theory. I am concerned, that is, to examine practices as nouns, rather than practice as a verb. In Chapter 6, I combine the discussions on substance and practice to shed some light on the historical development and impact of logics. I stress here the emergence of logics over time, casting some doubts on accounts of institutional change that telescope the process and attribute it to 'heroic' individual action.

In Chapter 7, I explore some further consequences of the view of institutional logics that is proposed. I examine the importance of materiality, the ways in which material objects and practices carry the logics that shape action. Using examples drawn in particular from the logic of play, I also explore the influence of logics on identities. Finally, in Chapter 8, I reflect on some of the limitations of logics. While a valuable tool for analysis, they have to be used in conjunction with the other categories of social analysis, such as gender, class and ethnicity. I pay particular attention to the need to set logics in particular historical contexts, where they often reinforce each other. I conclude with some observations of the power of the institutional logics approach when combined with some of the resources of social theory and history.

References

Archer, M. (1979) *Social Origins of Educational Systems*, London: Sage.

Archer, M. (1995) *Realist Social Theory: The Morphogenetic Approach*, Cambridge: Cambridge University Press.

Berry, C. (2013) *The Idea of Commercial Society in the Scottish Enlightenment*, Edinburgh: Edinburgh University Press.

Biernacki, R. (1995) *The Fabrication of Labor: Germany and Britain, 1640–1914*, Berkeley, CA: University of California Press.

Friedland, R. and Alford, R. (1991) 'Bringing society back in: symbols, practices, and institutional contradictions', in Powell W. and DiMaggio P. (eds.), *The New Institutionalism in Organizational Analysis*, Chicago: University of Chicago Press, 232–266.

Friedland, R. (2009) 'Institution, practice and ontology: towards a religious sociology', *Research in the Sociology of Organizations*, 27, 45–83.

Friedland, R. (2012) 'Book review: Patricia H. Thornton, William Ocasio and Michael Lounsbury 2012 The Institutional Logics Perspective: A new approach to Culture, Structure, and Process', *M@n@gement*, 15(5), 582–595.

Friedland, R. (2014) 'Divine institution: Max Weber's value spheres and institutional theory', *Research in the Sociology of Organizations*, 41, 217–258.

Goffman, E. (1991) *Asylums: Essays on the Social Situation of Mental Patients and Other Inmates*, London: Penguin.

Gorski, P. (2003) *The Disciplinary Revolution: Calvinism and the Rise Of The State In Early Modern Europe*, Chicago: University of Chicago Press.

Greenwood, R., Oliver, C., Suddaby, R. and Sahlin-Anderson, K. (eds.) (2008) *The SAGE Handbook of Organizational Institutionalism*, London: Sage.

Mutch, A. (2009) 'Weber and church governance: religious practice and economic activity', *Sociological Review*, 57(4), 586–607.

Mutch, A. (2014) 'History and documents in critical realism', in Edwards P., O'Mahoney J. and Vincent S. (eds.), *Studying Organizations Using Critical Realism: A Practical Guide*, Oxford: Oxford University Press.

Mutch, A. (2015) *Religion and National Identity: Governing Scottish Presbyterianism in the Eighteenth Century,* Edinburgh: Edinburgh University Press.

Mutch, A. (2018) 'Practice, substance and history: reframing institutional logics', *Academy of Management Review,* 43(2), 242–258.

Selznick, P. (1957) *Leadership in Administration: A Sociological Interpretation,* New York: Harper & Row.

Selznick, P. (1996) 'Institutionalism "old" and "new"', *Administrative Science Quarterly,* 41, 270–277.

Sewell, W. (2005) *Logics of History: Social Theory and Social Transformation,* Chicago: University of Chicago Press.

Smith, A. (1999) *The Wealth of Nations,* London: Penguin.

Swidler, A. (1986) 'Culture in action: symbols and strategies', *American Sociological Review,* 51(2), 273–286.

Thompson, E.P. (1968) *The Making of the English Working Class,* Harmondsworth: Penguin.

Thompson, E.P. (1977) *Whigs and Hunters: The Origin of the Black Act,* London: Penguin.

Thornton, P., Occasio, W. and Lounsbury, M. (2012) *The Institutional Logics Perspective: A New Approach to Culture, Structure, and Process,* Oxford: Oxford University Press.

Whitman, J. (2013) 'The neo-Romantic turn', in Legrand, P. and Munday, R. (eds.), *Comparative Legal Studies: Traditions and Transitions,* Cambridge: Cambridge University Press, 312–344.

1   Critical Realism and Social Theory

Introduction

This chapter introduces some core concepts that underpin the subsequent discussion. Summarising what is a complex, extensive and sophisticated body of work is a challenging task, so what can be said necessarily prioritises certain aspects of the literature. In particular, I'm going to stress that critical realism is a philosophical tradition that sees itself as a conceptual underlabourer for more substantive theories. In that regard, it is strictly speaking incorrect to speak of critical realist theories of any phenomenon; rather, it is a meta-theory. For those reasons, after introducing some basic concepts from the work of Roy Bhaskar, this chapter concentrates on the work of Margaret Archer in social theory. Her work is a rich source of concepts and frameworks that can then be brought into play to look at institutional theory in general and institutional logics in particular.

Roy Bhaskar and Critical Realism

Roy Bhaskar (1944–2014) was a British philosopher widely taken to be the key figure in the development of the philosophical tradition that has come to be known as critical realism. Starting in the philosophy of the natural sciences, Bhaskar (1979) sought to shift away from the study and the common room to the world of embodied practices. The method of philosophical introspection that had its origins in Cartesian doubt of anything other than that the contents of thought had, he argued, meant that philosophy had come to be almost exclusively focused on questions of epistemology rather than ontology. That is, it sought to define ways in which the world could be known rather than the nature of that world. Bhaskar sought to reinstate the importance of ontology by making his starting point the practices by which scientists came to know the world. The undoubted success of such practices, as manifest in technological artefacts such as airplanes that fly and bridges that (generally) don't fall down, led Bhaskar (in my paraphrase) to ask 'what must the world be like for science to be possible?'

This led to the distinction between what he termed the 'intransitive' and the 'transitive' dimensions of the world. The intransitive world is that which exists regardless of our knowledge of it. For example, in 2011, a dreadful earthquake struck the city of Christchurch in New Zealand, resulting in 185 deaths and widespread damage to buildings. Its cause was movement in a previously unknown fault whose impact was magnified by the 'liquefaction' of tons of silt on which the city was built. The fault had always existed, and the consequences of its existence had always contained the potential to be activated, regardless of whether that potential was ever realised or known about. In that sense, its existence was and is a brute fact, forming part of the intransitive world that exists independent of human activity, which did not call it into being, or human knowledge, which could not prevent its consequences. Once known about, the fault then became a constitutive part of the transitive domain of human knowledge. Here it became amenable to the theories of disciplines directly concerned with the nature of the earth, such as geology and seismology. It also, of course, forced its way into other theories of the world, such as town planning and engineering, to say nothing of disaster management and response. Each way of viewing the world takes a different view conditioned by the questions that it asks about the phenomena that are related to the ultimate concern that animates the inquiry. Each perspective has its own methods for engaging with its object of knowledge. The insights they produce are provisional, subject to revision as a consequence of theoretical elaboration or new means of investigation. It was consideration of these practices of understanding that led to Bhaskar's foregrounding of ontology. His work at this stage can be broadly defined as containing three core commitments: ontological boldness, epistemological relativity and judgmental rationality.

Critical realism is a philosophy that places ontology centre stage (Collier, 1994; Lawson, 2003; Sayer, 2010). It does so derived from the history of scientific practice. This seeks to explore what lies behind the sense experiences that are a common feature of humans' embodied engagement with the world. These sense experiences can be powerful, but mistaken. To give a simple example, it would appear to be common sense that the sun rises each morning and sets in the evening and our language is constructed round such observations, which happen so regularly as to become an obvious part of our lives. But we know that these perceptions are wrong and what we are actually witnessing is the effect of our planet orbiting the sun on a regular course, one whose patterns can be ascertained and confirmed by detailed observations that can be predicted by theoretical models. However, what the scientific enterprise is dedicated to is not the mere recording of such patterns, but the discovery of the causal mechanisms that generate the observable patterns. The philosopher of science Karl Popper (1979) famously argued that the scientific method was based on falsification. On this basis, positive knowledge of any domain lay beyond our grasp; the best we could aim at was to seek to disprove our hypotheses. Accordingly, scientists ought to set up tests that would be likely to falsify their best predictions drawn from their theoretical apparatus. However, examination of what scientists actually do has suggested that hypotheses are not easily abandoned. Rather, Imre Lakatos (1978) argued, scientists operate with a 'programme', which consists of core hypotheses surrounded by, as it were, a protective buffer of auxiliary hypotheses. Failure to validate hypotheses could be attributed to problems with the auxiliary buffer, thus preserving the core commitment. This tenacious adherence to a core explanatory framework suggested strongly that the scientific enterprise was a search for the real in the mechanisms that caused the effects that had been revealed through research methods.

Insights drawn from scientific practice suggested to Bhaskar a threefold division of the nature of the world that was under investigation: the empirical, the actual and the real. The familiar association of reality with the material existence of objects, as when Samuel Johnston refuted the idealist conjectures of Bishop Berkeley by kicking a stone, is thus rejected.[1] The power of scientific investigations has shown that the outward appearance of physical objects, seemingly fixed and permanent, can in fact conceal the movement of elements that are held in stasis only under a certain range of conditions. So the focus on the measurement of those aspects of the world available to our sense experience associated with forms of inquiry labelled as 'positivism' is roundly rejected. Behind the empirical lies what actually exists, but this does not exhaust the real but simply reflects its existence as the consequence of the mechanisms that bring such effects into being. These mechanisms are often best described as tendencies rather than laws. They operate under a certain range of conditions and while those conditions obtain, tend to produce particular outcomes. These mechanisms are a property of the world, operating regardless of our knowledge of them. It follows that they may be operating without producing discernible effects, either because their effects are negated by other contending mechanisms or because the conditions in which they can be triggered have yet to be encountered. Holding to this view of the real suggests that our investigations have to be concerned with the search for causal mechanisms that may only be inferred from the effects that they produce.

However, these investigations also have to take account of another way in which the world is stratified, which draws on the important idea of emergence. Emergence refers to the way that phenomena emerge from mechanisms that operate at one level of existence but, once emergent, cannot be reduced back to those mechanisms. Thus, at the level of physical phenomena, the discipline of physics has pointed to the complex interaction of particles governed by the mechanisms of quantum physics (Norris, 2000). These still mysterious processes, about which there remains considerable debate, have been inferred from the construction of theoretical models that posit the presence of entities that are not directly observable. Their interactions produce outcomes that then provide the basis for chemical interactions, interactions that in turn form the grounds for biological processes and sensate beings. Work in the science of the brain has indicated the complexity of processes at work at this level of existence (Rose, 1993). Studies of the brain indicate that areas are specialised for particular tasks. However, examinations of individuals who have experienced trauma in specialised areas have found that they retain capacities for the sorts of action that the specialised areas are thought to control (Damasio, 1995). In other words, the brain exhibits properties of a self-organising system, one which is capable of spreading its functions to new areas. This suggests that mechanisms operating at the biological level cannot be reduced to combinations of chemical properties. In other words, properties of one level of existence might emerge from an underlying level, but they cannot be reduced back to that level. Once combined at the new level of existence, the properties form part of a system proper to that level. Arguments that there can be a science of everything, based on the fundamental laws of physics, run onto the rocks with this recognition of the stratified nature of existence. It is not just physicists who make such claims; analysts of the social also seek to apply the lessons of quantum physics to the level of the social. In the study of technology, for example, Karen Barad (2007) has, with her 'agential realism', sought to argue for the 'constitutive entanglement' of the social and the material, as expressed in the neologism 'sociomaterial'. I have argued that this does not help in the analysis of the specifically social dimension of existence. As the critical realist Christopher Norris has argued

> it is preposterous in the strict sense of that term – an inversion of the rational order of priorities – when thinkers claim to draw far-reaching ontological or epistemological lessons from a field of thought [such as quantum mechanics] so rife with paradox and lacking (as yet) any adequate grasp of its own operative concepts.
>
> (Norris, 2000: 5)

As I have argued elsewhere, even if matters were settled here, critical realism would suggest that it is an illicit move to jump from the level of microscopic physics to the social without taking into account the notions of stratification and emergence (Mutch, 2013). For example, Daniel Nyberg (2009) uses the example of the atomic composition of coffee mugs to argue for the mutual entanglement of the material and the social. Nyberg uses it to suggest that there are no distinct boundaries between the elements that make up a customer service interaction. However, I would suggest that this is confusing levels of analysis; what is useful and appropriate at the level of micro physics is inappropriate at the level of the social. Here the arrangement and behaviour of atoms is beside the point; it is the inter-relations between specific configurations of the material and the social, and the perceptions that these give rise to and shape them, that are the object of analysis. This assertion is based on the stratified nature of reality.

From the biological emerges the psychological and the 'hard problem' of consciousness (Damasio, 2000). For critical realists, consciousness emerges from particular biological structures but cannot, once emergent from them, be reduced to them. A particular argument here is that against genetic determinism, the notion that it is particular genes that directly cause specific aspects of human behaviour (as in the discredited search for a 'gay' gene). What seems clear is that genes operate in combination, so that not only do their effects depend on the co-presence of other genes but also the activation of their properties is strongly conditioned by the context in which they operate. That context includes not only the embodied properties of the human who carries them but also that person's interactions with others. Those interactions form the basis for the social world, a world that requires the concepts of social theory for explanation.

Much of the discussion within and drawing on critical realism has been on the elucidation of ontological questions; indeed, many interventions in substantive debates in a wide range of disciplines have been concerned with challenging and clarifying the ontological basis of existing theories. This can sometimes make critical realism seem to be a rarefied, abstract form of approach. However, the emphasis on ontological questions is designed to help clarification of the epistemological issues involved in investigating the object of inquiry. It follows from the stratified and emergent nature of reality that the questions that are asked of it and the methods used to answer them will dependent on the assumptions made about the nature of the particular slice of the world that is being examined (Sayer, 2010). Putting methods first, as in the standard division between the so-called quantitative and qualitative methods is regarded as putting the epistemological cart before the ontological horses. There is a tendency to assume a philosophical position based on the methods adopted, whereas the methods ought to be related to the nature of the question being asked of a particular slice of the world (Edwards, O'Mahoney and Vincent, 2014). Many accounts drawing on the critical realist tradition have sought to explain large-scale problems using what are termed qualitative forms of inquiry. This is not, however, because techniques based on counting and numerical analysis are thought to have no place. Rather, that place is thought to be a limited one, restricted to conditions where there are widely accepted 'facts' or, better, states of the matter, which are amenable to enumeration and where that enumeration, as in the case of demographic data, can be illuminating (Williams, 2014). Where there are doubts about the application of more sophisticated statistical techniques is not just a question of data availability and definition. It is more do with the rejection of the notion of causality as the constant conjunction of empirical observations. Although such regularities might be found in empirical manifestations, these can only, at best, be pointers towards the mechanisms that require investigation.

The classic means of investigation in the natural sciences is the experiment. Here, an artificial condition of closure of a selected part of the world is constructed with a view to isolating hypothesised mechanisms. The range of conditions under which mechanisms are actualised can then be tested by expanding the constraints of the experimental situation. However, whether such experimental conditions then accurately mimic the world in which the mechanisms are found under natural conditions is a problem that indicates a further commitment of critical realism: to the world as an open system. Closed systems, where mechanisms operate in isolation from other factors and regulate their own performance are extremely rare in natural circumstances. Closed systems, such as a thermostat regulating a heating system according to measurements of states of the world can be created artefactually, but in most contexts mechanisms operate in concert with others. This means that mechanisms can fail to be actualised or their effects can be negated by other contending mechanisms. This commitment to the world as an open system is also of vital importance when we move from the natural to the social domain. Here such a commitment means that our talk is of tendencies rather than laws.

The world is therefore stratified into levels where the real is the mechanisms that produce effects in an open system. This is the claim to ontological boldness; that a mind independent world exists to which we have no direct access except through our provisional and imperfect theories. The second claim is that of epistemological relativism (Sayer, 2010). The claim is that our means of investigation have to be proper to the level of the world that we are seeking to investigate and to the questions we are seeking to ask of it. Thus, attempts to understand the strange nature of basic physical elements depend on the construction of mathematical models that hypothesise the existence of bodies that cannot be directly observed, but that can be tested for by artefacts such as the Large Hadron Collider in Switzerland. While the experimental method is valid for a large range of contexts, biological phenomena, such as the familial interactions of the chimpanzees studied by Jane Goodall, can only be studied through the careful observation of behaviour in natural settings (Rose, 1994: 49). The range of justified means of investigations means that ontological considerations are paramount. That is, it is necessary to first explicate the assumptions about the nature of the slice of the world that is to be examined before proposing the methods that will, however imperfectly, access its properties. That access cannot be direct but is always mediated by our imperfect theories, drawing our attention to the importance of conceptualisation.

That importance, however, raises important questions about the 'truth'. In some perspectives, mostly those associated with the label of postmodernism, the attempt to search for any form of truth is doomed to failure because of the known difficulties in gaining certain knowledge. The response of the feminist philosopher of science Hilary Rose, influenced by critical realism, is that 'Perhaps truth in the strong sense used by Rorty et al. never exists outside the certainty of "true forme", which I get when I read a poem or a novel' (Rose, 1993: 25). In other words, the project is better understanding of a given situation in order to furnish explanations, explanations that are always provisional and revisable. However, it is claimed that there is the possibility of better explanations. The third commitment is thus to judgmental rationality.

What, then, is the test for the better fit of our theories to the world they purport to describe and explain? Against arguments that what counts is intersubjective agreement or utility, critical realists argue that the test is the world. Ideas that theories should correspond to the world they examine came under sustained attack. These attacks are against the notion that somehow there is direct access to the world, in which theories act as if they were mirrors, reflecting a world that lays before them. However, it will be seen from the preceding discussion that critical realists reject the notion of direct access to the world. Our theories are always imperfect and provisional forms of access to that world, something we can observe from the history of science. That history, however, records successive series of attempts to more closely approximate to their object of study. It is such attempts that lead Douglas Porpora (2015: 80) to argue for a weak form of correspondence theory.

Bhaskar's work originates in the philosophy of science. While the implications for social science have been touched on above, the commitment to a non-reductionist approach means that the distinctive features of the social world have to be taken into account. As well as the understanding that the social world is an open system in which action has unpredictable and unintended consequences, social scientists have to recognise what the British social theorist Anthony Giddens (1984) calls the 'double hermeneutic'. Derived from the Greek word for reading, hermeneutics starts from the necessity of interpretation in understanding the social world. There is not, that is, a simple one-to-one correspondence between our theories and the world, as if the world were reflected in a mirror. Rather, we know the world through our imperfect theories and the phenomena we observe have to be understood in the light of those theories. Hence, natural states of the world have to be interpreted, although their nature does not change as a result of such interpretations. (That is not to say that they may not be changed by our interventions in the world in search of better knowledge of phenomena, and such changes have to be accommodated in our interpretations.) However, the social world contains living participants who are making their own interpretations. Indeed, often our object of study is precisely those interpretations. Those interpretations are based on theories of the social world, even if they are disguised as 'common sense' and so not regarded as theories. As theories, they are amenable to change, especially if influenced by the theories that emanate from the very people studying them. So the study of the social world is irretrievably an interpretative endeavour involving a complex relationship between the interpretations of those we study and our own.

With this in mind, Bhaskar (1979), drawing on, amongst others, the work of Giddens, proposed his Transformational Model of Social Activity (TMSA). One of the most enduring debates in social theory has been and remains the relationship between structure and agency. The TMSA was an attempt to tackle this relationship. People, argued Bhaskar, operate in a pre-existing content, one that has been created by the activities of those who have gone before them. Society is thus activity dependent, but that activity is not necessarily that of the current actors. Rather such actors operate within the constraints of a social world bequeathed to them. Refinement and development of the TMSA has continued in the work, in particular, of Tony Lawson (2003) in economics and Philip Faulkner and Jochen Runde (Faulkner and Runde, 2013) in the study of technology. Bhaskar himself continued to develop his own thinking but recognised the critique of his own reliance on Giddens in the work of Margaret Archer. Accordingly, the balance of this chapter will look at her work in more detail. Before doing so, it is worth noting two considerations that arise from this very brief and compressed account of Bhaskar's sophisticated, complex and extensive body of work. One is to reiterate that it operates on the plane of philosophy, providing meta-theoretical insights that can be used by others. Its aim is thus to be a 'conceptual underlabourer' for the development of substantive theories of a range of phenomena. It is thus formally incorrect to label any approach a 'critical realist analysis of *x*', although this is a shorthand that is widely and understandably encountered. It is shorthand to express the informing of domain-specific theories by the broad thrust of Bhaskar's ideas. Those theories, however, need to take account of the specific ontological features of their domain of study and the epistemological challenges of studying them. The present study is thus best characterised as a morphogenetic approach to the explication of institutional logics.

The second consideration is that Bhaskar has continued to develop his work, often in directions that have given pause to those who found his early work persuasive. He developed a form of 'dialectical critical realism', developed in a series of books of often difficult and obscure arguments. In particular, his later focus on spirituality and an attempt to marry the philosophical traditions of the East and West caused some debate within the broader community of scholars working in the critical realist tradition (Bhaskar, 2002). There has also been debate about the claims to emancipatory intent in critical realism, with some arguing that there was a lack of attention to political, as oppose to philosophical, argument (Frauley and Pearce, 2007). These debates mean two things. One is that there is an 'orthodox' or 'wave one' reading of Bhaskar's work, and it is the earlier work that often informs those, like Archer, who have gone on to use it to shape their own theorisation. The second is that there are debates, often sharp debates, within the ranks of those who share the same orientation to the world. Critical realism, that is, is not a monolithic set of ideas, but one that continues to generate debate. One of those debates is about how to approach the study of the social world.

Margaret Archer and the Morphogenetic Approach

Although others have used aspects of Bhaskar's work to explore the social world, such as Rob Stones (1996; 2005), Derek Layder (1990; 1997) and Andrew Sayer (2000; 2010), the principal focus of this book is on the work of Margaret Archer. She has produced an influential series of books from the 1990s onwards that draw upon the resources of critical realism to develop and apply a framework for social analysis. Although the detailed discussion of her ideas that follows draws on a series of books, it is useful to consider briefly the development of her work, in order to put some of her enduring concerns into context. Her work began as a sociologist of education, in which context she worked with both Pierre Bourdieu and Basil Bernstein. This gave her concerns about the way in which the relationship between agency and structure was handled in approaches influenced by practice theory. This resulted, as the title of one early article has it, in the consideration of 'process without system', that is, of abstracting human activity from the systems that condition and constrain it (Archer, 1983). This remains an enduring theme throughout her work. She produced in 1979 an analytical history of the *Social Origins of Educational Systems* (Archer, 1979). This traced the fate of educational initiatives in four countries – England, Denmark, France and Russia – from the late seventeenth century onwards. The four countries were selected because of the 'the diversity of history, culture and social structure in these countries', in particular their political systems – decentralised in the case of the first two, centralised in the others (Archer, 1979: 42). This difference, she argued, conditioned the relative success of initiatives to change educational practices. Already there was attention to the conditioning role of pre-existing contexts on social action. In particular, she was concerned with the status of culture, and this produced her first major statement in social theory following her engagement with critical realism. Her book on the relationship between *Culture and Agency* first appeared in 1988, that is, before the *Realist*

Social Theory that remains her most cited work and in which she first presented her morphogenetic framework (Archer, 1995). *Culture and Agency* (Archer, 1996) was then revised to align with the new framework, but it is important to remember that the focus on the problem of conceptualising culture came first.

Before looking at the formulation of the morphogenetic framework, it is useful to review briefly Archer's subsequent work, because this makes clearer that her aim is not to present some sort of revised framework for structural analysis but to tease out the conditions under which humans are capable of responding to and changing the context that they find themselves involuntarily placed in. In particular, much of her work has been in examining the formation and operation of agential reflexivity (Archer, 2000a). She did this by exploring the nature of the 'internal conversation' (Archer, 2003). Drawing on a detailed engagement with American pragmatist thought, she has argued that persons reflect on the projects they form in line with deeply held values, but they do so in different ways dependent on how they carry on their conversations. In turn, such differences in forms of conversation give rise to different forms of reflexivity (Archer, 2007a, 2010, 2012). It is useful to stress this focus as it provides a counterbalance to the earlier work, which can be seen as just the start of a broader project. However, the most influential area of her work remains her morphogenetic framework.

Archer (1995) suggests that there have been two dominant and equally one-sided approaches to the relationship between structure and agency. The first is to focus on structure and to argue that all activity is simply the consequence of the working out of structural conditions. In its strongest form this results in structural determinism, as in the economic determinism that is seen to characterise some of the cruder traditions of Marxism. People are reduced to being simply the bearers of the working out of historical processes that are beyond their power to change. She terms this form of analysis 'downward conflationism'. It is an approach where people and their activity are simply folded into structural properties, where the task of the analyst is simply to identify such structural practices and then, as it were, 'read off' human activity. Revolting against this are those approaches that see social structures as mere epiphenomena of activity, where the unit of analysis is the individual person. This 'methodological individualism' privileges psychology and social interaction. It produces the impoverished view of the social that Archer associates with the rational actor models promoted by mainstream economic approaches (Archer and Tritter, 2000). Here, decisions are taken by weighing up choices in order to maximise individual utility, failing to recognise that both the choices available and the value that is placed on outcomes are both shaped by forces broader than the individual actor. Archer terms this form of analysis 'upward conflationism' and argues that it fails to account for the enduring aspects of the social world – aspects like the political ideas and systems that she explored in the context of educational history.

As an alternative to these two poles, Archer identified a number of thinkers, notably Pierre Bourdieu and Anthony Giddens, who sought to remove the tension through their deployment of practice theory. Archer focused most of her attention on Giddens, in part because of his influence on the TMSA. As Tim Edwards (2016) points out, Giddens' work has been a significant influence on institutionalist thinking. It forms, for example, the core of Richard Scott's (2008) influential expression of new institutionalist theory. Stephen Barley and Pamela Tolbert (1997) suggested a rapprochement between institutional theory and structuration theory in an article that expressly discounted an Archerian approach. Citing her critique, amongst others, they note

> Because Giddens argues that institutions exist only insofar as they are instantiated in everyday activity, critics have charged that he 'conflates' structure with action [...]. Conflation concerns the problem of reducing structure to action (or vice versa) and the difficulty of documenting the existence of an institution apart from activity. Unless institutions and actions are analytically as well as phenomenologically distinct, it is difficult to understand how one can be said to affect the other.

However, despite this they persist with structuration theory to argue for the need to examine repeated cycles of interaction between institution and action. Here, they note that Giddens, 'models are only implicitly temporal, since he usually treats duration as a background assumption rather than a focus of attention' (Barley and Tolbert, 1997: 100). Given that these strictures result in a presentation that seems to accord more with Archer's approach, it is worth reviewing her critique in some detail. We will turn to the work of Bourdieu a little further on.

The development of structuration theory needs to be set in the context of broader intellectual trends. Giddens' early work sought to present some of the classic thinkers in social theory and rescue what he saw as their enduring strengths from subsequent accretions. In *Central Problems of Social Theory*, he outlined the contributions of Marx, Durkheim and Weber (Giddens, 1979). As well as rescuing social theory from the functionalism that was the legacy of Talcott Parsons (and which constituted the orthodoxy in the 1960s), he sought to provide an alternative to the significant intellectual prestige that attached to Marxism in the United Kingdom in the 1960s. The revival of a humanist Marxism had occurred in the wake of the suppression of the Hungarian Revolution in 1956. There was a mass exodus from the Communist Party and the growth of new intellectual currents, especially around the journal *New Left Review*. A renewed interest in themes within Western Marxism followed, which took two main forms. One was an adherence to the structuralist ideas of Althusser, resulting in works within sociology such as Carter's (1979) historical sociology of farm life in north-east Scotland. The other, much more rooted in the powerful British Marxist school of historical inquiry, issued in a trenchant challenge to structuralist ideas from, above all, E.P., Thompson (1968; 1977). Placing stress on the key category of class as a process of emergence from struggle, rather than a reified category of social analysis, Thompson's work was widely influential. As Giddens glosses it 'human beings act purposively and knowledgeably but without being able either to foresee or to control the consequences of what they do'; this focus on practical consciousness and activity is a powerful influence on later practice-based approaches to organisational life (Giddens, 1984: 217–218).

While recognising the enduring value of some of Marx's categories, Giddens subjected them, especially in their structuralist guise, to critique in his *Contemporary Critique of Historical Materialism* (1981). In parallel, he had engaged with the currents in sociology represented by symbolic interactionism, especially the work of Goffman and Garfinkel. This led him to a much more phenomenologically informed approach to sociology, one centrally concerned with meaning-making activities. This was to issue in structuration theory, presented in full in 1984's *The Constitution of Society*. The overall project of this was to develop a theory of social action that overcame the dualistic thinking represented by the focus on structure and agency. What Giddens was particularly concerned with was how actors made sense of the world in which they found themselves. This was informed by a strong sense of actors as reflexive, capable beings as opposed to the 'cultural dopes' that seemed to ensue from strong forms of structuralism. 'Human agents,' he argues, 'always know what they are doing on the level of discursive consciousness under some description' (Giddens, 1984: 26). This might not necessarily be based on propositional knowledge, but rather takes the form of 'practical consciousness', in which actors know 'the rules and the tactics whereby daily social life is constituted and reconstituted across time and space' (Giddens, 1984: 90). Given this anthropology, then the focus is on how such practical consciousness is formed.

Giddens presents his discussion of the shaping of such consciousness using the neologism 'structuration'. The framing of structures as rules and resources in this account raises a central tension in Giddens' work, which is to do with the definition and nature of structures. While at times he refers to structures as resources, which suggests that they might take enduring and material form (as in, for example, technologies, buildings and other material resources), at other times he speaks of structures as memory traces that are instantiated when they are drawn upon in action. It is this rather weaker sense of structure – 'structure exists only as memory traces, the organic basis of human knowledgeability, and as instantiated in action' – that gives rise to accusations of voluntarism (Giddens, 1984: 377).

Concern about how Giddens approaches structures has been expressed by thinkers other than Archer. The historian William Sewell, in a broadly sympathetic critique of Giddens' conceptualisation of structures drew attention to the importance of the material. Considering Giddens' idea of resources as virtual untenable, Sewell argued that 'it is ... hard to see how such material resources can be considered as "virtual", since material things by definition exist in space and time' (Sewell, 2005: 133). The sociologist Rob Stones has sought to retain what he sees as valuable in Giddens' account by developing what he terms 'strong structuration theory'. A similar concern with the status of structures is shared by Stones (2005). He draws on much of the work in critical realism more generally (notably the work of Andrew Sayer (2000)), so this is not the cause of his disagreement with Archer. Rather, he feels that, while her strictures on the treatment of structures are fair, she exaggerates her critique and fails to note the positive aspects of structuration theory. He suggests that there is indeed need for a stronger conception of structures than Giddens supplies, referring here to the macro and enduring features of social life.

Archer, however, presents a much more trenchant critique of Giddens, arguing that his formulations prevent us gaining any purchase on the interplay of structure and agency over time. She draws, in particular, on the work of the British sociologist David Lockwood, who drew a distinction between what he termed 'system integration' and 'social integration'. Archer characterises this as the 'parts' and the 'people'. That is, while there is a need to examine the relationship between activity and structures, this is best done by the method of 'analytical dualism'. This recognises that aspects of a system might be integrated and complementary, but that social interaction might be laden with contradiction and conflict – or vice versa. This insight drew on her prior work on the status of culture, where she was anxious to challenge what she saw as the 'myth of cultural integration', in other words the world of ideas presented an all-enveloping and consistent set of mutually interlocking and supporting propositions that shaped the resources available to actors. From these ideas, and her engagement with critical realism, she accorded a much stronger ontological form to both culture and structure, arguing that, once emergent from human activity, they took upon an existence that provided the context in which action took place. She christened this her 'morphogenetic framework'. The term morphogenesis derives from Greek terms for change and agency. As Archer explains, 'The 'morpho' element is an acknowledgment that society has no pre-set form or preferred state: the 'genetic' part is a recognition that it takes its shape from, and is formed by, agents, originating from the intended and unintended consequences of their activities' (Archer, 1995: 5). It is contrasted to 'morphostasis', which is a recognition that actions in the social world often (indeed, perhaps usually) reproduce and confirm existing social arrangements. The focus on the relationship between structure and agency means that this is seen as a dynamic approach in which history needs to be fully considered. Archer provides a summary:

> every morphogenetic cycle distinguishes three broad analytical phases consisting of (a) a given structure (a complex set of relations between parts), which conditions but does *not* determine (b), social interaction. Here, (b) also arises in part from action orientations unconditioned by social organization but emanating from current agents, and in turn leads to (c), structural elaboration or modification – that is, to a change in the relations between parts where morphogenesis rather than morphostasis ensued.
>
> (Archer, 1995: 91; emphasis in original)

As illustrated in Figure 1.1, concrete social analysis needs to consider the whole period between points T^1 and T^4. Where those points are drawn depends on the nature of the problem we are examining, for, as Archer argues,

> Analytical dualism can be used by any researcher to gain theoretical purchase on much smaller problems where the major difficulty of seeing the wood from the trees becomes much more tractable if they can be sorted out into the components of temporal cycles of morphogenesis – however short the time-span involved may be.
>
> (Archer, 1996: 228)

If analysis is limited to the factors that obtain at T^2, that is, subsequent action is simply read off structural conditions, then we turn humans into zombies or cultural dopes. By contrast, much social analysis that eschews history and focuses just on present activity during T^2 and T^3 ignores the forces shaping that activity, forces that might not be apparent to those engaged in action. To provide complete analysis, argues Archer,

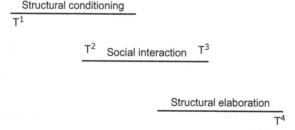

Figure 1.1 The Morphogenetic Framework, from Archer (1995).

we need to consider the outcomes of activity, as they provide the context for further rounds of the inter-relationship of structure and agency: new T^1s, in short.

As we have already noted, Archer began her major series of books with an examination of the relationship between culture and agency. The ideas she developed about the need to distinguish between the cultural system and socio-cultural interaction were in turn revised to align with the subsequent elaboration of the morphogenetic approach. Her work on culture (Archer, 1996) started with what she styles the 'Myth of Cultural Integration'. She sets the development of ideas about culture in the context of anthropology, where mistaken notions of cultural homogeneity were developed. Such ideas can be seen in notions of organisational culture as 'shared' systems of meaning, in which the focus is on explication of the myths and stories that circulate. Archer seeks to challenge this focus on homogeneity by bringing the same tools of emergence and analytical dualism to bear on culture as she deploys on social structure. The significant influence here is Karl Popper's (1979) ideas about *Objective Knowledge*. In this work Popper suggests three 'worlds' of knowledge. World One is the world of physical sensations. World Two is our embodied perceptions of and reaction to the world. World Three is the domain of abstract theory, theory that by being written, as it were, in the 'library' of human knowledge, transcends the conditions of its production and becomes a resource to be drawn upon. In being so divorced from its conditions of production, Archer argues, it contains logical relationships between elements as a system in its own right, regardless of whether these connections are recognised by or acted upon by any particular human actor.

Archer uses this idea of objective knowledge as one that transcends contexts, knowledge without a knowing subject, to suggest that we use analytical dualism to conceive of culture as the relationship between socio-cultural interaction on the one hand and a cultural system on the other. The cultural system is the result of cultural interaction but items once written into the cultural system form objects of relationship with other aspects. These relations can slumber unnoticed for generations, either because they fail to attract attention or because they lack champions with sufficient heft at the level of cultural interaction. However, they continue to exist and either when new elements enter the cultural system, thus forming new relations with them, or when their existence is noted by new groups at the level of socio-cultural interaction, they can be activated. Thus, much of what is the focus of investigation in the domain of organisational culture, the myths, metaphors and narratives, are for Archer at the level of socio-cultural interaction. Excessive focus here fails to take into account the way in which the cultural system provides a formative context. That formative context is specified by the particular sets of relationships that exist between items in the cultural system.

Clearly, for logical relations at the level of the cultural system to have an impact, they need to be seized upon and articulated by groups at the socio-cultural level. It is here that we can bring in social and material interests, as groups from the social system seize upon aspects of the cultural system to seek to further their ends. However, Archer is anxious to see that ideas are no pale or simple reflection of such interests. For as groups positioned in the social system take up ideas from the cultural system, they cannot avoid also taking on the situational logic that the whole system of ideas brings with it. Such groups cannot simply take up one part of a related complex of ideas; they must also inherit the bundle of logical relationships that has been created in the cultural system. Thus, those rulers who sought to utilise Christianity to cement their social standing also took on the challenges of censoring or hiding the uncomfortable aspects of classical thought that came with it in the nature of constraining contradictions. When these contradictions were seized upon by new social groups, groups that had emerged thanks to developments in the social system, then they were developed into competitive contradictions through the conflicts of the Reformation.

The two earliest books in which Archer combined her knowledge of social theory with ideas drawn from critical realism produced a framework for analysis that paid due attention to the impact of both culture and structure in providing the context in which actors found themselves involuntarily placed. The involuntary aspect arose from their being born into situations that they did not chose, and which provided certain situational logics that conditioned their actions. Conditioned, however, is not determined. For Archer is anxious to argue that actors can go against what seem to be their 'objective' interests, provided they are prepared to pay the opportunity costs of so doing. It is often easier to go with the grain and conform to the logic of action that is suggested in a particular context. This is particularly so when the course of action appears to be 'natural'. Actors are not confronted directly by the logics embedded in culture and structures but by the effects of those logics. These manifest, as we will examine in more detail later, in the practices that actors engage in. However, Archer's development of her framework is not the end point, but rather the clearing of the ground in preparation for a detailed examination of the reflexivity exhibited by persons. As Archer herself observes, much attention has been paid to the explication and conceptualisation of forms of structure but what 'we have omitted to examine is why people do not respond in uniform fashion under the same circumstances' (Archer, 2007b: 20).

As we have already noted, Archer is firmly opposed to the impoverished view embodied in the rational actor model, placing considerable emphasis on the emotional commitments of the person (Archer and Tritter, 2000. This person is conceived of as a strong evaluator of moral projects. The focus is, then, on ends not means as the prime concerns of

persons, who engage in and reflexively monitor personal projects. The
form of evaluation is the internal conversation, in which persons engage
in debate on their concerns (Archer, 2003). This notion is developed
from the American pragmatist tradition. Emirbayer and Mische (1998:
974) also suggest that such conversations are central to the exercise of
agency; 'we ground this capacity for human agency', they write, 'in the
structures and processes of the human self, conceived of as an internal
conversation possessing analytic autonomy vis-a-vis transpersonal interactions'. Rick Delbridge and Tim Edwards (2013) have sought to combine the work of Archer and Emirbayer and Mische in their discussion
of agential reflexivity in institutional theory. They endorse the value of
the analytical dualism that Archer suggests in an approach that is complementary to that essayed in this book, although they do not consider
the nature of broader institutional logics. The commitment to analytical
dualism in the specification of agential reflexivity stands in contrast to
the work of another social theorist, Pierre Bourdieu. The concept of the
field, as a structured set of positions, has been extremely influential in
institutional theory. Although often not directly based on Bourdieu's
formulations, the ultimate derivation is from his work. However, of
more significance has been his concept 'habitus', a term used to express
the shaping of dispositions to think and act by social structures. In arguing that different solutions to the construction of 'fairness' in long-term
contracts between suppliers and customers in the American and German
automotive industry were shaped by the reflexive deliberations of agents
Hyeong-Ki Kwon (2004) draws on Bourdieu for support. However, how
the habitus actually manifests itself in these deliberations, as opposed to
the way in which opportunities for reflection were shaped by the different forums available for such deliberations, is never explicated. Indeed,
more consideration of the nature of the habitus suggests its limitations
and the potential that Delbridge and Edwards (2013) see in Archer's
ideas for the study of 'inhabited institutions'.

   Building on early ethnographic work with the Kabyle people of Algeria,
Bourdieu devised a tripartite framework of field, capital and habitus, a
framework applied to subjects such as education and, most famously, the
sociology of taste (Bourdieu, 1984; Bourdieu and Passeron, 1977). His
focus was on the nature of practice, practice that took place in fields.
Fields were collections of objective relations in which distinctive forms
of capital appropriate to success in the field were accumulated. Success in
the field was produced in practice by the habitus, structured dispositions
to act that produced appropriate performances. Expressed in typically
elliptical form, Bourdieu explains

> The conditionings associated with a particular class of conditions of
> existence produce habitus, systems of durable, transposable dispo-
> sitions, structured structures predisposed to function as structuring

structures, that is, as principles which generate and organize practices and representations that can be objectively adapted to their
outcomes without presupposing a conscious aiming at ends or an
express mastery of the operations necessary in order to attain them.
Objectively 'regulated' and 'regular' without being in any way the
product of obedience to rules, they can be collectively orchestrated
without being the product of the organizing action of a conductor.

(Bourdieu, 1990: 53)

These formulations were seen as a way of escaping from the determinism of structuralism without collapsing into an unrestrained individualism in which rational actors took optimal decisions. For Archer,
however, this was no solution. Rather it was, she argued, a form of
central conflationism, in which structures were collapsed into agency,
allowing for no purchase on the interaction between the two. Although
Giddens was her main interlocutor in developing her critique of central
conflationism, we have already noted that in her work on educational
systems that Archer found that Bourdieu's focus on practice caused him
to develop ideas that did not acknowledge their origins in a particular
context, in his case the strong centralising state traditions in France
(Archer, 1983). Much later in her project, however, it was the concept
of habitus that draws her fire.

What is intuitively appealing about the notion of habitus is its embodied nature. The dispositions to act are not only, or even primarily, cognitive ones, but can also be expressed in the haughty sneer of the aristocrat
or the stocky stance of the peasant. The dispositions are thus manifest in
a way of being that has been shaped by involuntary initial positioning in
a particular social and cultural context. The problems with is formulation, however, are twofold. They can be expressed in linked form by asking the question about Bourdieu's own career. How, in LiPuma's (1993)
words, can we explain Bourdieu? 'There is no account,' LiPuma argues,
'of why internalization of the habitus is relative, of why it permits some
individuals to transcend their habitus (for example, Bourdieu himself)'.
How is it that a postman's son from a remote peasant area of France, the
Bearn in the south-west of the country, can ascend to the heights of Pari-
sian academic life and proceed to write in such detail about the academic
habitus? The two related concerns are these: how is the habitus formed
and how can it explain change? From the formulation presented above, it
can be seen that Bourdieu envisages all those in the same objective social
circumstances to have a shared habitus. For the sociologist of education
Basil Bernstein

Habitus is described in terms of what it gives rise to, and brings, or
does not bring about. It is described in terms of the external underlying analogies it regulates. But it is not described with reference to

the particular ordering principles or strategies, which give rise to the formation of a particular habitus. The formation of the internal structure of the particular habitus, the mode of its specific acquisition, which gives it its specificity, is not described. How it comes to be is not part of the description, only what it does. There is no description of its particular formation.

(Bernstein, 1996: 136)

Bernstein himself once described his own project as writing 'grammars' for the formation of particular thought styles through the education process. Closely linked to this lack of explanation of how particular dispositions emerge is the problem of change. Put crudely: if patterns of thought are established through tacit acquisition at an early stage, if such patterns of thought are durable and transferable, and if they reflect and reproduce existing patterns of social structure, then how are they to change? If the existing social structures are made possible through patterns of thought that have their inevitability built in to the very bodily positions adopted, how can they be changed, other than by exogenous shocks? (Douglas, 1996: 160). How can patterns of thought emerge that challenge existing modes of thought, at a macro level, or how can individuals, at a micro level, escape the habitus that they have acquired? An exemplification of these difficulties can be seen in the way that commentators have tried to escape their tensions. As an illustration of the sort of difficulties we can get into, it is interesting to examine Brubaker's (1993) essay on 'Social Theory as Habitus'. In this, he argues for the existence and necessity of a sociological habitus, a collection of dispositions that encourage one to see the world sociologically. A prime component of this habitus is, or should be, a conscious reflection on these dispositions. Of course, we have already seen that habitus is distinguished by its early acquisition, in largely tacit fashion. As a result, it is both embodied and largely unconscious. It represents a series of inter-related durable and transposable generative practices that are generalised across contexts. Recognising this leads to Brubaker to argue for a stratified habitus: 'The sociological habitus, then, is a tertiary or higher-order habitus, overlaid on, transforming without superseding, a primary familial and a secondary scholastic habitus' (1993: 226). But if this is the case, do we not lose what seems to be central to the concept, the durability and transferability of practices? We risk the creation of one, two, many habituses and so splintering the concept beyond recognition.

For Archer, habitus could, at best, be thought to obtain in the world explored by community studies, a world of settled occupational categories, familial structures and gender roles (Archer, 2010). In such a setting, perhaps habits of thought have become sedimented and relatively unchallenged. But the multiplication of situational opportunities provided by shifts in social and cultural settings challenge the efficacy of habitual action. Habitual action is, in any case, inimical to the focus on agential reflexivity that Archer espouses. Building on her explorations of the internal conversation, Archer suggests that it takes very different forms and so leads to different forms of reflexivity. She suggests four categories of reflexivity, although one category is marked more by the relative absence of reflexivity (Archer, 2003). These forms of reflexivity are shaped by the interplay between 'context' (that is, the social situation) and 'concerns' (that is, the personal concerns of agents). This is, then, a sociological conception of reflexivity, albeit one underpinned by the cognitive affordances possessed by embodied agents. As part of this formation, the differential access to resources such as, crucially, language may be of considerable significance, although this is not a point pursued by Archer (Mutch, 2004).

For some the internal conversation needs to be completed in the context of others. Concerns, that is, have to be verbalised and shared with others in order for resolution to be obtained. This group are the 'conversational reflexives', and their engagement with the world is characterised by measures to maintain continuity of context. In this they will tend to avoid contact with structures or work 'with the grain', in sharp contrast to the 'autonomous reflexives'. The autonomous reflexive completes their own internal conversation in relative (and these terms are all relative) isolation from the concerns of others. As we will see, this has the potential to bring them into conflict with and seek to change the structures that surround them. This feature is shared to some extent by the third category, that of the 'meta-reflexive'. The meta-reflexive uses the internal conversation not only to monitor personal projects but also to reflect upon the process of reflection itself (thus more closely approaching Giddens' conceptualisation of reflexivity). This does not necessarily lead to broader change, however, so much as to the dissatisfaction of the person with the nature of the world and their efforts in it. The final category is that of the 'fractured reflexive', the person who, for some reason, never acquires the ability to conduct a satisfactory internal conversation. These are society's victims, never able to achieve their personal projects and remaining in the position of what Archer would term 'primary agents', that is, with their life chances determined to a significant degree by their involuntary positioning. What Archer has gone on to explore is the contention that the conditions of modernity suggest greater scope for the creation of and exercise of both autonomous and meta-reflexivity. She suggests that the situational logic of opportunity that is characteristic of late modernity, by providing a much wider range of cultural and structural opportunities, provides the context for the fostering of much greater meta-reflexivity. Our current concern, however, is not with the adequacy of this project, but with how we can use these concepts to illuminate the notion of institutional logics.

Summary

This chapter has provided us with some meta-theoretical concepts and some concepts derived from social theory that will help our discussion. From Bhaskar came some core commitments: to the stratified and emergent nature of the real, conceptualised as the mechanisms that produce the social contexts and practices that we study. From Archer, we have a framework for analysis, one which focuses on the unfolding relationship between agency and structure over time. That relationship involves the use of agential reflexivity to navigate the opportunities and constraints provided by situational logics. We still have much to do in considering how such logics are presented to actors. We will need to consider further the nature of these actors. Archer's framework also suggests the importance of history, which we have yet to consider in detail. However, before so doing, we need to see what light the ideas we have considered can shed on the constitution of society and the place of institutions in that society. That is the task of the next chapter.

Note

1 George Berkeley (1685–1753), Bishop of Cloyne in Ireland, advanced the idealist theory that what we take as physical elements of reality were simply ideas in the minds of those perceiving them. Samuel Johnson (1709–1784), English literary critic and dictionary complier, subject of a famous Life by James Boswell, is said by the latter when faced with Berkeley's ideas to have struck a large boulder until his foot bounced off it.

References

Archer, M. (1979) *Social Origins of Educational Systems*, London: Sage.
Archer, M. (1983) 'Process without system', *Archives Europeenes de Sociologie*, 24(4), 196–221.
Archer, M. (1995) *Realist Social Theory: The Morphogenetic Approach*, Cambridge: Cambridge University Press.
Archer, M. (1996) *Culture and Agency: The Place of Culture in Social Theory*, Cambridge: Cambridge University Press.
Archer, M. (2000) *Being Human: The Problem of Agency*, Cambridge: Cambridge University Press.
Archer, M. (2003) *Structure, Agency and the Internal Conversation*, Cambridge: Cambridge University Press.
Archer, M. (2007a) *Making Our Way Through the World: Human Reflexivity and Social Mobility*, Cambridge: Cambridge University Press.
Archer, M. (2007b) 'The ontological status of subjectivity: the missing link between structure and agency' in Lawson, C., Latsis, J. and Martins, N. (Eds.) *Contributions to Social Ontology*, London: Routledge, 17–31.
Archer, M. (2010) *Conversations About Reflexivity*, Abingdon: Routledge.
Archer, M. (2012) *The Reflexive Imperative in Late Modernity*, Cambridge: Cambridge University Press.
Archer, M. and Tritter, J. (2000) *Rational Choice Theory: Resisting Colonization*, London: Routledge.

Barad, K. (2007) *Meeting the Universe Halfway: Quantum Physics and the Entanglement of Matter and Meaning,* Durham, NC: Duke University Press.

Barley, S. and Tolbert, P. (1997) 'Institutionalization and structuration: studying the links between action and institution', *Organization Studies,* 18(1), 93–117.

Bernstein, B. (1996) *Pedagogy, Symbolic Control and Identity,* London: Taylor & Francis.

Bhaskar, R. (1979) *The Possibility of Naturalism,* Hemel Hempstead: Harvester.

Bhaskar, R. (2002) *Reflections on Meta-Reality: A Philosophy for the Present,* New Delhi/London: Sage.

Bourdieu, P. (1984) *Distinction: A Social Critique of the Judgement of Taste,* London: Routledge.

Bourdieu, P. (1990) *The Logic of Practice,* Cambridge: Polity.

Bourdieu, P. and Passeron, J-C. (1977) *Reproduction in Education, Society and Culture,* London: Sage.

Carter, I. (1979) *Farm Life in Northeast Scotland 1840–1914: The Poor Man's Country,* Edinburgh: John Donald.

Collier, A. (1994) *Critical Realism: An Introduction to the Philosophy of Roy Bhaskar,* London: Verso.

Damasio, A. (1995) *Descartes' Error. Emotion, Reason and the Human Brain,* London: Picador.

Damasio, A. (2000) *The Feeling of what Happens: Body, Emotion and the Making of Consciousness,* London: Vintage.

Delbridge, R. and Edwards, T. (2013) 'Inhabiting institutions: critical realist refinements to understanding institutional complexity and change', *Organization Studies,* 34(7), 927–947.

Douglas, M. (1996) *Natural Symbols,* London: Routledge.

Edwards, P. and O'Mahoney, J. and Vincent, S. (eds.) (2014) *Studying Organizations Using Critical Realism: A Practical Guide,* Oxford: Oxford University Press.

Edwards, T. (2016) 'Institutional theory: reflections on ontology', In: Mir, R., Willmott, H. and Greenwood, M. (eds.) *Routledge Handbook of Philosophy in Organization Sciences,* London: Routledge, 2016, 1–26.

Emirbayer, M. and Mische, A. (1998) 'What is agency?', *American Journal of Sociology,* 103(4), 962–1023.

Faulkner, P. and Runde, J. (2013) 'Technological objects, social positions and the transformational model of social activity', *MIS Quarterly,* 37(3), 803–818.

Frauley, J. and Pearce, F. (2007) *Critical Realism and the Social Sciences: Heterodox Elaborations,* Toronto: University of Toronto.

Giddens, A. (1979) *Central Problems in Social Theory,* London: Macmillan.

Giddens, A. (1981) *Contemporary Critique of Historical Materialism,* Stanford, CA: Stanford University Press.

Giddens, A. (1984) *The Constitution of Society: Outline of the Theory of Structuration,* Cambridge: Polity.

Kwon, H. (2004) *Fairness and Division of Labor in Market Societies: A Comparison of the U. S. and German Automotive Industries,* New York: Berghahn.

Lakatos, I. (1978) *The Methodology of Scientific Research Programmes,* Cambridge: Cambridge University Press.

Lawson, T. (2003) *Reorienting Economics,* London: Routledge.

Layder, D. (1990) *The Realist Image in Social Science,* London: Macmillan.

Layder, D. (1997) *Modern Social Theory: Key Debates and New Directions,* London: UCL Press.

Mutch, A. (2004) 'Constraints on the internal conversation: Margaret Archer and the structural shaping of thought', *Journal for the Theory of Social Behaviour,* 34(4), 429–445.

Mutch, A. (2013) 'Sociomateriality – taking the wrong turning?', *Information and Organization,* 23, 28–40.

Norris, C. (2000) *Quantum Theory and the Flight from Realism: Philosophical Responses to Quantum Mechanics,* London: Routledge.

Nyberg, D. (2009) 'Computers, customer service operatives and cyborgs: intra-actions in call centres', *Organization Studies,* 30(11), 1181–1199.

Popper, K. (1979) *Objective Knowledge: An Evolutionary Approach,* Oxford: Clarendon Press.

Porpora, D. (2015) *Reconstructing Sociology: The Critical Realist Approach,* Cambridge: Cambridge University Press.

Rose, H. (1993) 'Rhetoric, feminism and scientific knowledge or from either/or to both/and', in Roberts. R. and Good, J. (eds.), *The Recovery of Rhetoric,* London: Bristol Classical Press, 1993, 203–223.

Rose, H. (1994) *Love, Power and Knowledge: Towards a Feminist Transformation of the Sciences,* Cambridge: Polity.

Rose, S. (1993) *The Making of Memory: From Molecules to Mind,* London: Bantam.

Sayer, A. (2000) *Realism and Social Science,* London: Sage.

Sayer, A. (2010) *Method in Social Science: A Realist Approach,* London: Routledge.

Scott, W. (2008) *Institutions and Organizations: Ideas and Interests,* London: Sage.

Sewell, W. (2005) *Logics of History: Social Theory and Social Transformation,* Chicago, IL: University of Chicago Press.

Stones, R. (1996) *Sociological Reasoning: Towards a Past-modern Sociology,* Basingstoke: Macmillan.

Stones, R. (2005) *Structuration Theory,* Basingstoke: Palgrave macmillan.

Thompson, E.P. (1968) *The Making of the English Working Class,* Harmondsworth: Penguin.

Thompson, E.P. (1977) *Whigs and Hunters: The Origin of the Black Act,* London: Penguin.

Williams, M. (2014) 'Probability and models', in Edwards, P., O'Mahoney, J. and Vincent, S. (eds.) *Studying Organizations Using Critical Realism,* Oxford: Oxford University Press, 2014, 282–299.

2   Institutions

Introduction

Although the ideas reviewed in the previous chapter provide us with helpful guidance on the concepts that we might use to frame our investigations and a framework in which to conduct them, they are in no sense a substitution for the tasks of investigation. In order to do this, we have to create what Cruikshank (2003) describes as domain-specific ontologies that can form the basis for the substantive theories that we use to shape our investigations. A key starting point here is with existing theories of that world. An immanent critique of such theories, setting them against what we have assumed about the world in order to identify gaps or unrealised potential, is a vital first step towards producing a more adequate account. In this chapter, I start by providing an overview of the hints that Archer provides about institutions and their place in the constitution of society. I then set these conceptions against the key features of new institutionalist theory. Given the volume of material produced under the aegis of this label, I have perforce to concentrate on some major contributions. Given what was said in the last chapter, my main focus is on how they handle the relationship between structure and agency. What emerges as a major concern is the ambiguous status of the term 'institution'. I seek some clarity here by drawing upon some other domains, such as economic sociology and the sociology of conventions. This leads me to argue for institutions as societal phenomena and an engagement with the way that the logics they manifest have been conceptualised as a combination of substance and practices by Rodger Friedland.

Archer on Institutions

For Archer, contradictions between institutions are a central part of the analysis of society, although she is resistant to the notion of defining what these 'core' institutions might be (Archer, 1995: 218). However, there are a number of arguments why the effort essayed in this book might be thought to be important, not least for her own project of 'social ontology'. While she specifies how interinstitutional complementarities and contradictions might provide the situational logics for social action at an abstract level, the practical task of social analysis requires that we have some sense of what these institutions are in particular conjunctions of time and place. As we will see in this chapter, other social theorists have suggested such constellations of institutions and engagement with their work demands that we have some sense of how we might arrive at candidate institutions. Without such consideration, as we will see, impoverished views of what institutions consist of are drawn up, based on the nature of the topic under consideration. In other words, the promise of broader social theories such as that supplied by Archer needs to be converted into guides for practical social analysis. Accordingly, and despite Archer's injunctions, the central thesis of this book is that it is possible and important to specify what we take institutions to be. As we will see, that process involves processes of abstraction from the historical record for analytical purposes, and then the concrete location of the concepts so derived into specific historical contexts.

While Archer says little about the specific nature and development of institutions, a sense of how she positions them actually comes at an early stage of the work on *Culture and Agency*. Here she bemoans the fact that 'there is no ready fund of analytical terms for designating the components of the cultural realm corresponding to those which delineate parts of the structural domain (roles, organizations, institutions, systems, etc.)' (Archer, 1996: 1). In a much later work, she, together with her collaborator Pierpaulo Donati, revises this list to be 'roles, networks, organizations, institutions, systems, etc.' (Donati and Archer, 2015: 157). Although she does not develop this list, there is an implied hierarchy here, a nesting of concepts. In particular, institutions are seen as separate to organisations. If one takes the spirit of levels of existence, emergent from prior levels but not reducible to them, then institutions are seen to be both 'above' organisations and to be part of wider constellations, here labelled as 'systems'. It is consistent with the later arguments in the book to see society as a cluster of interdependent, interrelated but relatively autonomous institutions.

A significant part of Archer's arguments about how culture might be analysed relates to her concerns with what she terms the 'myth of cultural integration'. This myth, which takes various forms, sees culture as an internally consistent force that envelops the social. She takes particular aim at Marxist accounts, especially those that operate with a notion of a 'dominant ideology'. Building on some statements in Marx, this argues first that ideas are a reflection of the material interests of dominant social groups, second that such groups are not internally divided and third that the ideas that are produced are equally coherent and consistent. All these claims, she shows, are flawed. There is not a one-to-one correspondence between ideas and material interests, with some important areas of culture, such as religion, clashing with the material interests of the powerful. In addition, such powerful groups are, she suggests, far from homogeneous, with the possibility of different fractions producing contending ideas. Finally, ideas, once produced, can come into logical contradiction with other propositions, as we have seen. She draws upon her own work in the sociology of education to challenge the notion that there could be some sort of immediate correspondence between the interests of powerful groups and educational practices. What this ignores, she suggests, are the features of educational systems that resist those attempts to mould and shape it, features that demand that we keep the cultural system and socio-cultural activity analytically separate in order to examine the interplay between them. It also indicated that the 'cultural system', just like the structural, is marked by potential contradictions and clashes. Here Archer returns to the institutional level, noting that 'the most macro unit of structural analysis is properly the 'institutional' for these are the parts between which contradictions develop – affecting the whole of society' (Archer, 1996: 278). She goes on to supply examples that are very pertinent to our later discussion:

> The institutional level in the structural field, where operations in one sphere can obstruct those in another, setting up inescapable strains and contradictions ..., have their parallel in the cultural domain. At what could be called the doctrinal level, then, social policies can be inconsistent with economic planning, religious doctrine can contradict defence programmes and educational knowledge can stand in logical opposition to legal rules.
>
> (Archer, 1996: 279)

The same can be true for what she calls 'the next floor "down"', the intra-institutional as opposed to the inter-institutional. Here again, she turns to an educational example, where the particular structuring of an institution 'generates distinctive strains between its component parts: a decentralized system suffers from semi-permanent anarchy amongst its highly autonomous components; a centralized system institutes a tension between the internal standardization of practices and the external diversity of educational demands' (Archer, 1996: 279). Archer thus gives us some working ideas about institutions. Societies consist of a number of institutions, comprising both structural and cultural properties, which can enter into relations of contradiction or complementarity. They provide the ever-present context for rounds of social activity. They are also internally differentiated, comprising, in Archer's terms, sets of organisations and roles that provide situational logics for such social activity. We will come to elaborate on this perspective during the course of this book, but the framework that has been outlined provides a useful yardstick against which to measure the key aspects of new institutional theory.

New Institutionalism

New institutionalist theory (so called to distinguish it from the 'old' institutionalism of Philip Selznick) was developed in the United States in opposition to the impoverished view of organisational action that was shared by both functionalist sociology and mainstream economics. Organisational action here was seen to be a response to competitive conditions, in which organisations responded in something akin to the action of a billiard ball when struck by the cue ball. In other words, reactions were predictable, measurable and carried out in line with 'objective' criteria. Similarly, the assumptions about individual actions were that they were utility-maximising (or, at least, optimising) and based on the objective scrutiny of the available information. All these assumptions were subject to challenge, with institutionalist accounts focussing in particular on legitimacy. The focus on legitimacy derived in turn from empirical observations of organisations that persistently seemed to disobey economic 'laws'. For example, many seemed to adopt practices that seemed to be against their 'objective' interests, ones that made little sense against an objective of profit maximisation. The reason was, suggested institutionalists, that organisations were embedded in cultural and social contexts that provided powerful constraints on their actions. Actions had to be seen not only to be about achieving growth or profit but doing so in ways that were seen to be legitimate by the broader society.

This sense of organisations being embedded in a context that shaped their actions and, indeed, provided the very measures of what constituted 'success', led to two approaches. One was to argue that in such cases organisations often complied with external demands by decoupling certain practices from their internal workings (Meyer and Rowan, 1991). On this reading, legitimacy was secured by symbolically adopting practices which met external demands, but that were buffered from internal processes. Such an approach put the emphasis on the broader factors inducing and shaping adherence to norms of legitimacy. Another approach was to examine the practices that organisations adopted, based on the observation that organisations in the same field of activity seemed to adopt very similar practices, even when those practices did not seem to make much sense in the context of organisational activities. The concept that Walter Powell and Paul DiMaggio (1991) suggested in a very influential account was that of 'isomorphism'. Drawn from ecological studies, where it referred to the phenomena of organisms occupying the same ecological niche developing the same adaptations, this posited that organisations might come to adopt practices that looked very similar. It is important to note (although it is frequently overlooked) that their framework did include the possibility that practices were responses to competitive pressures. However, the scale and nature of such responses was, they argued, considerably circumscribed and only to be found in specific contexts. More common, they argued, were responses to other pressures. Prime among these was the idea that organisations faced with uncertainty choose to adopt the response of what is perceived to be a successful organisation, that the mechanism was mimetic isomorphism (from the Greek for copy). We can see this in the widespread use of practices like benchmarking, with their associated notion of 'best practices'. Mimetic processes suggest the influence of fashion on senior decision-makers and it is important in suggesting that their decisions may not be 'rational' in purely economic terms. It is the need for legitimacy that may persuade such actors that it is safest to accept and adopt the 'best practice' regardless of whether such practice fits the needs of their organisation – indeed such 'needs' may in turn be shaped by what is perceived as common practice. However, an organisation may be in a position to enforce its practices on others in the same domain, through coercive pressures. This often is associated with the possession of particular resources that enable a particular organisation to insist on its way, for example, when the dominant organisation in a supply chain obliges its suppliers to adopt common practices. The final type of pressure suggested by Powell and DiMaggio was normative pressure, which was linked in particular with the sponsorship of particular practices by professional bodies. In this case, the need for legitimacy could be satisfied by adhering to the practices that professional bodies laid down as appropriate.

The research agenda established by, in particular, the work of DiMaggio and Powell has proved extremely influential, spawning an extensive body of work that is far too great to review in detail. Useful summaries are provided in the book by Scott (2008) and the collection of articles edited by Greenwood et al (2008). For our purpose, one of the values of work in the new institutionalist tradition is the attention it has drawn to the importance of practices, especially to the ways in which they are diffused and disseminated. However, there have been a number of concerns about the project, concerns that coalesce around the problematic status of agency. There has been a temptation to seek to measure the adoption of practices by counting their occurrence, an approach that can conceal the very different ways that practices come to be adopted. That is, there has been a tendency to focus on measurable outcomes, treating the organisation as a 'black box'. However, we know from studies that open up organisational working that in practice they are frequently more or less stable coalitions of interests, coalitions that may unite to adopt practices in different ways. The publicly available outcome, that is, may look the same, but the degree of commitment to that outcome may vary considerably depending on the forces mobilised during the adoption process. Another concern that emerged was related to the question of change. Institutionalist approaches were seen as being rather better at explaining situations of conformity and stasis, with institutions seen as totalising forces. In such a formulation, critics argued, where was the dynamic for change and who were the agents of such change?

Because of its focus on the broader factors that induce organisations to become the same, it has, according to some, neglected questions of agency, interest and change (DiMaggio, 1988). One response to this criticism has been the elaboration of the notion of the 'institutional entrepreneur'. These are seen as those who

> deploy the resources at their disposal to create and empower institutions. Institutional entrepreneurs serve as agents of legitimacy supporting the creation of institutions that they deem to be appropriate and aligned with their interests.
>
> (Dacin, Goodstein and Scott, 2002: 47)

One concern about such a formulation is that there is the danger of smuggling elements of the rational actor model back in through the back door, as it were. For example, Fligstein (1997) suggests that institutional entrepreneurs are those who display an array of 'social skills'. He suggests that 'the idea that some social actors are better at producing desired social outcomes than are others is the core notion that underlies the concept of institutional entrepreneurs', which seems to ignore issues about why it is that some rather than others either possess such skills or, more importantly, come to deploy them in the search for institutional change (Fligstein, 1997: 398). The focus on 'desired social outcomes' without a tighter specification of the nature of agency risks a retreat to a default model of rationally calculating actors and so a departure from the central insights of institutionalism about the embedding of agency in a network of existing institutional arrangements. Critics would argue that the focus on individual agents ignores what they term the 'paradox of embedded agency'. That is, if all actors are shaped by the same institutional environment, how is it that some manage to envisage opportunities for change? The outline already given by Archer of contending and contradictory tensions both within and between institutions already suggests part of the answer: the imagery of a totalising institutional environment is a misleading one.

An alternative approach that seeks to avoid these problems is the approach known as 'institutional work'. Here the focus is less on individuals and more on the practices that have to be engaged in to change or maintain institutions. Drawing on practice theory, authors in this tradition seek to surface 'the intentional actions taken in relation to institutions, [...] much of it nearly invisible and often mundane, as in the day-to-day adjustments, adaptations and compromises of actors attempting to maintain institutional arrangements' (Lawrence, Suddaby and Leca, 2009: 1). That is a welcome corrective to focus on heroic, 'muscular' individuals, focusing more on collective patterns of action, but, like the debate on institutional entrepreneurs, it begs the question of how we conceptualise institutions. If we conceive of them as taken-for-granted practices, that is, practices that have become 'institutionalised', then one can see how work has to be done to introduce and maintain them. The same might be said, although the timeframe will be longer, if we regard 'institution' as a substitute term for 'organisation'. However, if we adopt, as this book has done, Archer's conceptualisation of institutions as societal phenomena, then we have to question actor-centred accounts, given the endurance and stability exhibited by institutions such as religion and the family.

Now, it could be argued that the search for definitions is a quixotic endeavour, condemned to failure. On a strong version of this argument, concepts need only to be contextualised to the situation at hand, with the argument for their validity being confined to their usefulness for analysis. A weaker version would recognise the need for more clarity but prefer to hand it off to other disciplines and keep the notion of institution as a vague but helpful resource to be called upon as needed. As Greenwood et al. (2008: 14) note 'Much like the early days of organization theory, when a tacit agreement occurred to stop attempting to define "organization", there emerged an unwritten assumption that we intuitively know what we mean by institution and thus have no further need to define it'. They do, however, go on to suggest the need for the development of 'a more common vocabulary'. The danger of not having such a vocabulary is the snowballing of institutions, each adapted to a particular situation but with no common point of reference. This can get particularly problematic when we consider the question of change. As Rowlinson (1997: 86) observes, some new institutionalists tend to find 'institutions everywhere, from handshakes to marriages to strategic planning departments'. For others, he continues

> there is a tendency to reduce organisations themselves to institutions, given the extent of patterned behaviour that takes place within most organisations. This is evident in the work of Zucker, who treats organisations *as* institutions, and describes organisations as 'the preeminent institutional form in modern society'.

The conflation of institutions and organisations is not only to be found in everyday usages; it is also consistent with elements of the 'old' institutionalism. So, for Selznick (1957: 5), at some points, organisations are 'an expendable tool, a rational instrument engineered to do a job'. Institutions, by contrast, are suffused with value. But some organisations can turn into institutions over time:

> It is something that happens to an organization over time, reflecting the organization's own distinctive history, the people who have been

in it, the groups it embodies and the vested interests they have created, and the way it has adapted to its environment.

(Selznick, 1957: 16)

The problem with this conflation of (some) organisations with institutions is not only that there is no common point of reference when
talking about institutions but also that when talking about endurance
and change we are confronted with very different timescales at different
scales of action. Practices, that is, may be deliberately designed, maintained and changed in relatively short timescales, but other phenomena
are far more resistant to change. Accordingly, it is worth examining how
institutions are conceptualised in other investigations.

Institutions in Other Domains

The field of institutional economics, largely based on the work of Douglas
North, operates with a clear notion of institutions at a supra-organisational
level (Hall and Soskice, 2001: 9). However, it operates on a view of institutions as repairing market imperfections, tending to a view of institutions
as the regulations that condition economic activity. Institutions are seen
as embodying the 'rules of the game' in a fashion that emphasises intent
and design. This 'actor-centred functionalism', as Pierson (2004: 104)
terms it, is also to be found in political science. Here the focus is on 'formal institutions', such as constitutions and electoral arrangements and,
often borrowing from rational choice economics, institutions are seen as
amenable to conscious design and to be relatively plastic and so subject
to reform. Even where institutions, on this view, contain imperfections,
such problems can be ironed out through the mechanisms of learning and
competition. Pierson draws on the work of, amongst others, DiMaggio
and Powell, to challenge this focus on intentionality and design, pointing out that 'rather than competitive environments selecting institutions
that fit the needs of social actors, institutions, once in place, may "select"
actors' (Pierson, 2004: 152). While, therefore, the focus on institutions as
supra-organisational phenomena is consistent with Archer's approach, the
conceptualisation of institutions is too narrow.

A more socially aware model, but one that still has economic activity
as its prime focus, is the comparative business systems tradition (Whitley,
2000). This seeks to identify clusters of inter-connected institutions
that shape economic activity. Such clusters are associated with zones
of economic activity that might cross state boundaries. The institutions
that are focused on are 'the state, the financial, educational and training systems, the labour market regime and norms and values governing
trust and authority relationships' (Djelic and Quack, 2008: 304). These
clusters of institutions can form complementary wholes that are mutually reinforcing. Whitley suggests six systems: fragmented, coordinated

industrial district, compartmentalised, state organised, collaborative and highly coordinated. These systems map in some cases onto national boundaries but are most likely to relate to regional blocs. Although there are clearly mechanisms, such as multinational enterprises and management consultancies, that span these blocs, Whitley argues that national differences tend to persist. 'Technical and market factors,' he argues, 'are less significant in structuring these differences than are societal institutions and agencies' (Whitley, 2000: 22). What is valuable in this approach is the specification of institutions at a level of generality such that they are not bounded by one particular location, something that can be a concern in much of the work on institutional logics. However, the status of culture in this approach is something of a residual term. For example, Whitley notes that

> The peculiarities of the prevalent business system in Britain, for example, cannot be adequately understood without taking into account the combined consequences of the interconnected pre-industrial state and financial systems, their links with the development of the training 'system' and organization of labour markets, and the pervasive and long-established cultural norm of individualism.
>
> (Whitley, 2000: 55)

However, his treatment of that 'norm of individualism' proves to be rather thin when set against the historical record (Mutch, 2006). As Hotho and Saka-Helmhout (2016: 648) conclude in their overview of comparative institutionalist approaches,

> the varieties of capitalism approach (Hall and Soskice, 2001) and the business systems approach (Whitley, 1999), are unified by a shared concern with how the forms, outcomes and dynamics of *economic organization* are influenced and shaped by societal institutions and with what consequences (my emphasis).

That rather narrows the range of institutions, omitting, for example, important institutions like religion from consideration. However, what is interesting in the current context is Whitley's observation that Archer's morphogenetic framework provides a promising means of unifying insights from economics and sociology, given what he sees as her argument that 'social agents are constituted with certain powers and capabilities in distinctive ways in particular institutional environments' (Whitley, 2003: 494). Although, therefore, these approaches are rather narrow, their focus on the complementary nature of institutions and their formulation in an abstract level that escapes national boundaries is something to be carried forward into our later discussion.

An alternative to approaches founded in economics is that presented by Boltanski and Thevenot (2006) in their work on justification. This proposes a number of 'orders of worth' and has been influential in the French school examining the sociology of conventions (Cloutier and Langley, 2013). They propose a number of such orders of worth or 'worlds': these are inspired, domestic, fame, civic, market, and industrial. They suggest that each is drawn upon when persons justify their actions, giving them a sense of worth and identity. In order to derive these orders of worth, they contrasted ideas drawn from classics of political philosophy, such as Augustine's *City of God* and Adam Smith's *Wealth of Nations* with 'behavioral handbooks designed for businesses' (Boltanski and Thevenot, 2006: 17). Recognising that this might narrow the focus to economic life, they argue that their results indicated broader applicability. A similar method was employed in Boltanski and Chiapello (2007), who also used management texts to argue for a 'new spirit of capitalism'. In this new spirit, as derived from passages in management books, they find the qualities valued

> autonomy, spontaneity, rhizomorphous capacity, multitasking (in contrast to the narrow specialization of the old division of labour), conviviality, openness to others and novelty, availability, creativity, visionary intuition, sensitivity to differences, listening to lived experience and receptiveness to a whole range of experiences, being attracted to informality and the search for interpersonal contacts – these are taken directly from the repertoire of May 1968.
> (Boltanski and Chiapello, 2007: 17)

As noted by Martin Parker (2008), there is a strange neglect of popular music in this account, perhaps because it is not seen as producing direct resources for critique. However, the impact of music in shaping the broader outlook of a whole generation, and crucially of those coming to places of influence and power, surely merits more serious consideration. They note, for example, almost in passing, that in developing artistic critique the 1968 critics drew upon themes 'already pervasive in the United States in the hippie movement' (Boltanski and Chiapello, 2007: 170). Management texts are unlikely to point us to this important dimension of social life, just as they restrict potential orders of worth in the earlier work. This narrowing of the sources from which meaning and justification might be derived is an artefact of the research method. It means that the orders of worth presented are too narrow, as the authors themselves recognise, noting as they do that 'the model of justification we have presented here in its broad outlines does not claim to account for the behavior of actors in any and all situations they may encounter' (Boltanski and Thevenot, 2006: 347). Importantly, they note that

The act of bypassing justice and behaving only as one pleases, without being burdened by the requirement to explain, is the defining act of violence. But by the same token, such acts fall outside the scope of our research.

(Boltanski and Thevenot, 2006: 37)

Justifications, that is, draw on positive representations of appropriate conduct of humans towards each other. That is to neglect the rather darker sides of human conduct that are manifest in historical accounts and which, in the form of phenomena such as the military and the nation state, have been central to the development of economic and social life. While the orders of worth approach is valuable in drawing our attention to the rhetoric of justification, which is important when actors draw upon such notions as 'community', the focus is too narrow to do justice to the full range of practices and ideas that shape social and organisational life.

Logics and Institutions

A much broader perspective, and one that has gained in influence, is that presented by Friedland and Alford in the same influential collection that Powell and DiMaggio edited in 1991. Their starting point was a desire to 'bring society back in' as the title of their contribution announced. That society, they argued, was one comprising a number of institutional spheres, each with their own logics and possessing relative autonomy. This is important as presenting an alternative to more materialist interpretations of society drawing on interpretations of Marxism that operated on a widely discredited model of base and superstructure. In this, cultural constructions were built on a material base and, in the crudest forms, were simply a mirror of material interests. Friedland and Alford (1991) were anxious to preserve autonomy for their institutional spheres, whilst recognising inter-connections. There are parallels, that is, with the formulations that Archer presents. It is also important to note that this was a view from outside the world of organisational studies, indeed one in which religion and the lessons derived from its study were of considerable importance. It therefore presents a much richer and broader view of the logics at operation in society. For Friedland and Alford (1991), institutions are combinations of symbolic constructions and material practices that give meaning to the ways in which people engage in their social and organisational life. They are few in number, operate at the societal level, and are enduring in character. Society, they suggest, consists of a set of institutions, each with their own logics and possessing relative autonomy. Institutions display a logic that gives meaning to the practices that organisations and individuals engage in, forming the 'laws of motion' of a particular order. Friedland and Alford give us a list of institutions – capitalist market, bureaucratic state, democracy, nuclear family, and Christian religion – which they quite clearly label as features of 'the contemporary capitalist West' (Friedland and Alford, 1991: 232). They do not, however, provide us with any criteria by which they selected these as institutions, preferring to elaborate on their notion of the logics that such institutions display.

The application of the notion of institutional logics began to gain traction in the organisational literature quite slowly. A key landmark was the study of higher education publishing by Patricia Thornton, appearing in book form as *Markets from Culture* in 2004. Building on Friedland and Alford she starts from the perspective that 'The main institutional sectors of society – the family, the religions, the professions, the state, the corporation, and the market – provide a distinct set of often conflicting or complementary logics that form the basis of institutional conflict and conformity' (Thornton, 2004: 49). It should be noted here that two new categories – the professions and the corporation – make their appearance, although the development of these is not explored. Rather, the emergence of a form of market logic within the higher education publishing field is contrasted with an editorial logic. Under an editorial logic, decisions about publishing were in the hands of editors, whose specialist assessment of the offering determined publication and who accordingly had status in publishing organisations. Under a market logic (which could be either one that privileged decisions on financial grounds or one that privileged marketing considerations) the role and status of editors was diminished, with commercial considerations coming to the fore. Thornton then seeks to link these logics to the 'societal-level logics of the professions and markets', using Friedland and Alford as a supporting citation (even though these authors never referred to professions as embodying a distinct societal logic). Thornton does not provide any details of the organised bodies that she cites from Friedson (2001) as being a key marker of professions. Indeed, her own evidence, albeit tucked away in an endnote, notes 'publishing [as having] the description of a quasi- or accidental profession' (Thornton, 2004: 154). Although the analysis of the impact of the differing industry-wide logics is illuminating, therefore, the link to societal logics is a little tenuous.

Another example of a shift in logics is provided by an examination of changes in the brewing industry in the United Kingdom from 1950 to 1990 (Mutch, 2006). The industry was dominated by six large firms, who controlled a high proportion of both the beer brewed and the outlets for selling it. Over the forty-year period there was a secular shift exhibited by all these companies from a production to a retailing logic. Under a production logic, which had characterised the industry from the nineteenth century onwards, the focus was on the brewing of beer, with the outlets for its distribution being of secondary importance. The key figure was the head brewer and decisions were taken on the basis of production volumes. Under this logic, retail outlets ('public houses' or 'pubs') were generally run at arms-length, rented by nominally independent tenants who were, nevertheless, obliged to stock the company's products. By contrast, the retailing logic that emerged with force in the 1950s, in part in response to broader changing social practices such as home-centred leisure based on the expansion of television, reversed the previous logic. Under a retailing logic, the central focus became the establishment of customer preferences through the pub. Decisions were now more about marketing and brand development. Pubs were frequently brought under central control through the replacement of tenants by salaried managers in order to foster a consistent retail offering. The shift from production to retailing could be observed in all the major companies, although with significantly different degrees of commitment. These degrees of commitment owed much in turn to the specific history of the company, with some being much more able to make the switch than others.

The logics used to explain this shift, however, were not those characterised as 'institutional logics'. Rather, the literature drawn on was that drawn from the strategy literature in the form of the 'dominant logic'. Prahald and Bettis first presented their notion of dominant logic in 1986. For them it 'is a mind set or world view or conceptualisation of the business' (1986: 491). In this sense it can be seen as a 'horizontal' form of logic akin to debates on 'business models': an inter-related set of practices joined together by an underlying logic that suggests the focus for the business. However, in contrast to much of the work on business models, the idea of a 'dominant' logic at the very least implies the possibility of alternative logics and the possibility of contestation. For Prahald and Bettis, the dominant logic observed within an organisation is formed over time through the activities of the senior decision makers of the organisation. Whilst it can be a source of advantage, it can also be used inappropriately when, for example, the firm diversifies into unrelated areas. Prahalad and Bettis suggest that historical exploration of the development of such a logic is one important analytical approach (1986: 499), and that point was valuable in examining the shift from production to retailing in the UK case.

It is possible, therefore, to deploy the language of logics without resorting to that of institutional logics and that raises two important points. One is that it is worth distinguishing between institutional logics and *institutionalised* logics. The concept of a 'logic', a set of interconnected relations that condition activity, is a valuable one that can be used for a range of social situations. When the logics that Prahald and Bettis discuss within organisations become taken-for-granted we may claim that they have become institutionalised, just as we might make the same assertions when examining, for example, the field. However, for this discussion we need to distinguish such taken-for-granted logics from institutional logics. Just in the same way, these logics provide meaning to actions but at the scale of societies. They provide the situational logics for action at the scale of the field or the organisation but are relatively enduring in character. Just as with the example of UK brewing, what Thornton examined was the operation of logics at the level of an industry and the organisations within it. Here the second point is that much of the discussion of institutional logics in the literature is actually concerned with field-level logics. The field is an important term in new institutionalist approaches, one whose use is widespread. Its value is to suggest that organisations do not just operate in an industry 'sector' that is somehow 'given' but that they shape the very parameters of that field. Ultimately derived from the work of Bourdieu, the notion of the field is that activity does not just involve the organisations offering a particular product or service. Rather it also includes means of disseminating practices between such organisations, involving bodies such as trade associations, professional bodies and media outlets. For Bourdieu, the field was also structured, in part through the classifications and boundaries that powerful organisations were able to impose. That means that not all players in a field are of equal status, but that they can possess different forms of capital as appropriate to the field. The possession of such forms of capital – economic but also social or cultural – leads to fields being distinguished by central players and those on the margins. Much has been made of such distinctions in new institutionalist accounts to suggest how change occurs, either driven by central incumbents because of their control over key resources or introduced by marginal actors because of their relative freedom from embedded ideas. For the purpose of the current discussion the point is not to adjudicate on these debates, but to point out that when reference is made to institutional logics we are frequently referring to *field* level logics. Thus, in an otherwise exemplary examination of the mechanisms by which two contending logics are negotiated in the insurance business of Lloyds of London, Smets et al (2015) draw on a distinction between a 'community' logic and a 'market' logic. However, what they refer to as a 'community' logic refers not to how such a term might be defined (if indeed it can be) at societal level, but to the demands and expectations of a specific occupational 'community', that of the brokers and dealers who comprise the key players in the insurance business. The logics they identify, that is, are logics proper to that particular domain of activity, which we can term a 'field'. They are not societal logics that operate at a supraorgisational level.

Defining Institutions

Drawing in large measure on work done following Thornton's lead, Thornton, Ocasio and Lounsbury (2012: 66) suggest an expanded list of institutions: family, community, religion, state, market, profession, and corporation. In developing this list, they quite clearly have in mind some criteria for definitions, if these are only presented in negative fashion, by drawing attention to what they see as weaknesses in the Friedland and Alford discussion. For example, in reviewing the Friedland and Alford (1991) formulation they point out that 'The influences of the professions, which both Meyer and Rowan ... and DiMaggio and Powell ... so clearly laid out, are mysteriously absent' (Thornton, Occasio and Lounsbury, 2012: 66). Of course, as we have already noted, Friedland and Alford were working in the traditions of social theory, in which consideration of the professions might not be considered as so salient in the broader setting of society as opposed to a focus on organisational life. Much of the work in the new institutionalist tradition has indeed drawn attention to the importance of professions, but, as we have seen in the context of Thornton's work on academic publishing, 'profession' is a tricky term. In his influential exploration of professionalism, Friedson (2001: 127) suggests a number of key dimensions of the 'ideal type' of professions:

1 specialized work in the officially recognized economy that is believed to be grounded in a body of theoretically based, discretionary knowledge and skill and that is accordingly given special status in the labor force;
2 exclusive jurisdiction in a particular division of labor created and controlled by occupational negotiation;
3 a sheltered position in both external and internal labor markets that is based on qualifying credentials created by the occupation;
4 a formal training program lying outside the labor market that produces the qualifying credentials, which is controlled by the occupation and associated with higher education; and
5 an ideology that asserts greater commitment to doing good work than to economic gain and to the quality rather than the economic efficiency of work.

He explicitly sets these against the models of organising to be found in the free market and the bureaucratic firm. For him, 'professionalism is conceived of as one of three logically distinct methods of organizing and controlling' work and the knowledge it draws on (Friedson, 2001: 179). But professionalism can also be drawn on as a form of rhetorical justification, as when actors use it to distinguish their commitment to a task as against the part-time 'amateur' performance of the same tasks. Boltanski and Thevenot (2006: 292) seem to be making this point when they note that 'a person's profession, considered to be a fundamental attribute in a great number of situations, remains a passageway between worths and an object of tension'. That is, for them, profession is a cross-cutting term that is deployed with different inflections in several of their 'orders of worth'. Thornton, Occasio and Lounsbury, in their critique of Friedland and Alford's characterisation of the state, note that Thornton

> further questioned the reasoning of qualifying the institutional order of the state as the "bureaucratic state". Isn't bureaucracy an organizational form used by the state to carry out its objectives. Couldn't other institutional orders be characterized as bureaucratic as well?
> (Thornton, Occasio and Lounsbury, 2012: 67)

That is a fair point, and it could be further argued that if we turn to the literature on the state that of rather more centrality is the notion of the 'nation state'. However, if we accept this point, then can we not turn the same argument back on the professions? That is, both bureaucracy and professionalism are contending logics of organising and so cut across institutions rather than forming institutions themselves.

Similar observations could be made about the appearance of both the corporation and community in the new list of institutions. 'Also absent [from Friedland and Alford] is the institutional order of the corporation' (Thornton, Occasio and Lounsbury, 2012: 66). But it could be argued that the corporation is a historically specific organisational form, one that, while powerful in its time, is open to replacement by other forms (Davis, 2009). Finally, the appearance of community is based on a review of the literature that doesn't appear to draw on the many critical observations about the limits of the concept. Back in 1976, Raymond Williams in his examination of *Keywords* pointed out that 'community' was one of the few words that had only positive connotations. It is widely used to cover very diverse groups such as the 'academic community' or 'the Asian community', which are in truth riven by differences. In these senses the rhetorical appeal is to small, closed groups such as those found in rural areas where there is an assumption of harmony and common purpose. Closer examination often finds these assumptions wanting, but there is a clear 'halo' effect where the desired attributes are carried over to the target grouping. In this sense, 'community' is much closer to a rhetoric of justification than to a societal institution. It is interesting to note that Boltanski and Thevenot (2006) do not deploy community as one of their 'worlds'; the closest they come to it is their 'civic world'. Perhaps this makes sense in the context of French life, in which a Cabinet minister for gender equality, Marlène Schiappa, could declare in 2017 that 'You know, in France, we don't think about "communities". We are a revolutionary French République. There is just one community' (Marsh, 2017). Here it makes no sense to talk about 'community' as an institution, as it is regarded as being coterminous with the nation state. For the social anthropologist Anthony Cohen, community is a mental construct, not 'a structure of institutions capable of objective definition and description' (Cohen, 1985: 19). It is drawn upon as part of sensemaking: 'people assert community, whether in the form of ethnicity or of locality, when they recognize in it the most adequate medium for the expression of their whole selves' (Cohen, 1985: 107). If that is an accurate assessment, then it casts doubt on regarding community as a logic shaping action, rather than as an outgrowth of and justification for that action. Again, Richard Sennett draws our attention to the 'dark side' of community when he observes that a key feature of what he terms 'the intimate society' is 'destructive gemeinschaft' (Sennett, 2002: 220). By this, he was referring to the construction of community as a shared structure of feeling, defined against those who did not share such feelings, in which the focus becomes not on shared action and the content of action, but feelings and how they are expressed. This focus on community as feeling, he argued, had destructive effects on attempts to build relationships between unconnected persons.

> Myths of an absence of community, like those of the soulless or vicious crowd, serve the function of goading men to seek out community in terms of a created common self. The more the myth of empty impersonality, in popular forms, becomes the common sense of a society, the more will that populace feel morally justified in destroying the essence of urbanity, which is that men can act together, without the compulsion to be the same.
>
> (Sennett, 2002: 255)

It was such critiques that meant that, for Friedson,

> 'community' is an inadequate basis for ordering anything beyond a simple division of labor – certainly not a complex division of labor composed of many different discretionary specializations. The broad community of shared occupational identity is not enough: it must ultimately be organized into associations for representation and negotiation.
>
> (Friedson, 2001: 146)

There is room for doubt, at the very least, about some of the core categories that Thornton, Occasio and Lounsbury suggest, doubt that is reinforced by other aspects of their treatment of the issue.

One concern is the derivation of the categories that they deploy. As we have seen in their comment on the 'mysterious' absence of the professions in Friedland and Alford's account, some criteria are clearly being deployed in order to sustain the judgment, but it is not clear what these are. A clue can perhaps be found in their discussion of the derivation of community: 'we extend the ideas gleaned from the reviews of largely qualitative community studies' (Thornton, Occasio and Lounsbury, 2012: 71). Thus, what makes the absence of the professions from Friedland and Alford mysterious is the widespread focus in new institutionalist accounts of the impact of professions in, for example, shaping the normative pressures that contribute to isomorphism. However, it is surely plausible to argue that, given that Friedland and Alford (1991) were arguing on the terrain of social theory, not organisation studies, the professions and the corporation were not included because from an 'external' vantage point they were simply not significant enough. That is an argument to which we will have to return, but the derivation of institutions from the published work of those concerned with organisational life is likely to produce an impoverished set of institutions.

Thornton, Ocasio and Lounsbury (2012) present their framework of institutional logics in the form of a matrix representing Weberian ideal types of their selected orders. Thus, in concluding their discussion of community, they state that their illustrative table 'represents an ideal typical depiction of the inter-institutional system with the addition of a new entry on the X-axis, the community logic. We have derived the ideal types on the vertical Y-axis, that is, the categorical elements such as sources of legitimacy, authority, and identity, and the bases of norms, attention, and strategy from an interpretation of the research on community across the broad sweep of literatures previously discussed' (Thornton, Occasio and Lounsbury, 2012: 72). While Weberian ideal types are a valuable analytical device, they do, in this form of presentation, run the risk of the 'variablisation' of logics, something that tends to denude them of the historical depth and richness that will be argued is central to their operation. Particularly significant in this context is the argument that Thornton et al present of the possibility of the blending of elements of differing logics to form new logics. This focus on the modularity of logics returns us to the actor-centred accounts discussed above in which 'alternative institutional logics may serve as toolkits for action (Swidler, 1986)'. In the influential work of Ann Swidler (1986), cultural ideas are conceptualised as resources that can be taken up at will and combined. Such an approach underplays the often unconscious and unintentional introduction of logics, thanks to the selection of practices. A toolbox metaphor also downplays the extent to which ideas and practices are linked in complex relational webs. Practices are not independent objects that can be taken up or put down at will. As Porpora (2015: 174) argues

> in contrast with a toolbox, culture is not just an aggregation of independent objects. The ideational objects of culture bear objective relations to each other about which we can argue and converse and which, like differences in depth, can exert causal influences on us. All of that nature is missed by the toolbox metaphor and by what Archer calls the conflation of culture with action.

The toolbox metaphor also returns us to notions of agential choice. The focus returns to the skilled selection of options in response to the demands of the situation, without recognising that these choices might be tightly constrained by norms built into the institutional environment (Pierson, 2004: 152).

Friedland points to a further concern when he notes that Thornton et al 'tend to economize the logics, couching the "root metaphor" of the family, for instance, as a "firm", or that of religion as "Temple as a bank"' (Friedland, 2012: 585). From the perspective of the literature on organisations, where religion tends anyway to be rather neglected (King, 2008) perhaps seeing the root metaphor as 'temple as a bank' makes sense, but in a broader view it marks a drift away from the original ambition of Friedland and Alford to 'bring society back in'. It appears to rather diminish a cause that inspires devotion and a willingness to turn from the world. While the work of Thornton et al is valuable in stressing the need to examine institutional logics as societal phenomena, supplying meaning to actions within fields and organisations, the lack of clear criteria for determining what constitutes an institution gives the impression of a post hoc rationalisation of a disparate set of empirical investigations.

Friedland, by contrast, has taken the idea of institutional logic in a very different dimension, informed, in particular, by his work on religion. In his work with Richard Hecht on the tensions between Judaism and Islam at their shared scared space that is Jerusalem, he notes 're-ligions like Judaism and Islam, whose task is not the salvation of in-dividual souls or the provision of solace to persons in despair, but the production of moral compass and metaphysical mandate for an entire social structure' (Friedland and Hecht, 1996: 374). It is this focus on religion not as another variable in organisational environment but as all-encompassing value system that shapes his later formulation of insti-tutions as religious at their core, in the sense of involving belief in central values. Thus, the study of politicised religion shows that

> its political practices extend the institutional logic of religion, which derives authority from divine writ, grounds both individual and col-lective birth in divine creation, and locates agency in a self bound to God as opposed to an autonomous, self-interested monad.
>
> (2009: 49)

Extending this insight to other institutions, he draws on an Aristotelian notion of substance as 'the foundation, or essence, of a thing that cannot be reduced to its accidental properties that attach to it nor to the mate-riality of its instances' (Friedland, 2009: 55). For him, 'Institutions have logics. An institutional logic is a bundle of practices organized around a particular substance and its secondary derivatives from which the nor-mativity of those practices is derived' (Friedland, 2009: 61). Further, 'institutional substances cannot be directly observed, but are imma-nent in the practices that organize an institutional field, values never exhausted by those practices, practices premised on faith' (Friedland, 2009: 61). It is here that there is a connection with the focus on the centrality of values in Selznick's vision. 'Values do have a central place in the theory of institutions,' he argued. 'We need to know which values matter in the context at hand; how to build them into the organization's culture and social structure; and in what ways they are weakened or subverted' (Selznick, 1996: 271). That ambition was carried on into his manifesto for what he termed 'a humanist science', one in which values and ideas were central (Selznick, 2008). In his discussion of Arendt's focus on the centrality of meaning to human action, Finn Bowring points to her distinction between action 'in order to' and action 'for the sake of'. 'The carpenter cuts the wood,' he notes Arendt as arguing, '"in order to" realise the goal of making a table; but carpentry, as a vocational choice, is pursued "for the sake of" an ideal whose meaning demands to be honoured, not produced, chased after or acquired' (Bowring, 2011: 21). He relates this distinction to Weber's focus on the 'value rationality' of human action.

Here we can note the observation by Thornton et al that, to their surprise, Friedland and Alford did not reference aspects of Weber's work, notably his notion of value spheres. 'Weber', Thornton et al note, 'identified several life-orders or what he termed value-spheres, for example the economic, political, esthetic, erotic, and intellectual spheres' (Thornton, Occasio and Lounsbury, 2012: 66). Friedland has, indeed, returned to Weber's value spheres to argue 'that a theory of institution might be the basis for a religious sociology of passionate fields' (2014: 220). He quite specifically states in this discussion that he has no position on how many such fields exist, being more concerned with an argument about the centrality of love as crucial to the mobilisation of substances. However, his discussion points to the neglect of practices in Weber, derived in part from Weber's misunderstanding of the place of ritual in Protestant religions. For Friedland, the coupling of substance and practice(s) is essential:

> Material practices ground values; they manifest their actionability in an object world. Substances are not objects, but they depend on them. Practices – in law, exchange, accounting – are instrumental regimes whose actionability depends on substances, substances that are ontologically subjective, but whose objectivity as social forces depends on that practice. These regimes of routinized material practices are what enable participation in these spheres to proceed without passion, without possession, as a relation to what appear to be exterior objects in all their skeletal impersonality.
>
> (Friedland, 2014: 248)

There are not only intriguing parallels in this work with Archer's ideas, but also some departures. The parallels are principally in the conception of institutions as societal phenomena motivated by commitment to values. The idea of society as comprising a set of institutions, each motivated by a core value and entering into relations of contradiction or complementarity is consistent with her formulations. Also consistent with broader critical realist conceptions is the notion of a substance as ontologically real but never graspable, manifest in the practices that it animates. The focus on logics as supplying guides to action can be mapped on to Archer's ideas about the situational logics that condition, but do not determine, action. What is missing, perhaps, in Archer's morphogenetic approach is the importance of practices, and this is something we will return to.

Summary

This combination of Archer and Friedland gives us something of an agenda to pursue. In subsequent chapters, I will seek to provide criteria for establishing institutions, with a particular focus on belief. I will attempt to define the substances particular to each and the distinctive practices that each possesses. In order to do so, I will use the resources of history to suggest aspects of institutional development, maintenance and change. However, in order to do so, I need first to lay out some assumptions about the nature of the social world and of what history can bring to its study. That is the task of the next chapter.

References

Archer, M. (1995) *Realist Social Theory: The Morphogenetic Approach*, Cambridge: Cambridge University Press.

Archer, M. (1996) *Culture and Agency: The Place of Culture in Social Theory*, Cambridge: Cambridge University Press.

Boltanski, L. and Thevenot, L. (2006) *On Justification: Economies of Worth*, Princeton: Princeton University Press.

Boltanski, L. and Chiapello, E. (2007) *The New Spirit of Capitalism*, London: Verso.

Bowring, F. (2011) *Hannah Arendt: A Critical Introduction*, London: Pluto.

Cloutier, C. and Langley, A. (2013) 'The logic of institutional logics: insights from French pragmatist sociology', *Journal of Management Inquiry*, 22(4), 360–380.

Cohen, A. (1985) *The Symbolic Construction of Community*, Chichester: Ellis Horwood.

Cruickshank, J. (2003) *Realism and Sociology: Anti-Foundationalism, Ontology, and Social Research*, London: Routledge.

Dacin, T., Goodstein, J. and Scott, W. (2002) 'Institutional theory and institutional change: introduction to the special research forum', *Academy of Management Journal*, 43(1), 45–57.

Davis, G. (2009) *Managed by the Markets: How Finance Re-Shaped America*, New York: Oxford University Press.

DiMaggio, P. (1988) 'Interest and agency in institutional theory', in L. Zucker (eds.), *Institutional Patterns and Organizations: Culture and Environment*, Cambridge: MA: Ballinger, 1988, 3–19.

Djelic, M. and Quack, S. (2008) 'Institutions and Transnationalization', in Greenwood, R., Oliver, C., Suddaby, R. and Sahlin-Anderson. K. (eds.), *Sage Handbook of Organizational Institutionalism*, London: Sage 299–323.

Donati, P. and Archer, M. (2015) *The Relational Subject,* Cambridge: Cambridge University Press.

Fligstein, N. (1997) 'Social skill and institutional theory', *American Behavioral Scientist,* 40(4), 397–405.

Friedland, R. and Alford, R. (1991) 'Bringing society back in: symbols, practices, and institutional contradictions', in Powell W. and DiMaggio P. (eds.), *The New Institutionalism in Organizational Analysis,* Chicago: University of Chicago Press, 1991, 232–266.

Friedland, R. and Hecht, R. (1996) *To Rule Jerusalem,* Cambridge: Cambridge University Press.

Friedland, R. (2009) 'Institution, practice and ontology: towards a religious sociology', *Research in the Sociology of Organizations,* 27, 45–83.

Friedland, R. (2012) 'Book review: Patricia H. Thornton, William Ocasio and Michael Lounsbury 2012 The Institutional Logics Perspective: A new approach to Culture, Structure, and Process', *M@n@gement,* 15(5), 582–595.

Friedland, R. (2014) 'Divine institution: Max Weber's value spheres and institutional theory', *Research in the Sociology of Organizations,* 41, 217–258.

Friedson, E. (2001) *Professionalism: The Third Logic,* Cambridge: Polity.

Greenwood, R., Oliver, C., Suddaby, R. and Sahlin-Anderson. K. (eds.) (2008) *The SAGE Handbook of Organizational Institutionalism,* London: Sage.

Hall, P. and Soskice, D. (2001) *Varieties of Capitalism: The Institutional Foundations of Comparative Advantage,* Oxford: Oxford University Press.

Hotho, J. and Saka-Helmhout, A. (2016) 'In and between societies: reconnecting comparative institutionalism and organization theory', *Organization Studies,* 38(5), 647–666.

King, J. (2008) '(Dis)Missing the obvious – will mainstream management research ever take religion seriously?', *Journal of Management Inquiry,* 17(3), 214–224.

Lawrence, T., Suddaby, R. and Leca, B. (2009) (Eds) *Institutional Work: Actors and Agency in Institutional Studies of Organizations,* Cambridge: Cambridge University Press.

Marsh, S. (2017) "€5,000 would be a deterrent': the French minister who wants sexual harassment fines', *The Guardian, https://www.theguardian.com/world/2017/jun/24/marlene-schiappa-french-minister-sexual-harassment-fines [3 July 2017].*

Meyer, J. and Rowan, B. (1991) "Institutionalized organizations: formal structure as myth and ceremony" in Powell W. and DiMaggio P. (eds.), *The New Institutionalism in Organizational Analysis,* Chicago: University of Chicago Press, 1991, 41–62.

Mutch, A. (2006) 'The institutional shaping of management: in the tracks of English Individualism', *Management & Organization History,* 1(3), 251–271.

Parker, M. (2008) 'The Seventh City: Review of Boltanski and Chiapello', *Organization,* 15(4), 610–620.

Pierson, P. (2004) *Politics in Time: History, Institutions, and Social Analysis,* Princeton: Princeton University Press.

Porpora, D. (2015) *Reconstructing Sociology: The Critical Realist Approach,* Cambridge: Cambridge University Press.

Powell, W. and DiMaggio, P. (1991) *The New Institutionalism in Organizational Analysis,* Chicago: University of Chicago.

Prahalad, C. and Bettis, R. (1986) 'The dominant logic: a new linkage between diversity and performance', *Strategic Management Journal*, 7, 485–501.

Rowlinson, M. (1997) *Organisations and Institutions,* Basingstoke: Macmillan.

Scott, W. (2008) *Institutions and Organizations: Ideas and Interests,* London: Sage.

Selznick, P. (1957) *Leadership in Administration: A Sociological Interpretation*, New York: Harper & Row.

Selznick, P. (1996) 'Institutionalism "old" and "new"', *Administrative Science Quarterly*, 41, 270–277.

Selznick, P. (2008) *A Humanist Science: Values and Ideals in Social Inquiry,* Stanford: Stanford University Press.

Sennett, R. (2002) *The Fall of Public Man,* London: Penguin.

Smets, M., Jarzabkowski, P., Burke, G. and Spee, P. (2015) 'Reinsurance trading in Lloyds of London: Balancing conflicting-yet-complementary logics in practice', *Academy of Management Journal*, 58(3), 932–970.

Swidler, A. (1986) 'Culture in action: symbols and strategies', *American Sociological Review*, 51(2), 273–286.

Thornton, P. (2004) *Markets from Culture: Institutional Logics and Organizational Decisions in Higher Education Publishing,* Stanford: Stanford University Press.

Thornton, P., Occasio, W. and Lounsbury, M. (2012) *The Institutional Logics Perspective: A New Approach to Culture, Structure, and Process,* Oxford: Oxford University Press.

Whitley, R. (2000) *Divergent Capitalisms: The Social Structuring and Change of Business Systems,* Oxford: Oxford University Press.

Whitley, R. (2003) 'From the search for universal correlations to the institutional structuring of economic organization and change: the development and future of organization studies', *Organization*, 10(3), 481–501.

Williams, R. (1976) *Keywords: A Vocabulary of Culture and Society,* London: Fontana.

3 Bodies, Persons and History

Introduction

If we are to conceive of institutional logics as combinations of substance and practices emerging from embodied relations both between persons and between persons and the natural world, then we have to pay some attention to what we mean by persons. Drawing on critical realism, Christian Smith argues that social structures 'are real entities with causal powers generated through emergence from the tension created between human capacities and limits as given by the nature of the real world' (Smith, 2010: 18). Considering institutions as a key part of such structures means that we need to explore the capacities that critical realists argue form the bedrock of personhood and thus the building blocks of social structure. The first part of this chapter thus outlines some key features of that personhood. The structures that are built on these features emerge from distinctive aspects of what it is to be human. In order to address what Friedson (2001) calls the 'perennial problems' of human existence, we need to see them as historically emergent and, once emergent, relatively enduring. This means that we need to consider how to approach historical explorations, particularly in the search for substances immanent in practices. This poses some challenges, challenges that are explored in the second section.

The Emergence of Personhood

As we saw in the last chapter, critical realism suggests that reality is stratified, with phenomena emergent from but not reducible to the properties of a prior level. That emergence can be considered both synchronically and diachronically (Elder-Vass, 2010). Certain properties emerge from the embodied nature of human beings that are immediately and continuously emergent from particular biological properties. The most challenging of these is the capacity of consciousness, challenging because neuroscience continues to explore its emergence from the matter that constitutes the brain (Damasio, 2000). That emergence, for the practical purposes of social analysis, is immediate. The capacities that such synchronous emergence supplies are the building blocks of personhood but do not themselves constitute that personhood. They include, besides consciousness, the capacity for memory and language, on which other capacities, such as those of imagination and abstract conceptualisation, are built. (Smith, 2010 has an extensive list of these capacities.) Some of those capacities are shared with other animals, but it is the distinctive combination of these that makes for emergent personhood.

One key distinguishing feature from most animals is the time that humans take to reach maturity. This is not only in cognitive capacity. More fundamentally, humans lack ambulatory capacity and the ability to feed themselves for a much longer period than most animals, which makes human young uniquely vulnerable. They are dependent on collective social organisation from birth. The slow coming to maturity thus encompasses a diachronic form of emergence, in which learning features strongly. This initial learning, Archer (2000) argues in her discussion of ontogeny, proceeds before language acquisition. The human infant experiences the external world, both persons and objects, through touch, triggering the sense of me/not me. This realisation of an embodied existence independent of others gives rise, argues, Archer to a sense of self. This sense of self is prior to a concept of self. Such a formulation is consistent with the arguments of the neurophysiologist Antonio Damasio (2000). He argues that the constant, nonconscious monitoring of body states gives rise to what he terms a 'proto-self'. Consciousness arises when this monitoring encounters objects that prompt feelings, feelings that form the sense of self. In turn, this core consciousness is the basis for the extended consciousness that underpins the autobiographical sense of self. 'Autobiographical memory', he suggests, 'develops and matures under the looming shadow of an inherited biology. However, unlike the core self, much will occur in the development and maturation of autobiographical memory that is not just dependent on, but is even regulated by, the environment' (Damasio, 2000: 229). Building on such foundations, concepts of self, which can vary in time and space, are developed and shared through language. Such language is learned in social environments over extended periods of time. However, the sense of self that endures means that for critical realists persons are subjects, not the decentered objects of discourse that are proposed by the anti-humanist philosophies of continental Europe. As Smith puts it,

> By person I mean a conscious, reflexive, embodied, self-transcending center of subjective experience, durable identity, moral commitment, and social communication who—as the efficient cause of his or her own responsible actions and interactions—exercises complex capacities for agency and intersubjectivity in order to develop and sustain his or her own incommunicable self in loving relationships with other personal selves and with the nonpersonal world.
>
> (Smith, 2010: 61)

Joe O'Mahoney (2012) characterises such commitments as a form of 'weak essentialism', because of their focus on the emergence of person-hood from embodied capacities that are key features of the make-up of human beings. As he argues, perspectives that argue that human iden-tities are fragmented, fluid and shifting because they are products of discourses have to assume at least the capacity for language in order to make any sense.

Such capacities are, of course, profoundly shaped by the plurality of humankind. In her discussion of *The Human Condition*, the political philosopher Hannah Arendt (1958) distinguished between the plasticity of human nature and the brute facts of the human condition. In addition to the need to provide for biological survival at the level of the individual organism, politics, she argued, arose out of 'action, the only activity that goes on directly between men without the intermediary of things or matter, corresponds to the human condition of plurality, to the fact that men, not Man, live on the earth and inhabit the world' (Arendt, 1958: 7). A second form of diachronic emergence, therefore, is that which relates to the phenomena that emerge from human interaction over time but en-dure to shape future interactions. To such phenomena we give the name of social structure, the institutions that we examine here being a prime example. They arise when, Smith argues, the limits of human capacities run up against the extent of human desires, wants and needs. They en-able the accomplishment of more than finite individual capacities allow.

> The tensions arising between human capacities and human limits—between the vastly capable and severely finite in human life—give rise through emergence to creative patterns of lived practice that of-ten solidify into what we call social structures. Social structures are not agreed upon contracts made by autonomous exchange partners, nor are they illusions of facticity appearing falsely to socially con-structed and constructing actors as more real than they are. Social structures are real entities with causal powers generated through emergence from the tension created between human capacities and limits as given by the nature of the real world.
>
> (Smith, 2010: 18)

A tension arising out of this conception is between the essential charac-teristics of human beings that give rise to social structures and the tre-mendous flexibility of such arrangements. As Smith (2010: 117) argues, 'viewed from the vantage point of uniformity, human cultures are highly diverse. Viewed from the perspective of all the constructions humans could possibly produce, human cultures are in many crucial ways rela-tively similar.' For Selznick, the work of social anthropology indicates that 'all cultures have systems of family and kinship; all protect and discipline children; all distinguish fact from fantasy; all know how to perform elementary tasks of farming and animal husbandry; all have rules for determining ownership of land and chattel' (Selznick, 2008: 102). As he suggests 'anthropology teaches that all peoples have much the same biological capacities and limits. As the commonalities show, despite diversity, cultures are *human products*' (Selznick, 2008: 121). It is those relative similarities that suggest the possibility of identifying logics that emerge and develop over time and which, framed at an appropriate level of abstraction, can be thought to operate to condition human activity. Both Smith and Archer posit the existence of distinct domains of relatively autonomous social activity, each springing from a different aspect of human capacities. However, they do not provide a specification of what those domains might be. In order to make such an attempt, we need to consider further the embodied engagement of humans with the natural world and with each other.

Imagination and Reflexivity

One central argument of social philosophers has been that what distinguishes human beings from other animals is the capacity for imagination. Emerging from the existence of consciousness, building on the capacity for memory and enhanced by the ability to use language for not just communication but for conceptualisation, comes the capacity to imagine alternative states. As Karl Marx famously noted, the elaborate constructions that bees create put many a human architect to shame. 'But what distinguishes the worst architect from the best of bees is this,' he went on, 'that the architect raises his structure in imagination before he erects it in reality. At the end of every labour process, we get a result that already existed in the imagination of the labourer at its commencement' (Marx, 1976: 284). Henri Bergson, building on the insights of evolutionary theory, argued that there was a key distinction to be made between instinct and intelligence. Instinct is a reaction to situations, characteristic of animals, in which knowledge is tightly bound to activity. Two factors shape the evolution away from instinct in humans. One is embodied mobility, which puts humans in a variety of situations, the unfamiliarity of which challenges any instinctive response. The second is language, which means that such a variety of responses can be conceptualised. However, it is important that while the intelligence that is developed is distinctive, with its primary characteristic being thought as opposed to the activity of instinct, 'all concrete instinct is mingled with intelligence, as all real intelligence is penetrated by instinct' (Bergson, 1960: 143). However, intelligence possesses the key advantage of being mobile, while instinctive knowledge, although deeper and richer, remains tightly bound to its object. The former 'is characterized by the unlimited power of decomposing according to any law and of recomposing into any system' (Bergson, 1960: 165).Thus, when looking at the movement of an arm, intelligence, in the form of analytical science, breaks it down into a series of discrete points that can be mapped in space. However, no matter how sophisticated the measurement and how close together the points, this can never capture the movement itself. For this reason, argues Bergson, 'The intellect is characterized by a natural inability to comprehend life' (Bergson, 1960: 174), a true comprehension of movement and thus of evolution rested on intuition, a lived sympathy with the flow of consciousness. 'By intuition', says Bergson, 'I mean instinct that has become disinterested, self-conscious, capable of reflecting upon its object and of enlarging it indefinitely' (Bergson, 1960: 186). We see here the importance of reflection in the constitution of the person, something that Archer has stressed as the key defining characteristic of personhood.

The capacity for both imagination and abstraction gives rise to the search for meaning and the importance of belief. Belief is often associated with the key institution of religion, but it is, argues the theologian Graham Ward (2014), primordial, based on our embodied engagement with each other and the world. Drawing on both neuroscience and literature, he argues that belief is anterior to knowledge and, indeed, to faith. Although the work of a theologian, this is not a theological argument. Rather an inbuilt orientation to believe provides the capacity for religious faith, but also for other forms of belief. He relates this capacity for belief to intuition as an affective capacity associated with the right hemisphere of the brain, that part associated with feelings. He contrasts it to the emphasis in modernity on the left hemisphere activity associated with analysis and instrumental reasoning, with the activities Bergson characterised as intelligence. Belief is therefore linked to religion, but also to more. 'Religious faith', argues Ward (2014: 219), 'is therefore a specific orientation of the more primordial disposition to believe. It is not a different type of believing. It is the same disposition framed by and exercised within specific religious practices.' The same capacity for belief can also be found, he argues, in the exercise of imagination to produce works of art. '[P]oetic faith', he suggests, 'at the heart of imagination and making belief believable, inhabits the very possibility of apprehending the irreducibility of the real' (Ward, 2014: 157). Poetry is seen as a key means of making sense of the human condition in other thinkers. The eighteenth-century Scottish writer Adam Ferguson, for example, thought that '[t]he literary and liberal arts took their rise from the understanding, the fancy, and the heart. They are mere exercises of the mind in search of its peculiar pleasures and occupations; and are promoted by circumstances that suffer the mind to enjoy itself' (Ferguson, 1767:164). He noted in particular the prevalence of poetry in early attempts to seek meaning, noting that what he termed 'rude' civilisations 'delight in versification, either because the cadence of numbers is natural to the language of sentiment, or because, not having the advantage of writing,

they are obliged to bring the ear in aid of the memory, in order to facilitate the repetition, and insure the preservation of their works' (Ferguson, 1767: 165). Ferguson's observation is confirmed by the analyst
of orality Walter Ong (1982: 9) who notes 'human beings in primary
oral cultures, those untouched by writing in any form, learn a great
deal and possess and practice great wisdom, but they do not "study"'.
The rhythm that aided memory in the reproduction of poetic works was
greatly aided by the accompaniment of music. Noting the discovery of
bone flutes in both Slovenia and Germany that date from the Paleolithic
era, Steven Johnson observes that 'aeons before early humans started
to imagine writing or agriculture, they were crafting tools for making
music' (Johnson, 2016: 62). What this suggests is that the capacity for
seeking meaning in the world, whether that be in supernatural causes
or in making representations, is an important foundation out of which
institutions might emerge.

The combination of the capacity to make abstract conceptualisations
of experience, coupled with the expressive and communicative capacities
of language production, can be allied with the observation made above
about the slow growth to maturity of human beings. This necessitates an
extended period of care that can then be coupled with learning. That is,
thanks to conceptualisation, not every experience has to be encountered
directly to be shared and learned from. Over time, such learning fosters
the growth of specialised bodies of knowledge, which are so diverse that
they are beyond the capacity of individual persons. Encouraged by the
switch from orality to writing, a capacity for innovation and inquiry is
fostered. As Ong (1982: 155) suggests, 'these technologies of the word do
not merely store what we know. They style what we know in ways which
made it quite inaccessible and indeed unthinkable in an oral culture.'

The plurality of the human condition, we have noted in Arendt, gives
raise to differences of understanding and perception. Human capacities are unevenly distributed, giving rise to different perceptions of the
shared world. In addition, we know from the work of Kahneman (2012)
on heuristics that human beings are subject to a range of biases that
cause them, for example, to assimilate new findings to existing mental
models, models that might then not account for the full diversity of the
world. Drawing in particular on the experience of the ancient Greeks,
Arendt conceptualised the realm of politics as expressing the free play
of ideas, out of which contestation emerged understanding of the social reality that human actors had constructed. The free play of politics
was an ideal that in classical Greece was available only to a few and
which depended on the subordination of others. Violence as a means
of settling differences was an inferior means of operation. 'In Greek
self-understanding', she observes, 'to force people by violence, to command rather than persuade, were prepolitical ways to deal with people
characteristic of life outside the polis, of home and family life, where the

household head ruled with uncontested, despotic powers, or of life in the barbarian empires of Asia, whose despotism was frequently likened to the organization of the household' (Arendt, 1958: 26). While Boltanski and Thevenot (2006: 37) saw violence as an illegitimate means of settling disputes, had they consulted the works of Adam Ferguson as well as Adam Smith in their analysis of philosophical writers, they would have found a more positive estimation of violence as instantiated in military form. Ferguson, drawing on his own military service as a military chaplain with the Black Watch, argued that, '[t]he soldier, we are told, has his point of honour, and a fashion of thinking, which he wears with his sword. This point of honour, in free and uncorrupted states, is a zeal for the public; and war to them is an operation of passions, not the mere pursuit of a calling' (Ferguson, 1767: 144). Settling disputes by violence may bring about values inspired by belief however much of those outside the realm of violence might find them distasteful. Such beliefs, that is, need to be included in the range of beliefs that give rise to enduring social arrangements. An alternative to violence, both between persons and between the collectivities that they form, is the law. Here, treaties between states and contracts between persons take the place of debate or physical clash. In turn, the creation of law and its attendant practices can animate a belief in the procedures of the law in their own right.

Humans have, of course, to contend with the need of their bodies to survive, to reproduce and to cope with illness, disease and, ultimately, death. Arendt draws a distinction between labour and work. Many languages, she argues, have two different terms, with those equating to labour often associated with the menial and less valued. Labour she associates with the biological need for survival; its products are those almost immediately consumed. Work, by contrast, she links to the human capacity for innovation and fabrication. The products of work are therefore enduring. The impacts of such endurance go beyond the artefacts that have been produced. According to Arendt

> the things of the world have the function of stabilizing human life, and their objectivity lies in the fact that — in contradiction to the Heraclitean saying that the same man can never enter the same stream — men, their ever-changing nature notwithstanding, can retrieve their sameness, that is, their identity, by being related to the same chair and the same table.
>
> (Arendt, 1958: 137)

Out of the ability to construct artefacts that endure comes, suggests, Arendt, the public realm of the market place, where 'he can show the products of his hand and receive the esteem which is due him' (Arendt, 1958: 160). In his review of Arendt's work, Philip Walsh (2015) suggests that the distinction between labour and work is rather blurred in practice. Too great a focus on production tends to neglect the importance of consumption, especially of intangible experiences and services, which are such a feature of contemporary life.

If the market place, and all the theories about it that followed, emerged from the need to obtain subsistence and the capacity to devise artefacts that would go beyond mere subsistence to become desirable possessions in their own right, then the need to reproduce resulted in a different but no less enduring social structure. We have seen that human reproduction produced beings who needed a long period before they came to maturity, thus suggesting more or less stable support mechanisms. The process of creating such beings also involved a sexual act that generated meanings of its own, such that the desire for erotic satisfaction might exist alongside or ahead of a desire to procreate. Over time, these forms of relationship generated both stable social structures such as families and ideas about the nature of relationships crystallised in the shape of love. The notion of love, with its connotations of affect and desire, can, argues Friedland (2002), be seen at operation across institutions, providing a powerful motivation for commitment to the logic that powers the institution. The ultimate limitation human beings face is their finite existence on earth. The inevitability of death looms over all human endeavours, and the reality of sickness and diseases generates ways of relieving pain and staving off the inevitable. Out of such concerns emerges a specialised domain of medicine, complete with its own beliefs and value statements.

Reflexivity

This brief sketch of some of the embodied capacities of persons that give rise to institutions will be expanded on in subsequent chapters. There the transposibility of capacities such as belief and love across institutional domains will be explored in more detail. However, before that I wish to explore a little further the ideas about agential reflexivity that were introduced in Chapter 1. Archer (2003) sees reflexivity as both the key distinguishing feature of persons, emergent from the capacities that we have been examining, and the mediating factor between structure and agency. It shapes, she argues, the ways in which persons interact with social structures. Because of their need for familiar others with which to complete their reflections on their life projects, conversational reflexives will eschew opportunities to move from taken-for-granted contexts. By contrast, autonomous reflexives are more like the rational actors beloved by conventional economics, weighing up options and prepared to adjust structures to achieve their purposes. Meta-reflexives, in turn, are critical of broader social structures. Persons, Archer suggests, combine these forms of reflection, generated by their preferred form of internal conversation but exhibit dominant tendencies. This is, then a stress on the capacities of persons as subjects, able to form and evaluate their own projects and take action (or abstain from it) accordingly. Her approach, argues Walsh (2015), has considerable advantages over those that see, notably in Giddens, reflexivity as a set of social practices rather than as a property of individuals. So, reflexivity in modern life 'consists in the fact that social practices are constantly examined and reformed in the light of incoming information about those very practices' (Giddens, 1990: 38). For Giddens, then, reflexivity 'of course includes reflection upon the nature of reflection itself' (Giddens, 1990: 38). While such formulations do not address different capacities and modes of reflexivity, they do raise questions about Archer's formulations. In particular, it would seem that reflexivity for both conversational and autonomous reflexives is about reflection on courses of action to achieve ultimate goals, rather than reflection on the process of reflection itself, which is reserved for meta-reflexives. In their investigation of US university students, Porpora and Shumar prefer to investigate communicative and autonomous forms of meta-reflexivity, giving rise to four styles of individual reflection: un-reflexive, communicative, autonomous, and fully reflexive. They suggest that 'whereas Archer suggests that autonomous reflection is indicative of success in terms of mobility, our data suggests that autonomous reflection may be more basic and an ability to reflect communicatively a more developed skill' (Porpora and Shumar, 2010: 217).

Walsh further suggests that Archer's formulations are too orientated towards action, so missing out on thought that has no direct purpose. This 'deliberative bias', he argues, means that Archer does not recognise that 'many mental activities are reflexive but not deliberative, and many others are reflexive but seem often to act as barriers to acting' (Walsh, 2015: 74). This is perhaps a little unfair, given that Archer's overall project, which has to be traced through her entire series of books starting in 1995, is with the relationship of agency and structure. It does mean, however, that there could be a danger in not recognising broader categories of thought, not just those oriented to action. A more serious criticism, perhaps, is that in considering the way in which agential re-flexivity mediates the engagement with social structures she tends to downplay the extent to which such reflexivity is itself shaped by social structures (Mutch, 2004). In her small-scale qualitative study of a group of university students, she places most of her emphasis on the family conditions her subjects were born into and developed within for the form of reflexivity. The formation of her meta-reflexives, for example, 'stems directly from the particularities of their relational experiences in the family' (Archer, 2012: 207). This she links to broader changes in family life: 'Given the increasing rates of divorce, separation and re-partnering together with relatively novel arrangements such as living apart but together', she argued, more independent thinkers would be likely to be formed (Archer, 2012: 202). It is surprising that a sociologist of education should pay very little attention to the impact of forms of schooling, arguing that '[e]ven the traditional loci of socialization, the home and the school, are better viewed as introduction bureaux rather than as induction agencies' (Archer, 2012: 106). This is linked to a desire to downplay habitual forms of acting, something we will return to. What it does suggest, as Porpora and Shumar (2010) note, is a downplaying of the shaping of modes of reflexivity not by language alone but by differential access to different modes of linguistic performance.

One thinker who offers some ways of thinking about this is Basil Bernstein (although this suggestion is rejected by Archer). Bernstein was a sociologist of education who was concerned to investigate differential educational performance linked to social class. In a series of often difficult works, he suggested that the nature of the school curriculum, expressed in terms of control and classification, would have a powerful impact on modes of thought (Bernstein, 1977, 1990). Control related to the pedagogic process, for example, the degree to which it was teacher or learner centred. Classification referred to the content of what was taught, for example, with strong boundaries between different disciplines or holistic integrated problem solving. Differences in the combination of the two led to outcomes expressed as the acquisition of the rules of recognition and realisation.

Recognition rules relate to the ability of actors to recognise the context in which performances are to be produced. Some actors may lack the ability to recognise that the context exists and is different from other contexts. For example, Daniels (1995) looked at the production of Art and Maths statements across a number of schools with different classification and framing rules (that is, some made a strong distinction between subjects, others did not; some exercised strong control over what was to be learned when others were weaker). Some pupils could not recognise that the different subjects required a different sort of performance. Others could recognise that something different was required but lacked the means to produce a competent performance. In these terms, they lacked knowledge of the realisation rules. Other pupils could both recognise the nature of the context and produce the appropriate performance. The nature of the pedagogic process seemed to have an influence over the possession of realisation rules, but recognition rules seemed to come from outside the classroom. Similarly, Morais, Foninhas and Neves (1992) found that for those pupils who could recognise different contexts, changes in pedagogic practice could make a difference, but the possession of recognition rules was strongly related to class and race (with a weaker relation to gender).

Looking at Bernstein's work suggests ways in which reflexivity might be shaped, so that some capacities might be better developed by some experiences rather than others. Archer tends to neglect such approaches, with her focus being on broader changes in society, changes that, she argues, bring to bear the situational logic of opportunity, given the range of contending ideas and practices that persons are faced with. Although his criticism is perhaps a little unfair (because Archer does contrast the 1950s as the locus of traditional community studies with the present), there is some force to Walsh's (2015: 73) observation of Archer's 'relative lack of engagement with historical societies'. Accordingly, as something of a bridge to the next section in which we look at some of the problems of historical work in the context of practices, I want to look at reflexivity as indicated by some eighteenth-century diaries. As well as revealing some of the problems with historical evidence, these suggest the shaping of reflexivity by particular institutional logics, in this case by that embedded in a particular religious form. This serves as an illustration of not only how reflexivity enables persons to assess their relationship to structures, but also how that reflexivity is both shaped by broader logics and sustains those logics.

Diaries and Reflection

The discussion of reflexivity that follows is based on diaries, both published and unpublished, of Scots in the eighteenth century. There are, of course, limitations on diaries as a source, both in themselves and in their survival. Those that survive were often those that were designed for some form of publication. That publication in this case was determined by their spiritual content. The presbyterian minister Thomas Boston, for example, whose massive combined memoirs and diaries were published in 1766 (he died in 1732), noted in his preface that he had begun keeping a diary when he was 20, 'when, without a prompter, so far as I know, I began collecting of these passages, for my own soul's benefit: and they, being carried on, have often since that time been of use to me. For which cause I recommend the like practice to you'. He hoped, he continued, 'That my life may be more fully known unto my posterity, for their humiliation on the one hand, and thankfulness on the other, upon my account' (Morrison, 1899: 1, 5). Other diaries, however, were never intended for publication. The remarkable diary of Provost George Drummond of Edinburgh, for example, which contained both his reflections and those of his companion 'R.B.', contains the injunction that 'The present generation are not to see either her book or mine while we are on earth' and has never been published.[1] A similarly unpublished volume by the Scottish-born but London-based slater Samuel Kevan starts with an introductory note, added in 1829 to a diary that had been kept since 1788, that 'Down to my old age I still continue something of the kind – I have found it useful to myself for Humiliation, for Gratitude & thankfulness.'[2]

A number of features suggest themselves about these diary writers and others who could be cited. One is the range of occupations covered, from the minister Thomas Boston, to the public official and politician George Drummond and the slater Samuel Kevan. While the first two occupations had education as a qualification for entry (especially the church, which aspired to all-graduate entry), the facility with words of Samuel Kevan, from a working-class background, suggests the importance of basic education. The relative high levels of literacy in Scotland at that time, thanks to a relatively widespread network of elementary schools, developed the capacity to write (Smout, 1982). The form that writing took was shaped by practice in the church, which featured extensive record keeping of a form that is directly mimicked in Kevan's diary, with its marginal notes acting as an index of contents (Mutch, 2016). Kevan also gives us an insight into the labour involved in the practice of keeping a diary. In February 1799, for example, he records 'Growing dark I intended to write this but missed my Pen and could not see to make another – which rather ruffled me'.[3] In January 1800, he had considered renewing his covenant, but the house was too cold. George Drummond not only recorded his own reflections but transcribed those of R.B. as well. In July 1736, 'I caused her write the connection and the citations in a loose paper which is all that her bodily weakness will allow her to do'.[4] Diary keeping, that is, was an effortful accomplishment. It was a key religious practice by which adherents confirmed their spiritual attachments in writing. This was a continuous process that involved a constant watchfulness. In this, it was shaped by religious injunctions to self-examination.

In Scottish Presbyterianism, this was particularly the case when taking communion. Books were published offering guides to self-examination, and diaries were one technology to support this process. Diary keepers agonised over their suitability for taking communion. Having provided an extensive list of rules for self-examination in his diary, the Rev Thomas Love was still in doubt about his suitability to take communion. In 1775, he recorded

> With shame and difficulty, I came out of the church without going to the table: for I had felt myself inwardly touched at the time of the first table-service; and the minister had invited all who were abstracted from time, and from time's things. I came home. There I fell into carnal conversation – with regret, however, and not without saying some words boldly for the Lord. then retired; and there, while meditating on the fourth commandment, I felt the Lord's presence. I could not refrain from returning to the church, and applying to my grandfather for a token, who procured me one from the minister. I went to the table; and there I felt my soul go out in sweet willing consent, giving myself to the Lord, soul and body; and taking him, and triumphing and rejoicing in him.
>
> (Love, 1857: 65)

There is a sense of desire in some of these entries that is most striking in Drummond's diary. Here, we have two complementary entries. The first is from Drummond, who records in December 1736 that 'I sat 2 hours with her without being able to prevail with her to unbosom herself to me. I saw she was in a snare, but could not prevail with her to tell me what ailed her. Her distress adds to mine.' Meanwhile, R.B. recorded for the same date 'before G D came from the church, The enemy terrified me into a Resolution not to open my lips to him, of any thing that had been passing in my soul today, persuading me, if I did it, The Lord would confound me and sink me to hell'[5] These struggles over spiritual fitness provide the template for the type of reflection engaged in. As Mathew Kadane observes of the diaries of the devout English Nonconformist clothier Joseph Ryder, 'the practical consequence of the hermeneutics that justified spiritual diary keeping is that details typically didn't find written expression when God, the Devil, or salvational meaning couldn't be found to reside in them' (Kadane, 2013: 17). The structures of reflection were shaped by these ultimate concerns with the fate of the soul. Two particular themes structured much of the reflection in these diaries: providence and covenanting.

Much of the debate stimulated by Max Weber's Protestant Ethic thesis has centred on the protestant doctrine of predestination. Here, salvation is through the attainment of grace, not good works, and diaries record the struggle of the faithful to find the saving marks of grace in their own life and conduct. 'A believer should be an exact observer of the state of grace in his soul,' recorded the soldier Lieutenant Colonel Blackader in 1701 'whether it be making progress or decaying: He should be a careful observer of providences, and, like the bee, draw honey out of every dispensation' (Crichton, 1824: 159). But predestination was a difficult theological doctrine, even for adepts and, Kadane notes, a belief in divine providence, signs of an active interventionist God in the affairs of the faithful, was more likely to structure diaries. Worldly success was attributed to the working of providence: as Blackader recorded in 1705, 'Taking great pleasure in hearing a sermon on the Providence of God directing and disclosing all things. This is a comfortable doctrine to me, who am as great an instance of the care and kind conduct of Providence as any in the world' (Crichton, 1824: 235). This focus on providence often prompts what seems to be strange structuring of reflections, where any event is bent to the template of divine providence. So an entry in Boston's diary for 1717, when he was agonising about revealing controversial theological commitments to a wider church audience, notes 'O the wisdom and goodness that appeared in it, and in timing it and my wife's indisposition, and in making the rain to come on that day, whereby our purpose was broken! This was a most signal piece of the conduct of Providence towards me, of a most diffusive usefulness in point of practice, however it has been improved' (Morrison, 1899: 319).

The diaries are also frequently structured by commitment to a covenant, that is, a form of contract with God. Boston notes in 1699 'minding to renew the covenant with God, and subscribe it with my hand, I drew it up in writing' (Morrison, 1899: 83). The examples given in his book of signed covenants, both from him and his wife, reinforce the importance of writing as an expression of faith, a practice animated by belief in a supreme value that is immanent in the writing itself. His covenant is renewed at frequent intervals, as are those of several of the other diarists. So, for example, Samuel Kevan formally recorded and signed the renewal of his covenant in 1801.[6] Such actions were accompanied by a characteristic bout of self-examination at the end of each calendar year. In December 1735, for example, the schoolmaster of Glenmuick recorded

> This year being now at an end, I desire to acknowledge the Goodness of God towards me & mine with thankfulness, for he has not only spared our lives (which is a great mercy) but has Clothed us with health, strength, peace, and food & Raiment, and continued the Means of Knowledge and Grace with us; but alas, I must own, and O that I were suitable affected with it, that I have taken little heed to my heart and ways seldom or never minding the great end of my being, nor the early vows that I came under to Glorious God, I have lived in the neglect of many known &commanded dutys, oyrs I have gone carelessly & coldly about, not panting after Communion with Godin ym, nor being grieved at the tidings of his gracious fall from me. The Good Lord pardon me for Christs sake, & enable me to lay myself more & more out (if it be well to spare me) for thy names Glory, not only in mending my own Souls concerns, but for the Good of others in the Station I am placed & make my labours more & more Successful. Notwithstanding of my manifold failings & sinful departing from God, for wch I desire to be deeplie humbled, I adhere to the Covenant formerly entered into between God and my own Soul, and make a surrender of myself & all that I am & have to the Obedience & service of the Father Son and Holy Ghost. Lord enable me to depend continually upon thee for guidance, direction, through bearing &acceptance, and pour down thy blessing upon me and upon thy handmaiden & the Children.[7]

A brief outline of the practices of reflection recorded in the diaries of the religiously faithful in eighteenth century Scotland suggests the ways in which their reflections were shaped by the broader logic of the religion in which they were embedded. This logic selected both the content of the diaries and the categories that were used to shape reflection. To bring the story more up to date, Kwon's (2004) examination of responses to new forms of contract in the German and U.S. automotive industries points to the impact of differential conceptions of 'fairness' on the reflexivity of actors. Although faced with the same array of associations through which to articulate concerns about the terms that were being imposed by customers on suppliers, the response was different in each setting. In the USA, perceived unfair practices were deplored but accepted as the standard way of doing business. 'Many American suppliers', records Kwon, 'complain of the extreme pressure of price cuts, but they do not think that it is unfair. Although they feel that customers' opportunistic behavior is distasteful, many suppliers believe it is a customer's job to press prices down, while it is a supplier's job to try to endure' (Kwon, 2004: 72). By contrast, German suppliers used the forums available to them to press for rules to establish shared norms of fairness, drawing, perhaps, on a long tradition of codification of rules as we saw in Biernacki's (1995) account of nineteenth century textile workplaces. This was, Kwon argues, an active process, just as diary writing was for the religious Scots. Keeping a diary was more than a passive record; rather it was part of an active writing into faith. The example of diary writing suggests the value of historical material, but also some of the challenges in its use to explore the combination of substance and practice that constitutes institutional logics. Accordingly, the next section considers some aspects of historical investigations and evidence.

Looking for Practices in History

As we saw in our brief examination of diaries, examining practices in historical context poses distinct challenges. The nature of those challenges is exemplified by looking at how contemporary social scientists investigate practices (Decker et al., 2018). There is a stream of research that explores routines in organisations (Feldman, 2000; Feldman and Pentland, 2003; Pentland and Feldman, 2005). With the starting point that the performance of routines often departs from how they are laid down in procedure manuals, modes of investigation that prioritise qualitative, in-depth exploration of situated practices are employed. Some form of observation is often preferred, given that interviews are often imperfect means of teasing out the specificities of practices. Much performance is tacit in nature, meaning that participants might not be aware of the nuances that an observer might tease out. All these considerations pose challenges for the historical reconstruction of practices, given that access to observe is impossible. The closest, perhaps, that historians have come is in employing oral historical methods (Tosh, 2000: 193–210). Although they are subject to all the problems of faulty recall and forgetfulness that plague all retrospective accounts, oral history has proved to be of particular value in reconstructing work practices. It is often the very mundane practices that are best recalled, especially when they have been ingrained as part of daily activities. Sometimes this can be the only means of recovering practices that have not made it into the formal historical record. In the early twentieth century, for example, farm servants in the north of Lancashire were hired on an annual basis at hiring fairs.

These can be reconstructed from newspaper accounts, but such accounts do not reveal the 'runaway' hirings, at which those immediately dissatisfied with the bargain they had struck, especially if what had been offered did not live up to the initial promise, could legitimately seek a new place (Mutch, 1991). However, such accounts are dependent on living informants, which places severe limitations on historical reach. It might seem, then, that historical practices are beyond our reach.

There are, however, concerns about the exploration of routines in organisation studies that suggest that historical work still has much to offer. The resource intensiveness of observational techniques can mean that only relatively small sweeps of time can be explored. Sometimes the episodic nature of such inquiries raises doubts about whether the 'routine' element of practices is being missed. This is compounded by the focus on the unique nature of specific performances. As Sennett argues in his critique of Erving Goffman's sensitive observation of how roles are performed, '[e]ach of the "scenes" in is his purview is a fixed situation. How the scene came into being, how those who play roles in it change the scene by their acts, or, indeed, how each scene may appear or disappear because of larger historical forces at work in the society — to these questions Goffman is indifferent' (Sennett, 2002: 35–36). In addition, the observer, no matter how careful and sensitive, has access to only one aspect of a routine that by its nature involves a network of other actors and their material props. Informants, that is, may have only partial access to the social world that they inhabit. The reasons they give for particular aspects of that social world may be plausible but misleading. Comparative lawyers have debated the question of understanding legal systems from the outside. On one account, such attempts are doomed to failure, as the formal rules and practices evident to outsiders hide the informal understandings only available to insiders. However, against this, James Whitman (2013) has traced the history of dignitary law in the German legal system, contrasting it with U.S. equivalents. The focus on human dignity in German provisions has no equivalence in the USA, he notes. German jurists, when asked about the roots of anti-hate speech laws, point to the legacy of Fascism. However, Whitman, exploring the historical evolution of laws protecting human dignity in the German system, points to their origins in the aristocratic duelling culture of the nineteenth century. 'Interviewing local informants', he concludes 'is a very poor way of fully understanding what is going on in European dignitary law. The participants themselves do not understand where their system came from, nor why it takes the form it takes' (Whitman, 2013: 334).

The first quarter of the twentieth century saw something of a 'historical turn' in management and organisation studies. Renewed attention to the need to found organisational analysis on historical investigation was marked in the emergence, for example, of a significant stream at the annual colloquium of the European Group of Organization Studies (EGOS) and the publication of important books and articles advocating historical forms of analysis (Bucheli and Wadhwani, 2014; Mussachio Adoriso and Mutch, 2013; Rowlinson, Hassard and Decker, 2013). Much of this work has been concerned with conceptual discussion, especially to do with understanding the methods of the historian. In the rather sardonic observation of Daniel Raffa and Philip Scranton, '[o]ne might say that there is a lot of hortatory theory but not much practice yet' (Raff and Scranton, 2016: 4). That might seem a touch unfair, although one can note that the historical examples used by Thornton, Occasio and Lounsbury (2012: 111–112), such as the example of the Primitive Baptist roots of J.C. Penney's approach to organising, are rather thin illustrations rather than fully explored cases (Decker et al., 2018: 619). One of the problems is that the interlocutor for much of the discussion is a particular version of business history. The 'other' here is the commissioned company history, whose themes are often dictated by the need to celebrate success rather than provide balance, whose methods are confined to the digging up of 'facts' and that often present a founder-centred view of the world in which divisions within organisations are papered over. There is some truth in such observed problems, but also a downplaying of the conceptually founded histories of companies such as Unilever (Wilson, 1968) and ICI (Pettigrew, 1985), as well as efforts to compare and contrast the fortunes of companies in a common market sector, as with the examination of British merchant companies and their evolution by Geoffrey Jones (2000). The problem as perceived by critiques of standard business history is its intellectual reliance on economic history, leading to the neglect of broader cultural influences on business activities (Rowlinson and Procter, 1999). In turn, economic history is often powerfully influenced by trends in economics, with its focus on the construction of models. Thus, the term 'analytic narratives' has been rather colonised by game theory, indicating a very formalistic approach to history and evidence driven by the assumptions of economic theory. This is how the term has been critiqued by Rowlinson, Hassard and Decker (2013), but I will suggest shortly that there is another form of usage emergent from Archer's social theory. However, what such approaches to history lead to is the search for data sets that are amenable to analysis, even if such data sets are, at best, proxies for the lack of direct evidence that often bedevils historic inquiry. Sometimes this evidence is drawn from times when widespread collection of statistical data happens, leading to the anachronistic 'testing' of Weber's Protestant Ethic thesis, which is specifically about the fifteenth and sixteenth century, with data originating in the nineteenth century (Ekelund, Hébert and Tollison, 2006). It is, therefore, understandable that those who are looking to execute a historical turn are suspicious of such approaches.

However, history is much wider than business or economic history (setting aside for a time the fact that some historians in those domains, even if a minority, are open to broader perspectives). Accordingly, in what follows I have been more influenced by the growing body of cultural and social history, bodies of work that have been sensitive to and, sometimes, engaged in a dialogue with, the concerns raised by social theorists. Sewell (2005), for example, whose work we have already noted, engaged with the work of Giddens in order to contextualise it for use in historical investigations. This led him to contest the conceptualisation of structures in Giddens' work and turn his own work to the semiotic nature of practices. As we saw in the introduction, practices themselves convey messages in their action so that meaning is not confined to discursive formations. It is fair to note some gaps in cultural and social history in its turn, notably in the relative lack of consideration of the nature and impact of organisations. In looking at the evolution of public houses as a theatre for social interaction, for example, social historians have been rather deaf to the implications of changes in business strategy that shape those contexts for action (Mutch, 2004). The substitution of managers for tenants in the running of such venues, for example, might change the social dynamics of interactions. However, cultural and social historians can provide us with some help in suggesting how we might surface and explore taken-for-granted practices.

One interesting example of how a historian has risen to the challenge of finding evidence to shed light on historical practices is that supplied by the historian of English localities, Keith Snell (2006). He was interested in exploring the changing nature of identification with place, in particular, changes brought about by increased social and geographical mobility to the attachment to place in English rural life. In order to explore this, he hit upon an unusual source: memorial inscriptions on gravestones. Reasoning that carving letters on gravestones was an expensive operation and one involving limited space, he argued that this necessitated a selection process. The choice of words to describe the deceased could therefore give an indication of changing patterns of attachment to place. Inscriptions that gave a place of residence, or used phrases like 'of this parish', would seem to indicate a degree of attachment, a public statement that being from a place was worthy of commemoration. Using a sample of over 16,000 gravestones in 87 burial grounds, he was able to show that this attachment persisted until the turn of the twentieth century, when mentions of place began to be replaced by reference to more personal qualities, such as the relation to other family members. As he notes, memorial inscriptions provide evidence that 'People were once described, given an identity, and their behaviour even accounted for, by their place and their occupation in it, however parochial that might be' (Snell, 2006: 492). This imaginative use of what otherwise would seem mundane and taken-for-granted, of interest only to genealogists, indicates that historical sources can come in a range of forms. Often, for the historian, it is the mundane document, that which was produced as a by-product of operations, that is of particular value. Of course, much depends here on accidental survivals. In the eighteenth-century Church of Scotland, there was a practice of visitations. Here a committee would be formed to visit a parish to pose a series of questions to the minister, other church officials and heads of household. A complementary and integral part of this practice was the 'revision' of parish records. This involved the reading of parish registers, both of decisions made and monies spent, in order to produce a report. Often, we only have the summary of such inspections and the recommendations that ensued. On many occasions, it would appear that the results were given in verbal feedback that was not minuted, and so was lost to us. But in one case, a chance survival gives us considerable insight into not just the operation of the practice but also the wider logic that it embodied. Bound into the session register of Dailly in the presbytery of Ayr is a set of working notes, written in small script on scraps of paper. These clearly represent the thinking of those charged with revising session registers. The writer of the notes picked up 43 separate items of concern, all carefully cross-referenced to the pages of the register. He found 14 cases where the sederunt (that is, the record of attendance) had not been recorded and a further three where the session did not either open or close with prayer. In other words, these were matters of very detailed recording, as opposed to matters of principle, and one gets the impression of a very pernickety reviser. At one point, for example, it was observed that two elders were ordained without an edict being moved, but when one turns to the minutes, it is found that the edict had been served and recorded previously. The same obtains when four examples where communion had been intimated but it was not recorded that it had been celebrated were picked up. In a further eight cases, the reviser was concerned that sentences of discipline being satisfied were recorded without a session being constituted, although it would appear that this was often simply a record of the completion of a previously recorded decision. This level of attention to detail suggests something of what lay behind the bland notes about verbal representations. The revision of records, that is, could be a very thorough going process that must have played a part in engendering a particular style of record keeping, almost obsessive in its attention to detail (Mutch, 2015: 72).

The accidental survival of mundane documents that can throw light on broader logics also indicates some of the limitations of historical evidence. Not only are mundane documents more likely to be discarded when records are considered for retention, but the survival of records is patterned by social factors. Records pertaining to legal requirements or to property disputes are more likely to survive than insights into everyday domestic life. As one descends the social scale, so records become sparser. That is a factor behind the approach of many historians to be guided by the nature of the material that has survived and so to favour the illustrative example over the generalisable. So, as one observer of the work of the historian Keith Thomas observes, 'According to strict and even censorious critical criteria, these materials cannot stand as proof of any argument, since the reader is in the hands of the author and of what he has chosen to serve up as, strictly speaking, illustrations of his own contentions, it being, in principle, always possible to build up a different picture with the aid of different examples' (cited in Raff, 2013: 460). That awareness of the limitations of sources means that historians are, often rightly, suspicious of the attempts, often associated with economic historians, to build models based on proxy measures. Such measures may make models work, but at the cost of departing from real-world practices. However, the response from some historians is to stress the unique and ungeneralisable nature of the events they study. As one historian who engages in comparative analysis of European religious forms argues '[h]istory indeed is good at confounding and confusing labellers' (MacCulloch, 2004: 319). This slides into that suspicion of theory that characterises much of the work of mainstream historians, much to the exasperation of those who think that expounding assumptions is important. In the words of the medievalist Chris Wickham (2011: 221),

> Historians tend to avoid theorising; it is one of the most characteristic cultural features of the discipline, in fact. But it is also one of its major weak points, for the attachment of historians to the empiricist-expository mode only-too-often hides their theoretical presuppositions, not only from others, but from the writers themselves.

However, this is not true of all historians. Snell, for example, characterises himself as 'a social-science historian influenced by social history 'from below', whose main concern is with the quality of life and structures of human welfare. I have no problems in believing that the past was 'real', that much of that reality can be discerned and outlined and that certain themes, emphases, patterns, experiences, and consistent personal accounts emerge repeatedly from the documentary and quantitative evidence' (Snell, 2006: 26). However, as with many historians, he wears his theory lightly, weaving it into the exposition of his themes. As Sennet puts it, 'a dialectical inquiry means the argument is complete only when the book has come to an end. You cannot state "the theory" all at once and then lay it like a map over the historical terrain' (Sennett, 2002: 6). What you can do, however, is to use theoretical considerations to match out the terrain to be investigated and then, within the acknowledged limitations of the sources, engage in a systematic exploration of practices. So Snell, for example, examines 18,000 marriages from published registers to trace patterns of marriages within and across parish boundaries. 'I have picked', he informs us, 'clusters of parishes in disparate English regions, to check for national homogeneity, or to allow any possible regional patterns to emerge. Rural parishes rather than larger market towns were chosen so as to dilute earlier historiographical findings, and to give this study a rural coherence which it would lack if a fuller range of parishes across the whole rural-urban spectrum was used' (Snell, 2006: 168). Data analysis enables the discernment of patterns which can then be explored further using more qualitative sources.

Historians are frequently suspicious of comparative work, immersed as they often are in the contingencies of particular historical conjunctures. This is especially the case when comparative work, as in some economic history informed by econometrics, is associated with a positivist search for invariant laws (Steinmetz, 2014). As we have seen in our discussion of critical realism, while the search may be for mechanisms, such as institutional logics, these are manifest in the outcomes they produce. Mechanisms such as these, better described as tendencies rather than laws in open systems, may only be triggered in specific contexts or in conjunction with other mechanisms. Accordingly, formulating logics at a level of abstraction as essayed in the next chapter provides one basis for comparative work. However, there is another sense in which comparison is of value and that is in making the taken-for-granted strange. As the historian of classical antiquity, Paul Veyne, observes, 'if in order to study a civilization, we limit ourselves to reading what it says itself — that is, to reading sources relating to this one civilization — we will make it more difficult to wonder at what, in this civilization, was taken for granted' (Veyne, 1984: 7). We have already noted the difficulty of carrying out comparative work on legal systems, where the formal content of rules may have very different meaning in different legal systems. However, Lawrence Rosen argues that 'by immersing ourselves in others' laws we make our own systems appear just odd enough to grasp features we may otherwise have taken for granted' (Rosen, 2013: 508).

As an illustration of the value of comparing practices based on systematic sampling, an analysis of parish records in Scotland and England for the eighteenth century indicates an interesting variance in financial performance. In a contrast between two administrative units of the church, chosen because of their predominantly rural character, there was a sharp difference between the financial balances recorded in each country. In the Scottish example, of 347 annual balances examined, only 3 per cent were negative. In stark contrast, of 672 English balances recorded, 53.27 per cent were negative. (Further investigation of the Scottish records, with a total of 1,052 balances examined, confirmed the initial finding, with only 38, or 4.3 per cent being negative. A further 26 recorded a zero balance, 3 per cent of the total. Unfortunately, similar work on a larger sample has not been carried out for England, but the literature supports the broad contrast between the two countries). This detailed account of governance practices at the local level in the two countries does seem to suggest a contrast between two different logics of accountability: a systemic logic of accountability in Scotland and a personal logic of accountability in England. In Scotland, a national system of discipline was laid down, generating broad uniformity of practice. This practice was monitored by an active system of inspection, which involved checks and balances at all levels. In particular, these checks and balances operated by the definition of roles and the practice of detailed record keeping. These practices in their turn were made possible by the organisational framework, which provided for stability and durability of personnel. Accountability here relied not in trust in the personal characteristics of those entrusted with responsibility, but on the operation of a set of procedures whose operation could be traced through a detailed set of transactions, both written and numerical. By contrast, in England, no such uniformity obtained. The overwhelming feature was custom. Such guidance as was available at national level was the product of private enterprise, summarising the policies that emerged from such cases as made it to law. Accountability was a matter of personal responsibility, with considerable vagueness in the recording of transactions and much variability arising from personal competence and inclination. The inspection of such records was a matter for a small local elite, relatively undisturbed by either the incumbent or the broader processes of church discipline, which were broadly ineffective (Mutch, 2013).

Of course, there are limitations to the possibility of such comparative work. Indeed, the contrast between Scotland and England essayed above also reveals the richness and comparative completeness of the records that have been preserved in Scotland. The sheer survival of material in Scotland indicates something about the broader systems that produced and preserved them, just as the paucity of record survival in England reflects the very absence of system. However, such disparities mean that representative material is often difficult to obtain, leading historians to rely on vivid illustrations. It also means that detailed accounts of practices are often missing from the historical account. As Foucault observed

> it seems to me that the history of the pastorate has never really been undertaken. The history of ecclesiastical institutions has been written. The history of religious doctrines, beliefs, and representations has been written. There have also been attempts to produce the history of real religious practices, namely, when people confessed, took communion, and so on. But it seems to me that the history of the techniques employed, of the reflections on these pastoral techniques, of their development, application, and successive refinements, the history of the different types of analysis and knowledge linked to the exercise of pastoral power, has never really been undertaken.
>
> (Foucault, 2009: 150)

Foucault, of course, was not a historian in the sense of one who investigated archival sources. Indeed, he was rather disparaging about historians, however much he relied on their work (Mutch, 2017). He was reliant on secondary works for his exploration of social practice. The specific practice for his focus in his initial discussion of pastoral power was the confessional within the Roman Catholic church (Foucault, 2009: 171–195). This focus reveals some problems, for it was heavily dependent on the work of Lea, an American historian who produced a multivolume treatment in 1896 (Foucault, 2009: 195). Lea was not a dispassionate observer of his topic, although his treatment appears to have been thorough. His reason for exploring the confessional, he tells us in his introduction, was that 'the history of mankind may be vainly searched for another institution which has established a spiritual autocracy such as that of the Latin Church' (Lea, 1896: v). One problem is that reliance on this source led Foucault to neglect other disciplinary practices, such as the visitation. Another is that reliance on sources that seek to 'read off' actual performances from formal statements is problematic. Foucault relies on such formal statements to a large degree, such as the educational manual of the Brothers of the Common Life that forms such an important source in *Discipline and Punish* (Foucault, 1991). If we return to the example of Scottish accounting, the Church of Scotland was characterised by a plethora of programmatic statements. These sought, in particular, to lay down rules for governance at all levels in the church, resulting in the production of two important 'procedure manuals', *Overtures Concerning the Discipline and Method of Proceeding in the Ecclesiastick Judicatories in the Church of Scotland*, written by an anonymous author in 1696 (Anon, 1696) and *Collections and Observations Methodiz'd; Concerning the Worship, Discipline, and Government of the Church of Scotland* authored by the devout elder Walter Steuart of Pardovan in 1709 (Steuart, 1709).These were substantial documents, which sought to lay out in great detail how the church was to be run. However, one would search in vain for a specification of the practices of accounting that led to the detailed balancing observed above. While these practices were certainly in line with the spirit of the procedural guidelines and, beyond them, to the understanding of ecclesiology derived from a particular interpretation of the foundational religious texts, they evolved as a response to the practical needs of putting broader guidance into practice. Accordingly, if we are looking for connections between practices and substance, it is important not to simply read off either substance or practice from formal statements of belief.

Summary

That poses us with something of a problem in what follows, for, as in the case of English religious accounting practices, the substantive historical work has not been carried out. However, the focus on practices that is essayed here may be instructive in pointing to new lines of inquiry. Historical inquiry will always be dependent on the survival of sources and also requires an open mindedness to what might be found in those records that do survive, but the formulation of a conceptual apparatus first can suggest new places to look and, as with Snell, innovative ways of accessing practices. Archer suggests that the need is to create what she terms 'analytical narratives of emergence'. Based on the discussion of emergence and the morphogenetic framework for analysis that we explored in Chapter 2, she argues that

> analytical narratives of emergence can never ever be *grand* precisely because the imperative to narrate derives from recognizing the intervention of contingency and the need to examine its effects on the exercise or suspension of the generative powers in question — since outcomes will vary accordingly but unpredictably. On the other hand, *analytical narratives* are obviously distinct from any version of historical narration tout court, for although social realists in general have no difficulty in accepting the strong likelihood of uniqueness at the level of events, the endorsement of real but unobservable generative mechanisms directs analysis towards the interplay between the real, the actual and the empirical to explain precise outcomes.
>
> (Archer, 1995: 343)

With this watchword in mind, we can proceed to examine both substance and practices in historical context in more detail. This chapter has argued that institutions emerge from the embodied relations of humans with each other and the natural world that they inhabit. History provides a way of examining the enduring nature of the social structures that such relations produce and it is to an outline of such institutions and their associated substances that we turn next.

Notes

1 National Library of Scotland, WB. Dc.1.82 1736–1737, A Diary kept by Provost Drummond of Edinburgh, 26 July 1737.
2 British Library, London, British Library Add MS 42556, Autobiographical Memoir and Diary of Samuel Kevan, I, 15 August 1829.
3 Kevan diary, 17 February 1799.
4 Drummond diary, 31 July 1736.
5 Drummond diary 19 December 1736.
6 Kevan diary, 4 March 1801.
7 National Library of Scotland, Edinburgh, Rule of Glenmuick Adv. Ms.34.7.12, 31 December 1735.

References

Anon. (1696) *Overtures Concerning the Discipline and Method of Proceeding in the Ecclesiastick Judicatories in the Church of Scotland*, Edinburgh: George Mossman.
Archer, M. (1995) *Realist Social Theory: The Morphogenetic Approach*, Cambridge: Cambridge University Press.

Archer, M. (2000) *Being Human: The Problem of Agency*, Cambridge: Cambridge University Press.

Archer, M. (2003) *Structure, Agency and the Internal Conversation*, Cambridge: Cambridge University Press.

Archer, M. (2012) *The Reflexive Imperative in Late Modernity*, Cambridge: Cambridge University Press.

Arendt, H. (1958) *The Human Condition*, Chicago, IL: University of Chicago Press.

Bergson, H. (1960) *Creative Evolution*, London: Macmillan.

Bernstein, B. (1977) *Class Codes and Control Volume 3: Towards a Theory of Educational Transmissions*, London: Routledge & Kegan Paul.

Bernstein, B. (1990) *The Structuring of Pedagogic Discourse*, London: Routledge.

Biernacki, R. (1995) *The Fabrication of Labor: Germany and Britain, 1640–1914*, Berkeley: University of California Press.

Boltanski, L. and Thevenot, L. (2006) *On Justification: Economies of Worth*, Princeton: Princeton University Press.

Bucheli, M. and Wadhwani, D. (2014) *Organizations in Time: History, Theory, Methods*, Oxford: Oxford University Press.

Crichton, A. (1824) *Life and Diary of Lieutenant Colonel J. Blackader*, Edinburgh: H. S. Baynes.

Damasio, A. (2000) *The Feeling of What Happens: Body, Emotion and the Making of Consciousness*, London: Vintage.

Daniels, H. (1995) 'Pedagogic practices, tacit knowledge and discursive discrimination: Bernstein and post-Vygotskyian research', *British Journal of the Sociology of Education*, 16(4), 517–532.

Decker, S., Üsdiken, B., Engwall, L. and Rowlinson, M. (2018) 'Special issue introduction: historical research on institutional change', *Business History*, 60(5), 613–627.

Ekelund, R., Hébert, R. and Tollison, R. (2006) *The Marketplace of Christianity*, Cambridge: MIT Press.

Elder-Vass, D. (2010) *The Causal Power of Social Structures*, Cambridge: Cambridge University Press.

Feldman, M. (2000) 'Organizational routines as a source of continuous change', *Organization Science*, 11(6), 611–629.

Feldman, M. and Pentland, B. (2003) 'Reconceptualizing organizational routines as a source of flexibility and change', *Administrative Science Quarterly*, 48, 94–118.

Ferguson, A. (1767) *An Essay on the History of Civil Society*, Cambridge: Cambridge University Press.

Foucault, M. (1991) *Discipline and Punish: The Birth of the Prison*, London: Penguin.

Foucault, M. (2009) *Security, Territory, Population: Lectures at the Collège de France 1977–1978*, Basingstoke: Palgrave Macmillan.

Friedland, R. (2002) 'Money, sex, and god: the erotic logic of religious nationalism', *Sociological Theory*, 20(3), 381–425.

Friedson, E. (2001) *Professionalism: The Third Logic*, Cambridge: Polity.

Giddens, A. (1990) *The Consequences of Modernity*, Cambridge: Polity.

Johnson, S. (2016) *Wonderland: How Play Made the Modern World*, Basingstoke: Macmillan.

Jones, G. (2000) *Merchants to Multinationals: British Trading Companies in the Nineteenth and Twentieth Centuries*, Oxford: Oxford University Press.

Kadane, M. (2013) *The Watchful Clothier: The Life of an Eighteenth-Century Protestant Capitalist*, New Haven, CT: Yale University Press.

Kahneman, D. (2012) *Thinking, Fast and Slow*, London: Penguin.

Kwon, H. (2004) *Fairness and Division of Labor in Market Societies: A Comparison of the U.S. and German Automotive Industries*, New York: Berghahn.

Lea, H. (1896) *A History of Auricular Confession and Indulgences in the Latin Church*, Philadelphia, PA: Lea Brothers & Co.

Love, J. (1857) *Memorials of the Rev John Love*, D. D., Edited by the Committee Intrusted with the Charge of his Unpublished Papers, Glasgow: Maurice Ogle & Son.

MacCulloch, D. (2004) *Reformation: Europe's House Divided 1490–1700*, London: Penguin.

Marx, K. (1976) [1867] *Capital Vol 1*, Harmondsworth: Penguin.

Morais, A., Fontinhas, F., and Neves, I. (1992) 'Recognition and realisation rules in acquiring school science - the contribution of pedagogy and social background of students', *British Journal of Sociology of Education*, 13(2), 247–270.

Morrison, G. (1899) *Memoirs of the Life, Time and Writings of the Reverend and Learned Thomas Boston*, Edinburgh: Oliphant, Anderson & Ferrier.

Musacchio Adorisio, L. and Mutch, A. (2013) 'In search of historical methods', *Management & Organizational History*, 8(2), 105–110.

Mutch, A. (1991) 'The "farming ladder" in North Lancashire, 1840–1914: myth or reality', *Northern History*, 27, 162–183.

Mutch, A. (2004) 'Constraints on the internal conversation: Margaret Archer and the structural shaping of thought', *Journal for the Theory of Social Behaviour*, 34(4), 429–445.

Mutch, A. (2004) 'Shaping the public house 1850–1950: business strategies, state regulation and social history', *Cultural and Social History*, 1(2), 179–200.

Mutch, A. (2013) '"Shared protestantism" and British identity: contrasting church governance practices in eighteenth-century Scotland and England', *Social History*, 38(4), 456–476.

Mutch, A. (2016) 'Marginal importance: Scottish accountability and English watchfulness', *Church History and Religious Culture*, 96, 155–178.

Mutch, A. (2017) 'Governmentality and the historian: Scotland and the history of Protestant pastoral power' in McKinlay, A. and Pezet, E. (eds.) *Foucault and Managerial Governmentality: Rethinking the Management of Populations, Organizations and Individuals*, Abingdon: Routledge, 2017, 97–114.

O'Mahoney, J. (2012) 'Embracing essentialism: a realist critique of resistance to discursive power', *Organization*, 19(6), 723–741.

Ong, W. (1982) *Orality and Literacy: The Technologizing of the Word*, London: Methuen.

Pentland, B. and Feldman, M. (2005) 'Organizational routines as a unit of analysis', *Industrial and Corporate Change*, 14(5), 793–815.

Pettigrew, A. (1985) *The Awakening Giant: Continuity and Change in ICI*, Oxford: Blackwell.

Porpora, D. and Shumar, W. (2010) 'Self talk and self reflection: a view from the US', in Archer, M. (ed.), *Conversations about Reflexivity*, London: Routledge, 2010, 206–220.

Raff, D. (2013) 'How to do things with time', *Enterprise and Society*, 14(3), 435–466.

Raff, D. and Scranton, P. (2016) *The Emergence of Routines: Entrepreneurship, Organization, and Business History*, Oxford: Oxford University Press.

Rosen, L. (2013) 'Beyond compare', in Legrand, P. and Munday, R. (eds.) *Comparative Legal Studies: Traditions and Transitions*, Cambridge: Cambridge University Press, 2013, 493–510.

Rowlinson, M. and Procter, S. (1999) 'Organizational culture and business history', *Organizational Studies*, 20(3), 369–396.

Rowlinson, M., Hassard, J., and Decker, S. (2014). 'Research strategies for organizational history: A dialogue between historical theory and organization theory'. *Academy of Management Review*, 39(3), 250–274.

Selznick, P. (2008) *A Humanist Science: Values and Ideals in Social Inquiry*, Stanford: Stanford University Press.

Sennett, R. (2002) *The Fall of Public Man*, London: Penguin.

Sewell, W. (2005) *Logics of History: Social Theory and Social Transformation*, Chicago, IL: University of Chicago Press.

Smith, C. (2010) *What is a Person?: Rethinking Humanity, Social Life, and the Moral Good from the Person Up*, Chicago, IL: University of Chicago Press.

Smout, T. (1982) 'Born again at Cambuslang: new evidence on popular religion and literacy in eighteenth-century Scotland', *Past & Present*, 97, 114–127.

Snell, K. (2006) *Parish and Belonging: Community, Identity and Welfare in England and Wales, 1700–1950*, Cambridge: Cambridge University Press.

Steinmetz, G. (2014) 'Comparative history and its critics: a genealogy and a possible solution.' In Duara, P., Murthy, V. and Sartori, A. (eds.) *A Companion to Global Historical Thought*, Oxford: Blackwell, 2014, 412–436.

Steuart, W. (1709) *Collections and Observations Methodised, Concerning the Worship, Discipline and Government of the Church of Scotland*, Edinburgh: Andrew Anderson.

Thornton, P., Occasio, W., and Lounsbury, M. (2012) *The Institutional Logics Perspective: A New Approach to Culture, Structure, and Process*, Oxford: Oxford University Press.

Tosh, J. (2000) *The Pursuit of History*, Harlow: Longman.

Veyne, P. (1984) *Writing History: Essay on Epistemology*, Manchester: Manchester University Press.

Walsh, P. (2015) *Arendt Contra Sociology: Theory, Society and its Science*, London: Ashgate.

Ward, G. (2014) *Unbelievable: Why We Believe and Why We Don't*, London: I. B. Tauris.

Whitman, J. (2013) 'The neo-Romantic turn',in Legrand, P. and Munday, R. (eds.)*Comparative Legal Studies: Traditions and Transitions*, Cambridge: Cambridge University Press, 2013, 312–344.

Wickham, C. (2011) 'The problems of comparison',*Historical Materialism*, 19(1), 221–231.

Wilson, C. (1968) *Unilever 1945–1965: Challenge and Response in the Post-War Industrial Revolution*, London: Cassell.

4 Substance

Introduction

Institutions arise from the embodied relationships between humans and their natural world. They emerge from the multiplicity of human needs and demands running up against the finite limits of human capacities. They are organised around a central substance sustained by belief and immanent in practices. This chapter provides an initial outline of institutions and their substances. Clearly, as substance is immanent in practices, it is the relationship between the two that will have to unfold, but the present chapter provides a working outline to guide the subsequent discussion. Before providing an introductory outline of each institution and its substance, however, some preliminary remarks are in order.

Substance and Organisation

Although Roger Friedland (2009a) supplies us with an extensive discussion of the nature and relationship between substance and practice, it is not his aim to provide a comprehensive list of institutions, nor to provide us with the means of determining substance. His examples are illustrative ones, such as accountability. His argument is, however, couched at a more general level and so there are some additional considerations if we are to put his ideas to work. One is that he identifies not only a primary substance but also 'secondary derivatives' (Friedland, 2009a: 61). When we are searching for substance, therefore, our discussion will be complicated by the identification of these secondary derivatives. It is possible, too, that what is a primary substance for one institution features as a secondary substance in another institution. Friedland (2002), for example, makes much use of love in his discussion of what animates identification with a particular institution. Drawing on his wider work, love takes on an erotic cast, emphasising the desire that may fuel commitment. Here is a football fan, commenting on his passionate commitment to a football team, one that will feature in our later discussion of play as institutional logic. 'I still loved [Glasgow] Rangers', he lamented, following a poor run of form and off the pitch scandals, 'but we were no longer in love' (Duff, 2013: 122). As Tim Lomas argues, using ideas of love derived from either erotic or romantic senses seems to be stretching both beyond value. As he notes, the sort of love that might be attached to a football team is certainly stronger than 'like', 'respect' or 'appreciate' but appears to be of a different nature to the conventional uses. Accordingly, based on the analysis of a corpus of 'untranslatable' words (words, that is, that express a concept or a feeling that has no direct equivalent in the English language), he outlines 14 types of love, which he groups into four clusters (Table 4.1). Two of these are connected with interpersonal relations, where he distinguishes the type of caring love that characterises familial relations from erotic or romantic love. The remaining two categories of nonpersonal love are directed either towards such targets as places or objects, or love for abstract ideals. While in my later discussion I associate love as the substance connected with the institution of the family, it is the combination of these distinctive forms of love, coupled with belief, that manifest in forms of passionate attachment, at least among core adherents of institutional orders.

The discussion of love reminds us that attachment to a logic is not just, or even primarily, a matter of cognition, but also involves emotions and feelings. As Friedland (2018: 522) argues, institutions 'may have an emotional specificity, not just as vehicles or instruments of institutionalization, but as constituted through the practices characteristic of an institution.' Voronov and Vince (2012) suggest that institutional orders promote distinctive categories of acceptable displays of emotion that actors come to tacitly accept and need to produce for successful performance. One could suggest further that feelings offer a still deeper form of acceptance of logics, in that feelings of appropriateness may manifest in a sense of 'rightness' that underpins performed emotions. 'It is through feelings', argues Damasio (2000: 36), 'which are inwardly directed and private, that emotions, which are outwardly directed and public, begin their impact on the mind'. Later, for example, we will

Table 4.1 Forms of Love from Lomas (2018)

Experiences, objects, places	*Transcendent*
Experiential love	Compassionate love
Aesthetic love	Momentary love
Rooted love	Reverential love
People	*Romantic*
Friendly love	Passionate love
Self love	Playful love
Familial love	Possessive love
	Rational love
	Star-crossed love

discuss the role of rituals in their performance in sustaining institutional logics. An actor who has been used to sitting at prayer, for example, and so performing the logic immanent in the practice of prayer, may feel bodily discomfort if placed in the situation where adherents kneel to pray. As Friedland (2018:533) notes '[i]nstitutional logics mean in part through the specific ways in which we are moved. Take sovereign power: the bodies of citizens and noncitizens apprehend the gestures of soldiers and police kinesthetically, bodily movements which produce and are produced by affect, the circulation of fear and respect, by feelings that attend and animate offence'. That sense of rightness as manifest in particular practices might also be extended to when and where particular practices take place and with what material objects. The appropriate dress may mark the rightness of a particular occasion, and ceremonies may mark out the passing of time. In putting forward what she terms an 'aisthetic' perspective, Elke Weik (2018) draws attention to properties such as harmony and rhythm. 'Such properties', she argues, 'enable us to feel-perceive institutions immediately. This feeling-perception can explain institutional endurance to the extent that people, as a rule, will seek to maintain what they feel to be pleasurable and avoid what displeases them' (Weik, 2018: 11). That sense of rightness may then manifest in cognitive justifications for the performance, as elaborated on in the formal statements of belief and process appropriate to the field.

The second element that we need to add to Friedland is the organisation. As a sociologist of religion, he is not concerned with the organisational dimension of institutional life. As organisational analysts, we are interested in both how institutional logics might shape organisations across logics and how logics generate distinctive forms of organisation. So, for example, Protestant sects such as the Primitive Baptists developed organising models based on a commitment to the priesthood of all believers that then formed to-hand templates for business organisations (Thornton, Occasio and Lounsbury, 2012: 111–112). Churches are one distinctive form of organisation: we will consider others below. While Friedland's examples often operate with a direct connection between specific practices and the animating value, institutional theory would suggest the organisation as a key mediating factor. We can view organisations as particular bundles of practices, practices that are given more stability by being attached to defined positions. Those positions carry with them certain performance expectations and can be associated with authoritative relations over both people and material resources. Accordingly, the discussion below will bring organisations into explicit consideration.

Table 4.2 supplies a working guide to the discussion that follows. It is organised by three broad categories, based on the distinctive embodied relations that we explored in the previous chapter. There are the institutions that emerge from the human need to make sense of the

Table 4.2 Institution, Substance and Practice

Institution	Relation	Substance	Organisation	Practice
Religion	Existence	Faith	Church	Prayer
Play	Existence	Fun	Gallery	Game
Knowledge	Natural and social world	Curiosity	University	Experiment
Military	Intergroup relations	Honour	Army	Drill
Politics	Intergroup relations	General interest	State	Voting
Law	Interpersonal and group relations	Justice	Court	Pleading
Family	Reproduction	Love		Marriage
Economy	Production	Gain	Corporation	Transaction
Medicine	Embodied existence	Health	Hospital	Consultation

world: religion, play and knowledge. There are institutions that emerge from the regulation of relationships: military, politics and law. Finally, there are the institutions that derive from human subsistence and bodily limits: family, economy and medicine. There is a deliberate inversion here of the concern of much social theory with subsistence and the economy, one that is of particular salience for organisation theorists. Much of the discussion on institutional logics, as we have seen, has been concerned with the spread of, and resistance to, the logic of the economy into other domains of social life. Focus on these very important matters runs the risk, as Friedland (2012) points out, of 'economizing' logics. There is, therefore, a deliberate rebalancing of the discussion that is intended to stress institutions as meaning-providing systems.

There is an intriguing observation buried in the notes at the end of Patricia Thornton's account of the contending logics in operation in the American higher education publishing industry. 'American scholars', she contends, 'believe there is greater professional prestige and scientific value attributed to the development of theories that are universal, hence generalizable to other contexts, whereas European scholars tend to assume their theories are nation-specific' (Thornton, 2004: 152, note 9). From a European perspective, what is problematic is the assumption that work drawing on specifically American examples has automatic universal status. A similar complaint can be found in comparative law, where Lasser observes that by 'limiting observation to published French judicial decisions, and by adopting parochial US realist perspectives about the proper sources of law and about the evils of formalism, these analyses could not help but produce deeply dismissive – and often overtly negative – characterizations of the French civil judicial system'

(Lasser, 2013: 234). There are traces of a problematic universalisation of American experience even in Selznick's (2008) work, where he invokes the natural law tradition to counterpose the operation of reason in a legal system to will in the political system. Natural law had its origins in theology, with legal systems seen to be based on the natural laws handed down by God. Legal comparatists have shed considerable doubt on the ability to found legal systems on such principles, seeing them more as a key component of specific historical societies. So, argues Whitman (2013: 339), there is 'a vast and complex range of differences among human legal orders. Certainly, it would be a grave mistake to try to reduce all of those legal orders to any single set of natural-law principles.' However, this is not to rule out the comparative approach and the attempt to elucidate generalisable bases to the law. 'Nevertheless', he continues, 'while there is not a single natural law in the human world, it remains the case that normative legal orders generally address themselves to the same, relatively narrow, range of predicaments. Law is always roughly concerned with decisions about fates: who should die, who should profit, who should be subjected to the authority of whom' (Whitman, 2013: 339). In other words, sensitivity to such cultural differences does not mean that the task of comparative work should be abandoned altogether. Rather, it involves the search for anthropological constants of the type outlined in Chapter 3 (Walsh, 2015: 118). As Grossfeld (2013: 180) argues 'law largely grows from roots beyond our control that are partially universal'. The search for such roots rests on a firm grasp of history and the development of a wide range of solutions to the common problems posed by finite human capacities in a social and natural world.

Accordingly, the attempt essayed here is the initial abstraction from the historical record of what seems to be common responses to the 'perennial problems' of human existence. In doing so, we are inevitably simplifying. In particular, the search is guided by the desire to isolate common mechanisms that operate across historical contexts. This inevitably involves the simplification of complex reality in order to provide parsimonious analytical tools. It could be argued that in identifying nine broad institutions, I have already exceeded the bounds of such parsimony. There is also the danger that in, for example, aggregating the worlds of high art, organised sports and popular music, to take just a few important categories, under the common heading of 'play' that I am doing violence to the importance of each. However, the institutions suggested in Table 4.2 are broad headings, where some key features are abstracted from complex historical situations in order to provide analytical clarity. When these abstractions are then employed in concrete historical situations, as is essayed in Chapter 6, then we will see how we have to introduce complications, such as intra-institutional distinctions. For now, I am using 'institutions' as the 'headline' term to refer to the broad phenomena. When examining concrete instantiations, I will tend to use the term 'institutional order' to reflect the complex array of fields, organisations and practices that are orchestrated under the broad heading of the term 'institution'. I then take 'institutional logics' as the 'laws of motion' that link together the substance at the heart of each institution with the distinctive practices that it mobilises and animates.

In the table, the examples of organisations and practices are indicative only; further elaboration will follow in subsequent chapters. One blank cell in the table is worthy of comment. The family is the institution in which the relationship between the substance and the practices seems at its most immediate, relatively unmediated by other organisational forms, like platoons or congregations, which are proper to other institutions. There are plenty of such forces from other institutions seeking to mould the family, from law courts to church bodies, each claiming and contesting jurisdiction. But it seems difficult to conceive of the family itself as an organisation. At particular times in history and in particular places, however, one could argue the household is a form of organisation, especially when it contains unrelated members, such as servants. This is clearest in farming and craft environments, where workers and apprentices are housed under the same roof and treated as members of an extended family. However, I prefer not to consider the family as a form of organisation, even though much organising may be involved in its ongoing existence. With those qualifications in mind, I turn to examine each of the institutions in order, starting with religion.

Religion

Part of the reason for starting with religion is because it is one of the most commonly accepted institutions. It is also where Weber (1948 [1915]) started his exploration of value spheres, contrasting a number of spheres with the other-worldly nature of Indian mystical religion. The value spheres he identified were kinship; economic; political; aesthetic; erotic and intellectual. The detachment from the world that such religious traditions encouraged brought their relationship with other social domains into sharp relief. Not least here was the conflict with kinship, where religions strived to supply new forms of belonging in which, argued Weber, 'the faithful should ultimately stand closer to the savior, the prophet, the priest, the father confessor, the brother in faith than to natural relations and to the matrimonial community' (Weber, 1948: 329). However, another reason is that religion starts to introduce some of the complexities of examining logics, given that logics, as Friedland and Alford (1991) insisted, happen in particular conjunctures of time and space. There is the need, that is, to locate how a religious logic based in faith as its ultimate substance finds expression in particular forms, especially in particular practices.

For some, the very category of 'religion' is problematic, involving, Asad (1993) argues, the imposition of Western analytical categories on other societies. The sheer variety of spiritual expression makes the categories of the organised forms of religion to be found in the West to be problematic. As the editors of a collection on religion in China observe, although commentators 'raise serious concerns about the very applicability of the notion of "religion" to non-Western cultural contexts. [We]..., argue that it is nonetheless important to examine the contesting definitions of religion applied by different groups in modern China, along with the institutions they attempt to create, control, or struggle to maintain within the constraints imposed by these new discourses and related discourses of nationalism and modernity' (Ashiwa and Wank, 2009: 204). In similar vein, in his explorations of the cognitive bases of religious belief, Harvey Whitehouse (2004: 2), while recognising the force of Asad's critique, argues that religion is still a valuable concept, provided that its dimensions in any particular context are clearly specified 'and its existence should be explainable with reference to general capacities of our species, activated under generally specifiable conditions'. While for Whitehouse supernatural agency is a key component of religion, the sociologists Demerath and Schmitt (1998: 382), recognising the guides to spiritual action provided by faiths such as Buddhism, drop this requirement, arguing that religion be conceptualised as 'any mythically sustained concern for ultimate meanings coupled with a ritually reinforced sense of social belonging'. The second part of that definition opens the way for a focus on religion as a social practice that will inform our later discussion. However, the faith that animates these practices can also take form in the formal theological statements that religions produce.

Not all religions produce such documents. For example, in Daoism 'there is no single institutional framework for these ritual specialists. These Daoist ritual masters transmit their liturgical texts and practices to their sons and disciples in discrete, local lines of transmission' (Dean, 2009: 183). However, many religions do produce such statements that contain, often in documents regarded as foundational, the aspects of faith that set them off from other faith systems. What we have to recognise is the variety of these, even at the level of the great world religions, those which number their adherents in the millions and that have had influence extending beyond national boundaries. For a start, there is a distinction between monotheistic and polytheistic religions, that is, between faiths that have one god or goddess as their focus and those that feature many gods or goddesses. The most prominent version of the latter is often taken to be Hinduism, although it can be argued that the many gods and goddesses that are worshipped by adherents are manifestations of one god. The position is clearer, though, for the monotheisms of Judaism, Christianity and Islam. These have had significant influence on world history beyond their geographical origins and for that reason form the backdrop to much of the discussion that follows. Each, in turn, is internally divided: Judaism into Orthodox and Reform, Islam into Sunni and Shia, Christianity into Orthodox, Catholic and Protestant, to just adopt some very broad divisions. It follows that our consideration of practices has to attend to these internal differences, because they can produce very different outcomes. We can see this if we attend to the organisational forms that are characteristic of each.

It is not necessary for religions to take organisational form. For Demerath and Farnsley (2007: 202), 'there is nothing two Hindus do together that one Hindu cannot do alone'. That is, Hindu temples are shrines to particular deities rather than centres of organizing activity. Collins (2007: 33) notes that 'Islam is [...] a practice for everyday life, with a popularistic orientation rather than respect for hierarchy'. Thus, 'the mosque lacks a sense of full-blown congregational solidarity' (Demerath and Farnsley, 2007: 202). This is in distinction to Western Christianity, where much attention is paid to both central and local organisational forms, resulting in considerable attention being paid to ecclesiology, or the theory of church organisation. Western Christian denominations thus fall on a continuum of organisational types, ranging from Roman Catholicism at one end, featuring a strongly centralised hierarchy, to Congregational forms of Protestantism at the other, characterised by local autonomy. Each form has consequences for the practices adopted, especially in the degree of lay involvement in governance. Organisational considerations, that is, mediate the practices adopted and so the particular forms that the logic that has faith at its heart adopt. Such considerations remind us that logics need to be carefully contextualised to specific conjunctures of time and place. It is not sufficient to refer to a de-contextualised and abstract notion of religious logic, and the same holds for the other forms of logic that we investigate. Religion appears in most discussions of social theory because of its power in supplying meanings for human activities and its enduring influence. The same cannot be said for the next institution that we explore: play.

Play

In 1938, the Dutch art historian Johan Huizinga, who specialised in the history of the late Middle Ages, authored the book that was translated into English as *Homo Ludens: A study of the Play-Element in Culture* in 1949. It is interesting to note that Huizinga did not approve of this title 'because it was not my object to define the place of play among all the other manifestations of culture, but rather to ascertain how far culture itself bears the character of play' (Huizinga, 1949: i). In other words, where other social theorists, if they considered play at all, regarded as the rather marginal residual activities left over after the serious stuff of social life was considered, Huizinga saw it as fundamental to human existence. As Walsh (2015: 142) notes, drawing on Marcuse, 'Play, then, is not opposed to labour as a 'counterphenomenon' ..., but as belonging to a different ontological category.' So, for Huizinga play ranked in his argument alongside the other fundamental categories of human social life: law, war, knowing, religion, poetry, philosophy and art. At its heart, argued Huizinga was 'fun', a category that 'resists all analysis, all logical interpretation' (Huizinga, 1949: 3). For all that, historical work shows 'it is precisely this fun-element that characterizes the essence of play. Here we have to do with an absolutely primary category of life, familiar to everybody at a glance right down to the animal level' (Huizinga, 1949: 3). That difficult to define but clearly experienced sense of fun is at the centre of a variety of activities that we can broadly group under the heading of 'play'. For example, in the sport of football, one Glasgow Rangers supporter recalls of the time when his club, once dominant at the head of Scottish football, had to, following a number of off-field scandals, start again at the bottom, 'it was fun while it lasted. And fun was the key element' (Duff, 2013: 128). Very much earlier, the British writer and social reformer Havelock Ellis argued in the context of the fundamental importance of play to human life that

> Dancing is the primitive expression alike of religion and love — of religion from the earliest human times we know of and of love from a period long anterior to the coming of man. The art of dancing, moreover, is intimately entwined with all human traditions of war, of labour, of pleasure, of education, while some of the wisest philosophers and the most ancient civilisations have regarded the dance as the pattern in accordance with which the moral life of men must be woven.
>
> (Ellis, 1923: 34; see also Langer, 1957: 227)

For Ellis, dancing was at the root of expressive forms of art such as music and dancing, with building activities being at the heart of the plastic arts of architecture and painting. 'There is no primary art outside these two arts', he argued, 'for their origin is far earlier than man himself; and dancing came first' (Ellis, 1923: 33). Such is the justification for covering all forms of artistic expression under the broad heading of the logic of play animated by fun. Clearly, other secondary derivatives emerge over time, each proper to the emergent specialisations of artistic and sporting activity, but fun remains primary.

That is not to say that play is not a serious business. Through play, people learn serious lessons. 'Play', suggests Sennett (2002: 266), 'prepares children for the experience of playacting by teaching them to treat conventions of behavior as believable. Conventions are rules for behavior at a distance from the immediate desires of the self.' Learning about such rules through the flexible medium of play allows for the development of understandings that are vital for adult social life. 'Play', argues Sennett (2002: 266), 'is not art, but it is a certain kind of preparation for a certain kind of aesthetic activity, one which is realized in society if certain conditions are present'. Huizinga, we have seen, contrasts play to both art and poetry, and Weber considered the 'aesthetic' as one of his value spheres. I wish, however, partly in the name of parsimony, but more because of the huge importance of popular culture in more recent times, to incorporate the arts broadly defined under the heading of play, with a central substance of fun animating all the varieties of play, however, layered under subsequent accretions of meaning. That is a move which would not be welcomed by many social theorists, who see art as fundamentally having a serious purpose, one not available to popular culture. Hannah Arendt talks of 'mass culture which, strictly speaking, does not exist, but mass entertainment, feeding on the cultural objects of the world' (cited in Walsh, 2015: 133). Richard Hoggart (1971), in his sensitive exploration of working class cultural life in 1950s Britain, deplored the arrival of the American milk bar in a way which appeared to underestimate the power of the creativity unleashed in popular music during that decade. Constructing a binary between 'serious' high culture on the one hand and 'mere entertainment' associated with popular culture on the other tends to ignore the blurring of the two categories in a way that undervalues the impact of developed forms of play on social life. As Ken McLeod (2016: 227) observes, noting the centrality of the notion of 'play' to both sports and music, 'Given the near universal exposure to both sports and popular music, it would seem that all our identities are, at least in some small way, influenced by the confluence of these cultural forms'. Chapter 7 takes up some of these identities in these two domains in more detail.

There is value, then, in considering the myriad ways that the substance of 'fun' is enacted through practices associated with particular forms of the logic of play. In turn, taking play seriously might help to inform our study of organisations. Boltanski and Chiapello (2007), for example, argue that we are witnessing the birth of a new spirit of capitalism. In its espousal of autonomy and negation of hierarchy, this new form of justification for the economic order, they argue, builds on forms of social and artistic critique generated from the events of 1968. Popular music was a key carrier of such themes, and it may be here, rather than in direct critique, that the main impact is to be found. It also resulted in distinctive changes to practices that might be considered to have had much broader impact. In January 1964, Ian Macdonald records, the Beatles recorded German-language versions of their hits 'She Loves You' and 'I Want to Hold Your Hand'. 'The custom of recording special versions for foreign markets, standard practice at the time, was never afterwards bothered with by The Beatles and consequently fell into disuse', notes Macdonald (1995: 81). As he continues, 'the resulting promotion of the English language around the world is one of their most substantial, and least documented, achievements.'

Play is important then as exemplifying a particular form of logic centred on the substance of fun. It is one that features particular organisational forms. The club as organising sporting practices is one such form, one that can be contrasted with the idea of franchises. That is, a European form of organisation is seen as emergent from the sporting interests of both players and supporters. It mirrors, albeit often in distorted form, some idea about community and belonging. The contrast is with forms that import commercial logic, in which sports teams are franchises dominated by the logic of ownership, in which teams can be moved at will regardless of the desires and dreams of supporters. The tension is described by Tempany (2016: 329) in his contrast between German and English notions of football clubs in the era of the Premier League. 'The likes of Schalke and St Pauli', he argues taking two German examples, 'aren't political clubs so much as clubs that take their place at the heart of communities — enabling people of all ages, ethnicities and economic backgrounds to participate in the social and civic life of their town or city. In England, our clubs — like so many of our national assets — have been wrenched from their communities and turned into global brands' (Tempany, 2016: 329). While there might be argument about the accuracy of such claims, especially the deployment of the term 'community', his contention is a reminder that there can be passionate forms of attachment at the heart of the mass culture so disparagingly dismissed by commentators like Arendt.

Knowing

Both Weber and Huizinga posit forms of knowing as key domains of social life – Weber used the term 'intellectual', but Huizinga adopted the broader term 'knowing' and that will be followed here. A focus on forms of knowing as central to social life is merged into other logics in much institutionalist discussion, but I suggest that there is value in retaining knowing as a distinct form of logic with curiosity as its key substance. As we will recall, a distinctive feature of the human condition is that learning is a central part of the slow development and maturation of the person (Smith, 2010: 333). This is not just learning that one is a distinct centre of subjective experience but also the learning from generations of accumulated experience, such that one does not have to directly experience situations to know of their existence and of ways of comporting oneself in them. It is for this broader reason that I reject two key terms that are often used in social theory, for those of philosophy and science. This is not because of rejection of their importance, but because of the connotations of each, both of which might narrow our focus. In particular, both are closely associated with the university as a particular site of knowledge production and with particular practices.

Philosophy has connotations of introverted study expressed in obscure language by an exclusive body of scholars. That might be an unfair caricature, and we have seen how philosophers such as Bhaskar have sought to bring philosophy out of the common room and use it to further concrete investigations of the world, but it is a rather narrow sense of knowing. A form of knowing with considerably more social prestige, given its evident impact on the world, is that of science. Here, we have a convergence of meaning, from a continental European sense of science as any form of systematic study and the rather narrower sense of natural science that characterises much Anglo-American discourse. The problem with natural science, for all its achievements, is that its supporters see it as possessing the method, that of empiricism and the experiment, with which to approach the world. As we have seen, this is inadequate to the nature of the social world, but it is an approach that draws much prestige and many followers. Indeed, in some debates, the scientific method is presented as a form of belief system, especially when contrasted to the claims of religion (Collins and Evans, 2017: 78). At the heart of this belief is adherence to the notion of the disinterested study of the world, prompted by curiosity. 'The essence of science is the love of knowledge' argued Michael Polanyi 'and the utility of knowledge does not concern us primarily' (cited in Walsh, 2015: 118). That claim might be a counsel of perfection and has certainly been challenged by much of the work in the Social Studies of Science tradition (Collins and Evans, 2017). Associated in particular with the work of Bruno Latour (1987), this has looked at scientific practices in detail and has argued that, when one 'follows scientists around', one finds that their practical activities diverge rather sharply from the idealised picture of the scientific method. Here, questions of status and reward intrude, and results are reinterpreted to protect cherished hypotheses. Such accounts can lead to radical scepticism about the distinctive nature of science and to, on some accounts, reduce it to simply another form of storytelling. This had value in reminding us that commitment to curiosity is an aspiration that may never be achieved in practice, although it is one that animates many of the practices of science. However, radical scepticism about science carries with it considerable dangers, as one of the leading exponents of the social study of science, Harry Collins has recognised. In a polemic coauthored with Robert Evans, he argues that the commitment of scientists to the search for truth is something that needs to be sustained, despite that the studies of science which he and others have conducted show that it is a chimera, shaped and conditioned by all sorts of social pressures and assumptions. Commitment to the values of disinterested inquiry emerges, they suggest, from the practices that characterise the collective pursuit of scientific inquiry. Thus, they argue, 'it is the group aspirations and practice as a whole that give rise to the stability and identity of the form of life not the action tokens – the haphazard acts of individuals'

(Collins and Evans, 2017: 39). Sustaining this necessary myth is vital for society while recognising

> A good society would, of course, depend on many kinds of values other than those associated with science; there is a wider range of values than those exhibited by science and there are the aesthetics of taste and manners. While there is overlap between the moral values of science and of democracy, a good society needs also to draw from aspects of religion and a range of those secular institutions whose values have not yet been eroded.
>
> (Collins and Evans, 2017: 142)

Knowing, then is much broader than philosophy or science and has multiple sites of production. For Bourdieu and Passeron (1977), 'pedagogic action' can take place at a number of sites, most notably in the family. It is here that language in particular is acquired in a fashion that then conditions later encounters with more formal pedagogy. However, the emergence of a specialised group dedicated to pedagogical work sees the establishment of an educational system, one with its own internal logic and distinctive practices. For Bourdieu and Passeron, it is the construction of a self-perpetuating group that sets the educational system apart and causes it to both endure and be resistant to change. As they argue

> In the same way that, as Engels observes, the apparition of law qua law, i.e. as an 'autonomous realm', is correlative with the advances in the division of labour which lead to the constitution of a body of professional jurists; in the same way that, as Weber shows, the 'rationalization' of religion is correlative with the constitution of a priesthood; and in the same way that the process leading to the constitution of art qua art is correlative with the constitution of a relatively autonomous intellectual and artistic field – so the constitution of PW [pedagogic work] as such is correlative with the constitution of the ES [educational system].
>
> (Bourdieu and Passeron, 1977: 56)

What this specialised group do, argue Bourdieu and Passeron, is to impose a 'cultural arbitrary', a set of ideas that reinforces the existing state of affairs and which is implicitly adjusted to the capacities of those who bring the right aptitudes with them from their family formation. Education is thus a key transmission device solidifying the hold of dominant social groups. For Friedland, however, this is to downplay the importance of the substance that animates practices. 'Institutional logics are not', he argues, 'as in Bourdieu, first ordered by the distributive struggle over capitals that sustain the stake as an illusio, in which categorical oppositions are arbitrary transpositions of positional oppositions'

(Friedland, 2009b: 908). Hence while Bourdieu and Passeron's point about the educational system as relatively autonomous with a distinctive logic of its own is important, here the focus is on a wider logic, one animated, ultimately, by curiosity.

While the university that Bourdieu and Passeron examine in some detail is a central site for knowing, knowledge has contending locations. Since the nineteenth century, the corporation, in the form in particular of the research wings of companies in industries such as pharmaceuticals, has been a central site of knowledge as structured forms of discovery. Here, it is shaped by commercial imperatives, such that curiosity takes a back seat to more market-driven imperatives. Gaining momentum from later on, notably after the Second World War, has been the rise of the management consultancy as a site of processual knowledge. Often taking ideas from the academy and simplifying them for onward transmission, this has been a central means of innovating new managerial practices, such as Business Process Reengineering. Here, ideas drawn from the literature on fashion cycles have often been more applicable than that of curiosity-driven science (Mutch, 2008). Finally, as we noted above, the professions have also been a site of vocational knowledge, reminding us that knowing is not just about the production of new knowledge but also, and often more significantly, is about forms of learning, about the transmission of knowledge about how to perform adequately in particular roles. Those forms of learning differ significantly in the various professions, which is another reason to regard professionalism as a mode of organising that cuts across institutional logics, rather than being a logic in its own right. Often, those forms of knowing are in an uneasy relationship with academic knowledge. Here the status system of academic knowledge, with its privileging of abstract, general knowledge, often shaped by the cultural prestige of natural science, comes into conflict with the more instrumental form of knowledge valued by the professions. As new domains of work, such as teaching and nursing, seek the reputational rewards of professionalisation, involving the credentialisation of their knowledge by academic bodies, they are drawn into patterns of knowledge production that may sit uneasily with the accumulated experience of what works in practice.

What all these forms of knowing have in common is that they focus on formal, explicit knowledge. Much of the research engendered by the shift to what is often termed a 'knowledge economy' has revealed the importance of tacit knowledge. The emphasis on the importance of tacit, as opposed to explicit, knowledge first emerged in the work of the scientist and philosopher Polanyi (1958, 1967). For Polanyi, we know more than we can say. Certain forms of knowledge are acquired in an almost unconscious fashion and once learned can be used to produce an effective performance. However, such knowledge is not immediately accessible to us and can be difficult to communicate to others. The most well-known application of this to knowing in organisations has been the work of Nonaka and Takeuchi (1995). They suggest that much knowledge is held tacitly and can only be acquired through extensive periods of socialisation. There are parallels in this account with the stress in material on organisational learning on the importance of learning from experience. In their influential work on *Situated Learning*, Lave and Wenger (1991) draw on accounts of learning in apprenticeships to develop their notion of 'limited peripheral participation'. This refers to the learning that takes place when newcomers begin to participate in a 'community of practice'. What is important here is not the formal learning process but learning to act and talk as a member of the community. In such a process, tacit knowledge is acquired and shared. In the context of knowledge in organisations, this suggests that questions of identity are central. That is, rather than placing the emphasis on forms of technology, the focus should be on methods of socialisation into communities of practice (Gherardi, 2006). Again, we see the emphasis that is placed in both approaches on forms of knowledge that do not fit into conceptions drawn from formal models of theories and education. What the history of formal education points to is the way that frequently these forms of practical knowledge have been marginalised and downplayed in favour of more abstract and formalised knowledge. The focus that the work on tacit knowledge gives us is the importance of learning to *be* alongside learning content. The same focus can be seen in work on elementary education. The classic account here is that by Paul Willis (1977) in his ethnographic study of working class boys in *Learning to Labour*. These boys resist formal education by drawing on imageries of manual work and practical common sense. 'The rejection of school work by 'the lads' and the omnipresent feeling that they know better', suggests Willis (1977: 56), 'is also paralleled by a massive feeling on the shopfloor, and in the working class generally, that practice is more important than theory'. The rejection of formal education is thus an active process of identity construction, but one that, in its celebration of a particular form of resistance, is ultimately constraining, limiting the boys' life chances. We seem to have come a long way from the value of curiosity as expressed in Polanyi's formulation, but once again the value and importance of seeing knowing, broadly conceived, as a crucial social domain is reinforced by Willis's comment that 'The teacher is given formal control of his pupils by the state, but he exerts his social control through an educational, not a class, paradigm' (Willis, 1977: 67). There is a logic of knowing, that is, that manifests in distinctive practices that cannot be reduced to political or commercial imperatives.

Military

Huizinga noted that war is often conceived of as a game. 'The great wars of aggression from antiquity down to our own times', he argues, 'all find a far more essential explanation in the idea of glory, which everybody understands, than in any rational and intellectualist theory of economic forces and political dynamisms' (Huizinga, 1949: 90). Adam Ferguson also noted in the middle eighteenth century the role of play in preparing for conflict. 'His sports are frequently an image of war;' he claimed, 'sweat and blood are freely expended in play; and fractures or death are often made to terminate the pastime of idleness and festivity. He was not made to live for ever, and even his love of amusement has opened a way to the grave' (Ferguson, 1767: 28). While Boltanski and Thevenot (2006) rule out resort to violence as a justifiable means of settling conflicts, Ferguson presents a more positive view of the impact of the military calling. For him, the animating substance is *honour*: 'The soldier, we are told, has his point of honour, and a fashion of thinking, which he wears with his sword. This point of honour, in free and uncorrupted states, is a zeal for the public; and war to them is an operation of passions, not the mere pursuit of a calling' (Ferguson, 1767: 144).

Ferguson was drawing on his own military experience as chaplain in the Black Watch regiment of the British army to make a point about the value of military experience in the formation of an active citizenry (Neocleous, 2013). He was intervening in contemporary debates about the creation of a militia in Scotland, which he very much favoured over the alternatives of hiring mercenaries or creating a standing army. He recognised the growing occupational specialisation in societies that grew ever more complex. In general, the learning that such specialisation engendered increased the productivity of particular callings and so the prosperity of society as a whole. But the emergence of a specialised military had its dangers. While standing armies might be able to fight more effectively, thanks to the habits of discipline that could be instilled,

> When a people is accustomed to arms, it is difficult for a part to subdue the whole; or before the establishment of disciplined armies, it is difficult for any usurper to govern the many by the help of a few. These difficulties, however, the policy of civilized and commercial nations has sometimes removed; and by forming a distinction between civil and military professions, by committing the keeping and the enjoyment of liberty to different hands, has prepared the way for the dangerous alliance of faction with military power, in opposition to mere political forms, and the rights of mankind.
>
> (Ferguson, 1767: 256)

Ferguson's warning seems prescient in the light of the many military dictatorships that have come to take the place of both political and economic logics. Even when this is not the case, the growing refinement of the means of settling differences by violent means has been a key means of driving political and economic development. Thus, Giddens (1990) sees military power as a key institution of modernity (alongside capitalism, industrialisation and administrative power). It has, Giddens argues, its own logic and developments in military techniques shaped the emergence of the nation state. The development of military capacity involved the solving of complex problems of coordination such as at the naval dockyards of the Venice Arsenale, which then formed to-hand templates for economic activity (Zan, 2004). And the evolution of military organisations formed the basis of imageries that profoundly influenced the emergence of organisational disciplines such as business strategy. Such imageries often draw on a picture of military organisation that features tight central control and a rigid hierarchical structure: a 'command and control' organisation (Mutch, 2006). Even with the development of more flexible military structures, what remains common is the strong cultivation of identification with the home unit, through the centrality of artefacts such as the regimental history conveyed through symbols and stories, often centring on honour and loyalty. That loyalty might be to the local unit or the more abstract entity of the nation state, but loyalty is an important secondary derivative of honour.

Ferguson, for all his attachment to citizen involvement and martial virtue, recognised that societies advanced by replacing resort to violence to settle disputes by the advent of more peaceful means. However, such advances were not without their dangers. He observed

> Our ancestors, in rude ages, during the recess of wars from abroad, fought for their personal claims at home, and by their competitions, and the balance of their powers, maintained a kind of political freedom in the state, while private parties were subject to continual wrongs and oppressions. Their posterity, in times more polished, have repressed the civil disorders in which the activity of earlier ages chiefly consisted; but they employ the calm they have gained, not in fostering a zeal for those laws, and that constitution of government, to which they owe their protection, but in practising apart, and each for himself, the several arts of personal advancement, or profit, which their political establishments may enable them to pursue with success.
>
> (Ferguson, 1767: 57)

He here mentions the two alternative means of settling disputes, politics and the law, which supersede violence, certainly internal violence (military violence remains, but is turned outwards). The danger of a commercial society, though, is that actors turn away from civic engagement. Just as they leave fighting to the professionals, so they abdicate their public duties, duties that Ferguson, schooled in the examples of classical antiquity, regarded as central to the maintenance of public life.

Politics

In her characterisation of politics as the site of human freedom, Hannah Arendt (1958) also drew extensively on the traditions of classical antiquity. Her main focus was on the Greek polis, where, freed from the realm of necessity, issues were debated and solutions agreed. Of course, participation in the Greek agora was restricted to a small elite of men, with those who laboured and those who maintained the household being relegated to the realm of unfreedom, trapped in bodily necessity. The household was a realm of autocratic rule, where women and slaves were subordinate. A key feature of the human condition for Arendt was multiplicity and with this inevitably came a range of perspectives on the same issue. It was only by contrasting these perspectives and debating their merits that issues could be resolved. Human history was then marked by the introduction of more and more people to the sphere of political debate. That introduction of more perspectives means that politics is inevitably the most fissiparous of all the logics. By its nature it involves disagreement and debate, so identifying an animating substance is not so straightforward. From the times of the city states of Greek antiquity have grown much larger entities, with the key one being the nation state. From the discussion of the civic world in Boltanski and Thevenot, I borrow the notion of the 'general interest' as the animating substance of political practices. Drawing on Rousseau but, more especially one suspects, traditions of French Republicanism, they suggest 'persons are more or less worthy depending on whether they are viewed as individuals or as citizen members of the sovereign, that is, depending on whether the will that drives them to act is particular or on the contrary directed toward the general interest' (Boltanski and Thevenot, 2006: 114). Defining that general interest is, of course, a matter of considerable debate. It is often more a matter of emotional attachment than reasoned debate, as explored in Benedict Anderson's (1991) classic *Imagined Communities*. 'Imagined' in this case is not the same as imaginary but represents the imagery of bodies of people all doing the same thing in the name of a common entity, but not knowing each other. His account points to the importance of quotidian practices in embodying the entity. He points, for example, to the importance of schooling in providing a common shared experience: 'the government schools formed a colossal, highly rationalized, tightly centralized hierarchy, structurally analogous to the state bureaucracy itself. Uniform textbooks, standardized diplomas and teaching certificates, a strictly regulated gradation of age-groups, classes and instructional materials, in themselves created a self-contained, coherent universe of experience' (Anderson, 1991: 121). In similar vein, Steve Hindle (2000: 229) points to the symbolic importance of meeting places at local level in creating forms of national identity when he notes of local government meetings in sixteenth century England that 'whereas manor courts did not meet in parish churches (even though they were almost certainly the only buildings large enough for the purpose), vestries almost invariably tended to do so. The simple fact of this relocation rendered the presence of the state all the more tangible in the local community, for if Elizabethan vestries met in parish churches they did so in the presence of the royal arms' (the coat of arms which by royal decree was to hang in a prominent place in every church). The coat of arms thus displayed was an example of what Michael Billig (1995) has termed 'banal' nationalism. That is, he argues, what is important to an ongoing sense of national identity 'is not a flag which is being consciously waved with fervent passion; it is the flag hanging unnoticed on the public building.' Once again, it is the mundane and taken-for-granted practices that carry logics and perform them. National boundaries, argues Billig, are the taken-for-granted units of analysis of contemporary social science. As such they creep, unannounced and unnoticed, into all our forms of analysis. They cannot be escaped, but their presence can be acknowledged.

The importance of symbols in fostering emotional attachment tends to undermine arguments that see the logic of politics and its concomitant practices as reflecting the outcomes of deliberately directed interest. Paul Pierson (2004: 14) notes the prevalence of such arguments in political theory, terming them 'actor-centered functionalism'. In such conceptualisations, political outcomes such as, say, electoral systems, are explained in terms of the pursuit of particular interests by individual or, more likely, collective actors. Such actors design the systems to produce the outcomes they desire, outcomes that match their objectively determined interests. Pierson demonstrates the main problems with this approach from a historical perspective. Actors find it difficult to establish a clear link between their interests and systems designed to deliver them. Especially when multiple actors are involved, then it is difficult to meet all the shades of interest in one design, even assuming that agreement on the eventual design can be reached. More than this, designs may be buffeted by changes occurring elsewhere, changes that could not necessarily be foreseen. As Pierson puts it, 'actors may make rational design choices, but change in broader social environments and/or in the character of these actors themselves may markedly worsen the fit between actors and institutional arrangements after they are chosen' (Pierson, 2004: 108).

History, he suggests, presents us with a more persuasive account of institutional development (his institutions here being what he terms 'formal institutions' such as voting systems. This diverges from the perspective being taken here but is nevertheless pertinent and illuminating). Historical evidence, he suggests, shows how, once adopted, particular practices may be subject to reinforcing feedback mechanisms, which make such practices 'sticky'. While there might have been a universe of possible alternatives at the starting point, once selected, practices are reinforced by resource allocation and are embedded in a web of relations with other practices. Timing is therefore important: a practice that meets with success in one context may fail in another when introduced later. A striking example of this is given by Jacob Hacker in his exploration of the fate of national health insurance schemes in Britain, Canada and the United States. He notes the very different degrees of success in enacting such systems and attributes them to three factors: 'whether governments fail to enact national health insurance before a sizable portion of the public is enrolled in physician-dominated private insurance plans, whether initial public insurance programs are focused on residual populations such as the elderly and the very poor, and whether efforts to build up the medical industry precede the universalization of access' (Hacker, 1998: 128). When these three factors are found together, as in the United States, it proves extremely difficult to implement comprehensive insurance schemes, regardless of the political momentum that has built up behind them. Further than this, practices are not necessarily adopted because they meet 'objective' needs but for other reasons. Here he draws on new institutionalist accounts of practices being copied because they seem legitimate or because they are to-hand. In an analysis of the electoral systems operating in 166 countries having a directly elected parliament in 1995, Andre Blais and Louis Massicotte found three broad clusters of system: plurality, proportional representation and majority. While the biggest single group was those adopting plurality, the key factor here was British colonial rule where (as contrasted to French colonialism, where there was no such relationship) the template for elections in former colonies was derived from the imperial centre. By contrast, the prevalence of proportional representation in South America (which might be thought to be against the objective interests of powerful oligarchies) was imputed 'to the fact that South American constitutional lawyers were trained in continental Europe and looked to Europe as a model for the choice of an electoral system' (Blais and Massicote, 1997: 113). As Blais and Massicotte (1997: 117) conclude 'politicians may choose electoral institutions on the basis of their interests, but their perceptions of what institutions best suit them are likely to be shaped by the range of options debated at a given moment. Moreover, politicians sometimes make choices primarily on the basis of their views about what is good, just or efficient'.

Law

For some, the final logic that emerges out of the need to resolve disputes, that of the law, is simply a mirror of political or economic interests. Musacchio and Turner (2013), for example, note that much law is statutory in origin, thus reflecting political decisions. However, in arguing that historical work 'suggests that legal origins do not matter – they are not deterministic' they are holding to an extreme standard of causation, one that seems logically flawed (Musacchio and Turner, 2013: 536).

Legal origins can matter greatly when we examine the underlying logic that is mobilised through practices animated by the substance of justice. 'Law is not necessarily just', concedes Selznick (2008: 107), 'but it offers a promise of justice'. As we have seen with science, the ideal that the substance represents may never be achieved, but it is what animates those whose labours are shaped by a particular institutional logic. So, Selznick (2008: 107) continues, 'justice counterposes reason to will, including the will of a democratic legislature'. Adherence to the value of this substance gives the law an internal logic, one which can at times come into conflict with the political or economic interests that it is said to reflect. Support for this comes from the great Marxist historian E.P. Thompson, a source which might be expected to endorse the sort of deterministic relationship of the law with political economy that Musacchio and Turner envisage. In his study of the moral economy of crime in the eighteenth century, he argues

> The law may also be seen as ideology, or as particular rules and sanctions which stand in a definite and active relationship (often a field of conflict) to social norms; and, finally, it may be seen simply *in terms of its own logic, rules and procedures* – that is, simply as law. And it is not possible to conceive of any complex society without law.
>
> (Thompson, 1977, 260: my emphasis)

That was a controversial conceptualisation in the ranks of fellow Marxists, but it points to a deeper logic than a model of simple interest reflection (although, to be sure, such interests are important). The notion that there is an internal logic to the practice of law is also a topic of debate for legal scholars. Thus, it has been argued,

> Members in a professional group, such as lawyers, treat the law as belonging to their professional culture. Through it, they distance themselves from other groups. Among lawyers, reputation establishes authority. Reputation, in turn, depends on argument and invention according to the rules of legal debates, although those rules are implicitly established by participants in the game themselves. This is why lawyers claim to be solving problems by using a legal logic peculiar to their profession. Of course, lawyers are involved in political decisions. Nevertheless, their intellectual outlook does not necessarily depend on their political orientation.
>
> (Graziadei, 2013: 122)

That internal logic often refers to the form of the law, rather than its content. That is, formal rules may be transposed from one context to another, but their effect is heavily dependent on their insertion into existing ways of proceeding.

The importance of the internal logic of the law is amplified when one considers that much law is made outside the political domain, especially when it concerns contractual issues deriving from economic activity. Even when a framework has been provided by legislators, they often are unable to envisage how it will be applied in practical circumstances, many of which they could not foresee. In such circumstances, judges have considerable scope for interpreting what they consider to be legislative intention. Lauren Edelman, Christopher Uggen and Howard Erlanger (1999), for example, show how, over a 30-year period, judges in the United States evolved a body of case law that gave weight to internal organisational grievance procedures in cases involving the 1964 Civil Rights Act and other equal opportunities legislation. While the legislation offered little support for the notion that having such procedures would shield defendants from liability, over time a body of case law emerged that legitimated such procedures. In turn, the authors suggest the courts did so because grievance procedures 'look like the system of appeals available in the public legal process, a basic and well-institutionalized feature of a legitimate normative order' (Edelman, Uggen, Erlanger, 1999: 416) (even if, of course, in operation they might diverge wildly from the public standards.) What Edelman et al do not point out (because it was not their purpose) is that this historical process reflects the operation of a common law legal system. In such systems, typically found in Britain and its former colonies, law is based on the evolving precedents provided by previous legal decisions, giving considerable scope for judge-made law. The evolution of law, that is, depends to a great extent on whether cases are brought before the courts; if matters are settled out of court, then a point of legal principle may never be debated.

There are a large number of legal systems in the world, although much comparative law rests on the contrast between common and civil law traditions (Vranken, 2015). In turn, this owes much to the process of colonisation from the eighteenth century onwards, where legal systems were imposed on newly conquered territories in the furtherance of political and economic ambitions. Thus, the English common law is to be found in countries subject to British colonisation efforts, giving rise to, in particular, the important U.S. variant. In turn, the centrality of U.S. political, military and economic might in the twentieth century makes the common law tradition of central importance to the world system. Its chief rival for influence was then the civil law tradition of Continental Europe. Based on the codes of Roman law, Martin Vranken (2015) identifies three main forms, those obtaining in France, Germany and Scandinavia. The French and German systems have had the most global influence. Civil law, in contrast to common law, is formulated by jurists and legal scholars and is codified. It is this codification that marks it out as a distinctive form of logic. While both common law and civil law practices might be animated by the common goal of justice and the rule of law, the underlying logic is considerably different. So when, for example, Renate Meyer and Gerhard Hammerschmid (2006: 1003) refer to the legalistic nature of Austrian public sector management, they are referring to a civil law tradition in which laws are handed down in a hierarchical system and 'legal and procedural correctness prevails over performance and results'. If we were to refer to the United States as a legalistic society, we would have a different sense of legalism. Here, we would be referring to a propensity to litigation, led by the widespread availability and status of private lawyers. Underlying such differences, and with impacts on the broader society, is the difference between a flexible and interpretive tradition and one based on codification. Such differences in underlying logic animate specific practices and create particular identities. Of particular importance here is the distinction between substantive and procedural law. While the increasing importance of legislation in both common law and civil law jurisdictions has led to a level of convergence in formal prescriptions, major differences persist in the procedures that each system rests on. How law is carried out is therefore often more important than what law formally is. The distinction is often characterised as one between an adversarial approach in the common law and an inquisitorial one in civil law traditions. In the former, arguments are played out between the legal representatives of the contending parties, with judges acting as impartial mediators upholding the 'rules of the game'. By contrast, in an inquisitorial system, judges are an activist part of the search for the facts of the matter, especially in criminal proceedings.

These differences give rise to significantly different practices. Thus, Bernhard Grossfeld contrasts the style of judgments in the contending systems.

> In England, the higher courts traditionally give their opinions orally in a highly personal way. Even today, opinions in the House of Lords are called 'speeches'. In France, judges produce short and abstract written versions, 'more geometrico'. In Germany, they elaborate long written 'dissertations' in the particular grammatical style of the Latin-language tradition and, thus, quite often in bad German
>
> (Grossfeld, 2013: 160)

The focus on orality in the common law tradition is matched by the sense of drama in the courtroom. As the English lawyer Jeremy Lever (1999: 299) observed, in the common law tradition 'the judge or judges come in, the house lights are dimmed, the curtain goes up and the audience settles down to watch the play, though it may react from time to time to ensure that the rules governing the drama are observed and to clarify aspects of the action.' By contrast, in civil law traditions the court hearing is just one part of an overall process of discovery. 'On the Continent', notes Grossfeld, 'we see a continuing exchange of written texts, punctuated whenever necessary by proof-taking hearings, but with no dramatic climax' (Grossfeld, 2013: 176). Different legal systems, thus, generate distinctive practices and it is in those practices that the substance of the logic at the heart of each is manifested. We have to look beyond formal content, that is, in each of our logics to observe the mechanisms at work.

Family

Human beings have an imperative to reproduce. Our previous discussion about the embodied capacities of persons did not consider differential capacities based on biological sex. Many of those capacities do not differ but, in typical cases and before the advent of modern reproductive technologies, women have the capacity to bear children. There is no necessary ascription of social roles based on such differentiation, but the emergent social institution of the family often provides such roles (Fine, 2017: 87). It is also based on the long period needed for the nurturing of human children to full independence, a process that, as we have seen, involves considerable processes of learning. For all of these reasons, Smith (2010: 341) argues, 'in one form or another, in every place where humans are found, family social structure comes into existence'. That is not at all the same thing as asserting that the family has invariant universal forms. The classic division between the nuclear family, consisting of parents and their biological offspring, is one variant, the extended family, consisting of multi-generational households is another. Family can be extended to encompass others based on relations of dependence and loyalty. 'Should Mr Anderson ask you to be of his family', wrote the East India Company officer Allan Macpherson to his cousin's son in 1781 on his becoming political assistant to one James Anderson, 'do not by any means refuse, but if he should not, do not conduct yourself as if you felt a neglect' (Macpherson, 1928: 347). In such cases, loyalty might be a key substance animating conduct; in others, honour might be considered more appropriate. But it is possible to argue that these are secondary derivatives of the primary substance of love.

Love, as Lomas (2018) has pointed out, can not only take a variety of forms but could be regarded as in many cases a rather distant aspiration. Love, remarked Arendt caustically, was not found as often in real life as poetry would suggest. ('The common prejudice that love is as common as "romance" may be due to the fact that we all learned about it first through poetry. But the poets fool us; they are the only ones to whom love is not only crucial, but an indispensable experience, which entitles them to mistake it for a universal one' (Arendt, 1958: 242)). Love, also, takes a variety of forms in different historical contexts, from the courtly love of the European nobility in the Middle Ages to the romantic love beloved of popular culture through to the companionate love that might be a more realistic aspiration. This is not to speak of erotic love, which Weber saw as a key value sphere. It took its 'extraordinary quality', argued Weber, 'in a gradual turning away from the naïve naturalism of sex' (Weber, 1948: 344). Considerations of erotic love, which feature strongly in Friedland's (2002) work, emphasise desire, desire that can be at the heart of commitment to other institutional substances as well. It reminds us that commitment to such substances is as much, if not more, a matter of emotions rather than cognitions. It also suggests to us the dark side of logics for, as much feminist work in particular has shown us, families can be sites of oppression and dark desire. 'There's a thin line', Annie Lennox reminds us, 'between love and hate', and it is often the negative emotion that is mobilised, especially behind closed doors.

In addition, the family is, of course, not the only site for the expression of sexual desire and the need for companionate love. Indeed, many of the social movements that challenge traditional gender roles also reject the practices on which they seem to be founded. Marriage, for example, came under critique as a patriarchal practice cementing oppressive forms of interpersonal relationships. In many countries, this led to a long-term decline in the number of formal marriages. The movement for gay liberation further challenged traditional gender norms. However, much to the dismay of commentators like Foucault, who envisaged the creation of new forms of relationship, the move for equality for those identifying as LGBT meant assimilation to practices such as marriage. The demand for same-sex marriage was an important symbolic statement about equal treatment, but in many ways it simply reinforced the enduring nature of the family unit. While it is undoubtable that in many countries this has been subject to change, it has not disappeared as a key institution. The nonmarried couples tend to be in stable relationships and for all the many shifts in family composition, the family remains an important site of socialisation.

Economy

The human need for subsistence powers the beginning of economic relations, especially when conditions emerge for barter and exchange. Arendt (1958) distinguishes between labour, which is concerned with obtaining and consuming resources for bodily sustenance, and work, which involves the production of enduring artefacts. It is these artefacts that can be exchanged and which, she argues, produces a forum, the market, in which not only products are exchanged but reputations established, in parallel to the agora for political action. The challenge is to find a substance that covers the wide variety of economically motivated practices. 'Profit' is the classic answer, but this is subject to many definitional problems and, in practice, survival may be just as powerful a motivating force. I have suggested 'gain' as a term that encompasses a focus on both short-term profit and long-term market share, both approaches that can be found in different interpretations of economic activities. The problem is that there can be several routes to the achievement of this substance. In Thornton's (2004) work on higher education publishing, for example, she uses the term 'market logic', but in her detailed account there appear to be two variants of this logic. In one variant, the focus is on the rise of marketing as an internal function. In this case, the logic shifts from editorial control over the books published, based on an assessment of their worth in terms of content, to control by a marketing function that deals in perceptions of the demands of potential consumers. The second variant is focused more on the external integration of the companies into financial markets, where attention shifts from the books produced to 'the logic of Wall Street investment bankers and the increasing concern with profitability and market orientation common to other U. S. industries' (Thornton, 2004: 35). The two variants are connected but subtly different. Thornton introduces a further type of logic, that of the corporation, into the equation, spending a considerable amount of space discussing shifts in divisional forms of organisation. However, if we widen our horizons, we can see how contextually bound this form is. Richard Whittington and Michael Mayer (2000) carried out an investigation of corporate forms in Europe over a 20-year period and indicated the remarkable persistence of organisational forms that should have yielded to the superiority of the multidivisional corporate model. What this suggests is the importance of setting economic forms of organisation in the context of interactions with other logics, as we noted in the comparative business systems perspective.

As presented by mainstream economics, economic activity often operates with the assumptions of rational choice, uncoloured by the influences of culture. However, it is the core of the institutionalist project that not only are there cultural forces at work in society that overflow the rational calculations said to be indicative of economic activity, but also that economic activity itself is profoundly shaped by culture. The rationality of economic life, that is, is as much an artefact of the search for order by economists, themselves shaped by powerful myths, as it is a natural property of economic life itself. At the heart, just as with the other institutions, is belief. The philosopher of religion Mark Taylor has argued that in Adam Smith's work, God becomes secularised: 'God did not simply disappear but was reborn as the market' (Taylor, 2004: 6). The market then becomes the object of faith, in which practices, such as the granting of credit, take their efficacy from a belief in shared rationalised myths. This for Taylor then becomes a 'confidence game' in which economic activity is based not on real-world production but on belief in future states. Emil Kauder (1965) in his *History of Marginal Utility Theory* takes this analysis of the impact of religion on economic thought still further. Noting the central place of work as a justified activity in its own right in Calvinist theology, he suggests that Adam Smith, bathed in the Scottish Presbyterian literature, put labour in the centre of his account of value creation. By contrast, he argues 'moderate pleasure-seeking and happiness form the centre of economic actions' in Catholic traditions (Kauder, 1965: 9). One can doubt the specifics of this characterisation, given the focus of Scots Enlightenment figures on luxury. The debate about the supposedly adverse impacts of luxury consumption was a live one in the eighteenth century, but, on balance, Berry (2013) suggests that most Scots thinkers were in favour of modest consumption, on the grounds that it stimulated industry and provided employment. What such a debate suggests is the need to see the economy as profoundly shaped, just as with the other institutional orders we have considered, by beliefs.

Medicine

'Hospitals', writes Tim Winton (2014: 211), 'have their own surreal logic, their own absurd governance, their own uncanny weather, and the impotence and boredom they induce is hard to match anywhere else but prison or the military.' As a particular organisational form, the hospital is representative of our final logic, that of medicine. It emerges out of the limits on human life, especially the inevitability of death. For Winton, it 'seemed as if the aura of the institutional precinct brought out something different in people, something that altered them from their workaday selves, as if hospital didn't simply license them to behave differently but required it' (Winton, 2014: 212). As Friedson (2001: 167) points out in his study of professionalism, the 'transcendent values of the core disciplines, Health, Justice, and Salvation, are of nearly universal attraction and can gain broad support for privilege'. The inevitability of ill health for many and death for all help to make medicine the prototypical site for professionalisation, in which claims to specialist knowledge form barriers to access and corresponding rewards in both status and financial resources. Of all the professions, it is medicine that claims, in the form of variations on the Hippocratic oath, to a formal statement of the substance around which it is organised. Although 'first do no harm' has mutated into extensive statements of professional ethics controlled by representative bodies, the emphasis on a code of conduct that privileges patients sets medicine apart from the imperatives of other institutional orders. Apart from, but not uninfluenced by, as we saw in the case of the fate of health systems in the comparison of the United States of America, Great Britain and Canada. In the United States, in particular, commercial imperatives with an emphasis on individual action in a market were profound and enduring influences on the provision of healthcare (Hacker, 1998). As Andrei Markovits and Steven Hellerman

(2001: 46) in their consideration of American exceptionalism conclude, 'American sports are like American education and American religion: independent of the state, market driven, and ultimately subject to few, if any, regulating bodies outside those of their own creation.' They could here, based on Hacker's account, have added medicine. Further, Mary-Dunn and Candace Jones, in a historical account examining the period 1967–2005, show the impact of the logic of science on the education of the medical profession, bringing it into conflict with an ethic of care. 'In short,' they suggest, 'a science logic focuses on knowledge of diseases built through research and innovative treatments, whereas a care logic highlights physicians' clinical skills used to treat patients and improve the health of the community' (Dunn and Jones, 2010: 116). Their work draws our attention to both the conflict between logics within institutions and the relationship between the institutions, reminding us that the institutions we have been considering do not stand alone but form clusters of mutual influence. The contrast between such clusters only becomes clear when we engage in comparative analysis, a point to be returned to in the chapters that follow.

Summary

Institutions emerge out of the embodied relationship of human beings with each other and the natural world. Each generates distinctive practices, animated by belief in a core substance, a substance that is never reachable but is immanent in practices. This chapter has provided an outline of the substance at the heart of each of the suggested institutions and, in the course of so doing, has suggested some of the distinctive practices we might examine in more depth. The coverage accorded to each institution has not been symmetrical but in large measure reflects not their relative importance but the attention that has been paid to these practices in the literature. As noted in the introduction, the discussion of institutions has often been characterised by attention to formal bodies of doctrine or to organisational forms, rather than to taken-for-granted practices. Accordingly, the following chapter considers the nature of practices in a little more detail.

References

Anderson, B. (1991) *Imagined Communities*, London: Verso.

Arendt, H. (1958) *The Human Condition*,Chicago, IL: University of Chicago Press.

Asad, T. (1993) *Genealogies of Religion: Discipline and Reasons of Power in Christianity and Islam*, Baltimore: John Hopkins University Press.

Ashiwa, Y. and Wank, D. (2009) *Making Religion, Making the State: The Politics of Religion in Modern China*, Stanford, CA: Stanford General.

Berry, C. (2013) *The Idea of Commercial Society in the Scottish Enlightenment*, Edinburgh: Edinburgh University Press.

Billig, M. (1995) *Banal Nationalism*, London: Sage.

Blais, A. and Massicotte, L. (1997) 'Electoral formulas: a macroscopic perspective', *European Journal of Political Research*, 32, 107–129.

Boltanski, L. and Thevenot, L. (2006) *On Justification: Economies of Worth*, Princeton, NJ: Princeton University Press.

Boltanski, L. and Chiapello, E. (2007) *The New Spirit of Capitalism*, London: Verso.

Bourdieu, P. and Passeron, J. (1977) *Reproduction in Education, Society and Culture*, London: Sage.

Collins, R. (2007) 'The classical tradition in sociology of religion', in Beckford J. and Demerath, N. (eds) *The Sage Handbook of the Sociology of Religion*, London: Sage, 2007, 19–38.

Collins, H. and Evans, R. (2017) *Why Democracies Need Science*, Cambridge: Polity.

Damasio, A. (2000) *The Feeling of what Happens: Body, Emotion and the Making of Consciousness*, London: Vintage.

Dean, K. (2009) 'Further partings of the way : the Chinese state and Daoist ritual traditions in contemporary China' in Ashiwa, Y. and Wank, D. (eds) *Making Religion, Making the State: The Politics of Religion in Modern China*, Stanford, CA: Stanford General, 2009, 177–187.

Demerath, N. and Schmitt, T. (1998) 'Transcending sacred and secular: mutual benefits in analyzing religious and nonreligious organizations', in Demerath, N. Hall, P., Schmitt, T. and Williams, R. (eds.) *Sacred Companies*, New York: Oxford University Press, 1998, 381–392.

Demerath, N. and Farnsley, A. (2007) 'Congregations resurgent',in Demerath, N. and Beckford, J. (eds.) *The Sage Handbook of the Sociology of Religion*, London: Sage, 2007, 193–204.

Duff, I. (2013) 'We don't do walking away', in Franklin, S.,Gow, J., Graham, C. and McKillop, A. (eds.) *Follow We Will: The Fall and Rise of Rangers*, 2013, 121–129.

Dunn M. and Jones C. (2010) 'Institutional logics and institutional pluralism: the contestation of care and science logics in medical education, 1967–2005', *Administrative Science Quarterly*, 55(1), 114–149.

Edelman, L., Uggen, C. and Erlanger, H. (1999) 'The endogeneity of legal regulation: grievance procedures as rational myth', *American Journal of Sociology*, 105, 406–454.

Ellis, H. (1923) *The Dance of Life*, London: Constable.

Ferguson, A. (1767) *An Essay on the History of Civil Society*, Cambridge: Cambridge University Press.

Fine, C. (2017) *Testosterone Rex: Unmaking the Myths of Our Gendered Minds*, London: Icon.

Friedland, R. and Alford, R. (1991) 'Bringing society back in: symbols, practices, and institutional contradictions', in Powell, W. and DiMaggio, P. (eds) *The New Institutionalism in Organizational Analysis*, Chicago, IL: University of Chicago Press, 1991, 232–266.

Friedland, R. (2002) 'Money, sex, and god: the erotic logic of religious nationalism', *Sociological Theory*, 20(3), 381–425.

120 *Substance*

Friedland, R. (2009a) 'Institution, practice and ontology: towards a religious sociology', *Research in the Sociology of Organizations*, 27, 45–83.

Friedland, R. (2009b) 'The endless fields of Pierre Bourdieu', *Organization*, 16, 887–917.

Friedland, R. (2012) 'Book review: Patricia H. Thornton, William Ocasio and Michael Lounsbury 2012 "The Institutional Logics Perspective: A new approach to Culture, Structure, and Process"', *Management*, 15(5), 582–595.

Friedland, R. (2018) 'Moving institutional logics forward: emotion and meaningful material practice', *Organization Studies*, 39(4), 515–542.

Friedson, E. (2001) *Professionalism: The Third Logic*, Cambridge: Polity.

Gherardi, S. (2006) *Organizational Knowledge: The Texture of Workplace Learning*, Oxford: Blackwell.

Giddens, A. (1990) *The Consequences Of Modernity*, Cambridge: Polity.

Graziadei, M. (2013) 'The functionalist heritage', in Legrand, P. and Munday, R. (eds.) *Comparative Legal Studies: Traditions and Transitions*, Cambridge: Cambridge University Press, 2013, 100–127.

Grossfeld, B. (2013) 'Comparatists and languages', in Legrand, P. and Munday, R. (eds.) *Comparative Legal Studies: Traditions and Transitions*, Cambridge: Cambridge University Press, 2013, 154–194.

Hacker, J. (1998) 'The historical logic of national health insurance: structure and sequence in the development of British, Canadian, and U.S. medical policy', *Studies in American Political Development*, 12, 57–130.

Hindle, S. (2000) *The State And Social Change In Early Modern England 1550–1640*, Basingstoke: Palgrave Macmillan.

Hoggart, R. (1971) *The Uses of Literacy: Aspects of Working-Class Life, with Special Reference to Publications and Entertainments*, London: Chatto and Windus.

Huizinga, J. (1949) *Homo Ludens: A Study of the Play-Element in Culture*, London: Routledge & Kegan Paul.

Kauder, E. (1965) *History of Marginal Utility Theory*, Princeton, NJ: Princeton University Press.

Langer, S. (1957) *Philosophy in a New Key: A Study in the Symbolism of Reason, Rite, and Art*, Cambridge, MA: Harvard University Press, third edition.

Lasser, M. (2013) 'The question of understanding', in Legrand, P. and Munday, R. (eds.) *Comparative Legal Studies: Traditions and Transitions*, Cambridge: Cambridge University Press, 2013, 197–239.

Latour, B. (1987) *Science in Action: How to Follow Scientists and Engineers Through Society*, Cambridge, MA: Harvard University Press.

Lave, J. and Wenger, E. (1991) *Situated Learning: Legitimate Peripheral Participation*, Cambridge: Cambridge University Press.

Lever, J. (1999) 'Why procedure is more important than substantive law', *International and Comparattive Law Quarterly*, 48, 285–301.

Lomas, T. (2018) 'The flavours of love: A cross-cultural lexical analysis', *Journal for the Theory of Social Behaviour*, 48, 134–152.

MacDonald, I. (1995) *Revolution in the Head: The Beatles' Records and the Sixties*, London: Pimlico.

Macpherson, W. (1928) *Soldiering in India 1764–1787*, Edinburgh: William Blackwood.

Markovits, A. and Hellerman, S. (2001) *Offside: Soccer and American Exceptionalism*, Princeton, NJ: Princeton University Press.

McLeod, K. (2016) *We are the Champions: The Politics of Sports and Popular Music*, London: Routledge.

Meyer, R. and Hammerschmid, G. (2006) 'Changing institutional logics and executive identities - a managerial challenge to public administration in Austria', *American Behavioral Scientist*, 49(7), 1000–1014.

Musacchio, A. and Turner, J. (2013) 'Does the law and finance hypothesis pass the test of history?', *Business History*, 55(4), 524–542.

Mutch, A. (2006) 'Organization theory and military metaphor: time for a reappraisal?', *Organization*, 13(6), 751–769.

Mutch, A. (2008) *Managing Information and Knowledge in Organizations*, New York: Routledge.

Neocleous, M. (2013) '"O effeminacy! effeminacy!" War, masculinity and the myth of liberal peace', *European Journal of International Relations*, 19(1), 93–113.

Nonaka, I. and Takeuchi, H. (1995) *The Knowledge-Creating Company: How Japanese Companies Create the Dynamics of Innovation*, New York: Oxford University Press.

Pierson, P. (2004) *Politics in Time: History, Institutions, and Social Analysis*, Princeton, NJ: Princeton University Press.

Polanyi, M. (1958) *Personal Knowledge : Towards a Post-Critical Philosophy*, London: Routledge & Kegan Paul.

Polanyi, M. (1967) *The Tacit Dimension*, London: Routledge & Kegan Paul.

Selznick, P. (2008) *A Humanist Science: Values and Ideals in Social Inquiry*, Stanford, CA: Stanford University Press.

Sennett, R. (2002) *The Fall of Public Man*, London: Penguin.

Smith, C. (2010) *What is a Person? : Rethinking Humanity, Social Life, and the Moral Good from the Person Up*, Chicago, IL: University of Chicago Press.

Taylor, M. (2004) *Confidence Games: Money and Markets in a World Without Redemption*, Chicago, IL: University of Chicago Press.

Tempany, A. (2016) *And the Sun Shines Now: How Hillsborough and the Premier League Changed Britain*, London: Faber & Faber.

Thompson, E. P. (1977) *Whigs and Hunters: The Origin of the Black Act*, London: Penguin.

Thornton, P. (2004) *Markets from Culture: Institutional Logics and Organizational Decisions in Higher Education Publishing*, Stanford, CA: Stanford University Press.

Thornton, P., Occasio, W. and Lounsbury, M. (2012) *The Institutional Logics Perspective: A New Approach to Culture, Structure, and Process*, Oxford: Oxford University Press.

Voronov, M. and Vince, R. (2012) 'Integrating emotions into the analysis of institutional work', *Academy of Management Review*, 37(1), 58–81.

Vranken, M. (2015) *Western Legal Traditions: A Comparison of Civil Law & Common Law*, Sydney: The Federation Press.

Walsh, P. (2015) *Arendt Contra Sociology: Theory, Society and its Science*, London: Ashgate.

Weber, M. (1948) 'Religious rejections of the world and their directions', in Gerth, H. and Wright Mills, C. (eds.) *From Max Weber*, London: Routledge & Kegan Paul, 1948, 323–359.

Weik, E. (2018) 'Understanding institutional endurance: the role of dynamic form, harmony and rhythm in institutions', *Academy of Management Review*, In Press, https://journals.aom.org/doi/abs/10.5465/amr.2015.0050.

Whitehouse, H. (2004) *Modes of Religiosity: A Cognitive Theory of Religious Transmission*, Walnut Creek, CA: AltaMira Press.

Whitman, J. (2013) 'The neo-Romantic turn', in Legrand, P. and Munday, R. (eds.) *Comparative Legal Studies: Traditions and Transitions*, Cambridge: Cambridge University Press, 2013, 312–344.

Whittington, R. and Mayer, M. (2000) *The European Corporation: Strategy, Structure And Social Science*, Oxford: Oxford University Press.

Willis, P. (1977) *Learning to Labour: How Working Class Kids Get Working Class Jobs*, Farnborough: Saxon House.

Winton, T. (2014) 'In the Shadow of the Hospital', *Granta*, 124, 205–218.

Zan, L. (2004) 'Accounting and management discourse in proto-industrial settings: the Venice Arsenal in the turn of the 16th century', *Accounting and Business Research*, 34(2), 145–175.

5   Practices

Introduction

Institutional logics are emergent from our embodied relations with each other and the natural world. They arise from the finite limits of the human condition and are value driven, motivated by a substance that is immanent in practices. It is to those practices that we need to look to explore the workings of logics, for substances that are beyond our reach, manifest only in the practices that they have put in motion. From a morphogenetic perspective, practices are a part of the structural and cultural conditioning of action. However, practices as such figure little in that tradition, in part because of a reaction against practice theory. The distinction between practice, as a verb, and practices, as a noun, forms the first part of this chapter, which seeks to formulate a more detailed picture of practices in order to investigate them historically. To that end, the second part of the chapter distinguishes between conventions, rituals and routines. I focus on routines in particular, both because they are most often neglected in historical accounts and because of their centrality to organisational life.

Practices and Morphogenesis

To remind ourselves, here is the list that Margaret Archer (1996: 1) gives of key components of social structure: 'roles, organizations, institutions, systems'. Roy Bhaskar (1979), in his transformational model of social action (TMSA) uses 'position-practices' as a somewhat clumsy but nonetheless informative substitute for roles. There is something to be lost here that we need to be mindful of in our later discussion, the sense of performance that goes with the notion of 'roles'. This dramaturgical perspective on social life is seen most clearly in Goffman's notion of the front and back stage of social life, in which roles are accomplished performances. Something is lost, argues Sennett, when rituals are downplayed in the service of 'authenticity'. As he argues

> The question of play and what happens to play in adult life is important because the cultural evolution of modern times is peculiar.

It is unusual for a society to distrust ritual or ritualized gesture, unusual for a society to see formal behavior as inauthentic. The childhood energies of play are in most societies continued and enriched as
ritual, usually in the service of religion. Secular, advanced capitalist
society does not call upon, but rather works against, these energies.

(Sennett, 2002: 315)

There is clearly an important link in that statement to our earlier discussion of play, and that is something we need to be mindful of. However,
as Sennett himself points out, the consideration of roles as performance
can detach them from the rules that specify how the performance is to
be accomplished, rules that may be explicit or tacit and that change over
time. To this end, the importance of Bhaskar's formulation is that it links
particular practices to particular 'slots' in social structures, positions
that are given relationally by the logics, which have emerged historically.
The general in the military, the judge in the law, the referee in a football match are all positions that are specialised to a particular logic and
that are licensed to carry out specific practices in order to carry out the
requirements of their position. That such performances can be inflected
by the particular character of the individual actor is not doubted and
is a key part of concrete analysis, but the combination of position and
practices puts boundaries around performances. How those boundaries
are shaped and challenged over time is a key part of historical analysis
and of the development of institutional logics, but first we need to place
practices back into the morphogenetic framework.

Archer is somewhat ambivalent about the position-practice formulation. Her concern is that it occludes those encounters with social structure that do not rest on formal positions (Archer, 1995: 153). In this
regard, the position-practice formulation better fits the world of organisations than broader social encounters like the conventions we will
encounter shortly. But the problem is that Archer's adherence to roles
means that practices do not get the consideration they are due. As we
have seen, Archer (1996) develops her ideas at a high level, often covering large sweeps of time. Her discussion of cultural contradictions, for
example, draws heavily on Durkheim's account of the contradictions
involved in the contribution of Greek classicism, with its pagan roots,
to Christianity. For many years, Durkheim argued, these contradictions
were manifest only to a select group, who could supress knowledge of
their existence. However, changing social conditions made such suppression more difficult, meaning that more and more sophisticated attempts
to repair the contradictions had to be undertaken. Just as with other
social theorists, such as the work of Weber that we will consider in due
course, this means the focus is on grand ideas rather than more mundane
practices. The same could be said for *Realist Social Theory*, in which
Archer (1995) explicates her morphogenetic framework. Practices do not

feature explicitly here, although it is important to note Archer's (1996: 228) argument that the framework she proposes could be used at any scale of activity.

Elsewhere in her work we can find this attention to practical action, especially when she is resisting the claims to the priority of language. We have already seen her commitment to pre-linguistic understanding as prior in ontogenetic development. She also develops a theory of knowing based on an insistence that as embodied persons, humans have of necessity to engage with three orders of existence, the natural, the practical and the social. In her account of *Being Human*, the instructive chapter headings are, respectively, 'the primacy of practice' and 'the practical order as pivotal'. In this account, self-consciousness emerges from embodied interactions with the world. 'It is through the activities of embodied practice,' she argues, 'that we develop the powers of thought'. In the natural order it is the world that suggests practical actions, which are embodied as tacit knowledge, engaged in automatically' (Archer, 2000: 146). 'Most of us,' she suggests, 'were never taught to lean into the wind or incline our body-weight forward when climbing a hill, and backwards when descending, nor do we do it cerebrally – which is not to deny intentionality' (Archer, 2000: 163). In the practical order, where we get things done with the artefacts that are to-hand, much of our knowledge is tacit, gained from embodied experience and manifest in the form of skills. It is only in the social order that discursive knowledge becomes more central. What these extracts suggest is a focus on practice as action, one that leads to the downplaying of practices as elements of structural and cultural conditioning. This is amplified by her hostility to forms of practice theory, especially as found in the work of Bourdieu (1990). Before turning to that, we can catch something of the distinction if we turn to Archer's discussion of knowledge amongst the Roman Catholic faithful.

Here practice is seen as that which obtains as distinct from official formulations. That is, the focus is on what persons actually do, as opposed to what they are told to do or what they 'ought' to do. Thus, she contrasts what Roman Catholics do in relation to sexual practices (contraception, extra-marital sex) with the official position on such practices. She then goes on to question the degree to which membership of the Catholic faithful depends on shared knowledge or understanding of those official positions. 'Every Sunday,' she observes, 'it is the duty of the faithful to say the Creed but, were it broken down into its component propositions, the most diverse array of understood meanings would result' (Donati and Archer, 2015: 174). What I would argue is that it is the saying of the Creed that is the practice, and that the saying rather than the understanding is what is important. I think this only becomes clear when we take a comparative perspective. Creeds are a statement of official doctrines, boiled down from more abstruse theological debates. Other branches of Christianity also incorporate the recitation of such creeds into their liturgical practices, notably the Church of England in its Book of Common Prayer. In turn, this has to be seen in the context of a wider practice, which is that of a specification for conducting services of worship. To be sure, such practices can be contested, but the contrast has to be with other Christian denominations that reject both the recitation of creeds and tightly structured forms of worship. As opposed to creeds, those in the Reformed Protestant tradition have catechisms (Petterson, 2014). The faithful are expected to understand these, and indeed, to recite them, but not as part of an act of worship. Rather, they are used for education and, in particular, as a test for worthiness to participate in an important practice that we will consider in more detail later, that of communion. The opposition to structured worship then becomes an article of faith in itself, a badge of commitment to a particular set of beliefs and practices, as with the Presbyterian commitment to extempore prayers. This is not to say that such denominations do not have forms of structure in their services but, for the present purpose, the contrast points up the importance of specified practices in Roman Catholic liturgical practice.

The tendency in Archer to conflate practice with action and so to rather neglect practices is compounded by her strong critique of versions of practice theory, notably those associated with the work of Bourdieu. She is particularly concerned to reject his central concept of habitus, seeing it as conflating structure and agency and depriving persons of the capacity for reflexive engagement with the conditions in which they find themselves. Bourdieu's work is centrally concerned with the ways in which actors can produce structured outcomes through engaging in practical activity without strategic intent. Their mastery of the rules of the game, acquired unconsciously and through socialisation, means that they can produce effective performances that reproduce the field in which they are engaged without necessarily having an instrumental intention. Bourdieu (1990: 50) contends that,

> Practices can have other principles than mechanical causes or conscious ends and can obey an economic logic without obeying narrowly economic interests. There is an economy of practices, a reason immanent in practices, whose "origin" lies neither in the "decisions" of reason understood as rational calculation nor in the determinations of mechanisms external to and superior to the agents.

What regulates this 'economy of practices', making actors produce patterned and structured outcomes, is the habitus. Archer rejects such a perspective, focusing instead on agential reflexivity. To remind ourselves, rather than involving a lack of reflection, continuity between social structure and reflexivity would be a feature of conversational reflexivity, where the need for others to complete processes of reflection on ultimate values would indicate a desire to accommodate to existing contexts. However, this still, for Archer, involves considerably more reflexivity than would be consistent with notions of habitus. For Porpora (2015), the problem is that structure and culture are folded into activity. This activity is then seen as guided by habit, by largely unconscious dispositions that lead to the charge that persons are turned into 'zombies'. At best they are cultural dopes who are 'performed' by the practices they engage in. The counter to this is to stress the capacity of persons to engage in reflection fuelled by their ultimate values. In order to do this, the emphasis is against notions of habit as guides to action. Porpora, for example, spends some time describing his own morning routine, stressing how it involves reflection at each stage. There are two problems with this. While it ably defends the notion of reflexive persons it rather downplays the specification of practices by others. In the case of domestic routines, there is a strong degree of agential choice. However, Porpora has earlier endorsed an observation of Howard Becker about rules: 'differences in the ability to make rules and apply them to other people are essentially power differentials (either legal or extralegal). Those groups whose social position gives them weapons and power are best able to enforce their rules' (Porpora, 2015: 127). This is the situation that, as we will see, often obtains in formal organisations. It raises important questions about who makes the rules and who has the power to enforce them. That power is often, as Lukes (1974) would tell us, at its strongest when embedded in practices that are taken to be 'natural'. The second concern is the opening that the focus on creative performances gives to those who would focus on practices as patterns of behaviour. This has tended, in the organisational literature, to a focus on performance abstracted from the wider context that places limits on that performance. The emphasis here is on change in a way that exaggerates the degrees of room for manoeuvre that are on offer. Habits can be seen as individual forms of practices, subject to the vagaries of individual volition and formation. For the purpose of social analysis, we are more interested in social practice, that is, practices that involve relations between persons.

Forms of Practices

There is an amusing account in the work of popular social anthropology by Kate Fox (2005), *Watching the English*. She engages in a breaching experiment of the type pioneered by Garfinkel, one in which she fully anticipates the result, when she jumps a queue of people waiting for service. She anticipates the result of breaching the powerful social convention obtaining in British life of queuing in an orderly fashion where the rule is 'first come, first served'. The confirmation of the operation of this tacit social rule is the disapproving looks that she gets from breaching it. But the response of those appalled by her action is also revealing: they do not complain. At least their complaints are limited to *sotto voce* verbal utterances ('tut tut') or knowing glances exchanged by others whose place has been usurped. Fox's example is a strong one of a social convention in which rules are not formally expressed but are known by all participants native to the social setting. The rules have been learned through experience and emulation but have rarely been formally expressed except perhaps in childhood socialisation. The degree to which such social conventions are artificial and socially constructed only becomes evident when persons are placed in other social settings in which the conventions do not apply.

Conventions are then, one important form of practices, ones that are often only revealed in the work of social anthropologists. Their investigations are concerned with making the taken-for-granted strange, with denaturalising practices and so making them visible. Conventions are forms of social practice that remain largely tacit; by contrast, rituals and routines are often connected to formal bodies of knowledge and to power relations within organisations. One impulse behind the closer scrutiny of this couplet comes from the focus on mundane practices in new institutional theory. Another is the work of social theorists like Michel Foucault, who sought to examine the emergence of new forms of social practice. A key example in his work arises from the study of Christian, specifically Catholic, practice. He argued that religion had been studied largely as a matter of belief or as a history of organisational forms (Foucault, 2009: 150). Not enough attention had been paid, he argued, to the history of social practices, especially those that reinforced what he term 'pastoral power'. That is, he was concerned about the techniques whereby certain persons, in particular positions, could control the actions of others. The practice of auricular confession, that is the revelation of conduct classified by the church as forbidden conduct by word of mouth to a listening priest, the priest being in a position to absolve those sins, was Foucault's focus. Drawing on secondary work, he examined the development of this process, involving the training through manuals of those hearing confessions and the provision of a specific material technology, that of the confessional box to ensure a private one-to-one confession. He then used this as an example to suggest how techniques developed in the realm of religion could be taken up in secular life.

The specifics of this discussion are not our concern at this point, but it points to both the importance of religious ritual and some problems with its investigation. As Foucault himself recognised, the history of formal injunctions 'does not represent the massive and extensive real practice of confession since the sixteenth or seventeenth century' (Foucault, 1991: 191). He was quite aware that confession often represented a ritual on the part of those doing the confessing. Nevertheless, rituals are, as we have seen, a central part of the logic of religion. For Friedland,

> Religion appears to us as a distinctive kind of institution, replete with rite, that is, with practices — prayer, penitence, piety, pilgrimage, sacrament and charity — that have a non-arbitrary relationship to what they signify, that is, symbolic actions, as well as with

performative forms of speech, where use of language is a form of action, referring to the reality it itself produces. Both cleric and laity literally speak and act God's presence into existence, an ontological substance that can never be reduced to its attributes, nor to the practices that access or evoke it.

(Friedland, 2009: 60)

In his investigation of the cognitive psychology of religion, Whitehouse (2004) defines rituals as practices that display an excess over technical motivation and so invite exegesis. However, 'procedural competence is, therefore, somewhat disconnected from people's explicit concepts of why rituals take the form that they do' (Whitehouse, 2004: 8). As Asad (1993: 62) suggests, 'apt performance involves not symbols to be interpreted but abilities to be acquired according to rules that are sanctioned by those in authority: it presupposes no obscure meanings, but rather the formation of physical and linguistic skills'. That is, in many cases, it is perfectly possible to take part in rituals successfully and give accounts of that performance, 'constrained more by commonsense principles than by the kind of complex theoretical knowledge available to experts' (Whitehouse, 2004: 17). Hence, as Clark argues, arises the danger of seeking to construct ritual performances and their meanings from formal bodies of theology alone (Clark, 2004). Ritual is also important in making connections, connections that come from shared performance rather than, necessarily, shared values. So, observes Whitehouse (2004: 69), 'what it means to be a regular churchgoer is not to be part of a particular group but to participate in a ritual scheme and belief structure that anonymous others also share'. In turn, the rituals that are shared can become a powerful indicator of identity. Whitehouse (2004: 93) observes that although 'people who attend church regularly do not need to have quasi-theoretical knowledge of the links between standing and singing, kneeling and praying, and sitting and listening; such knowledge is bound to emerge over time'. Such knowledge can then articulate particular identities that are shaped more by the common performance of the ritual than by more abstract theoretical considerations. In his study of the religious influences on the cities of Boston and Philadelphia, Baltzell (1979: 367) recounts the story of an eminent Boston Unitarian commenting to an Episcopalian friend, 'Eliza, do you *kneel* down in church and call yourself a miserable sinner? Neither I nor any member of my family will ever do *that*!' (emphasis in original). By contrast, in his ethnographic study of converts to Islam, Daniel Winchester points to the importance of a different practice of prayer, that of praying in a prostrate posture as an act of submission to God. As he observes

In practicing saiat [ritual prayer], then, converts were restructuring their everyday lives according to cultural schemes of transcendent time and sacred authority, embodying these schemes, in turn, as durable dispositions of mindfulness and humility. These arbitrary schemes of culture became embodied as lived realities: submission to the authority of Allah was not just performed but felt, becoming, in and through practice, part and parcel of the embodied moral subject.

(Winchester, 2008: 1766)

I will discuss the more conceptual aspects of this discussion further shortly, but first I want to illustrate the point with another historical example drawn from Presbyterian practice, specifically that found in Scotland. This is the practice of seated communion. Communion is a central practice in most Christian denominations. It involves the partaking of bread and wine, blessed by a religiously sanctioned individual, symbolic of the meal that Jesus was said to have presided over before his death and resurrection, the Last Supper. Disputes over the meaning and nature of the communion were a central issue in the European Reformation that saw Protestant denominations split from Roman Catholicism. The debates over whether the bread and wine were actually transformed into the blood and flesh of Christ (the transubstantiation thesis) or were merely symbolic are not our concern, although much real blood was spilled over such debates. However, such debates transformed practices of taking and receiving communion. As opposed to the individual kneeling and taking the communion elements from a priest, a practice grew up in Scottish Presbyterianism of taking communion in collective form. Seated at a table, the bread and wine, having been introduced to the table by the minister with injunctions from the Bible, were passed round from participant to participant (Torrance, 2014). This practice was justified by a reading of the Biblical texts in an effort to mirror the Last Supper, reflecting in turn a commitment to return to the practices of the primitive church as recorded in the Bible. Now, there are good reasons to doubt the theological warrant for this practice. In many ways, it could be read as developed in opposition to its Catholic 'other'. Nevertheless, it persisted, engendering a collective form of worship that some argue has influenced American revivalism (Schmidt, 2001). That, in the eyes of some Presbyterian divines, was a cause for concern. Not only was obvious religious emotionalism rather frowned upon, but such practices, as memorably satirised in Robert Burns'. 'The Holy Fair' provided opportunities for unruly gatherings prone to more secular forms of satisfaction. What this meant over time was the shift from sitting at a table to the reception of communion sat in pews in the body of the church, a practice that did not involve movement and so was considered to be more conducive of order and decorum. Nevertheless, the practice of remaining seated for this most important occasion in the church calendar became a taken-for-granted practice, one that only loses that status when contrasted to practices in other denominations.

Rituals are an important part of the practices that carry other logics as well. The confirmation that an educational credential has been achieved can be conveyed by an impersonal written communication, but higher education organisations have evolved elaborate graduation ceremonies. The official confirmation of achievement may well be received, but it is played out in a public performance, replete with often arcane material objects (the ceremonial mace and mace bearer) and costumes designed to mark out actors from those outside the logic. Here the ritual is a form of acceptance into a particular community, but rituals can also be ways on confirming difference from other domains. The practice of military drill can have functional reasons such as inculcating a sense of discipline and obedience to orders, but it also serves to mark off a distinctive logic. This is particularly the case when the practice of drill is extended to public performance as in ceremonies such as the change of the guard in symbolically important places. While there is a technical purpose in changing personnel at the end of a tedious and taxing physical activity, the changing of the guard at Buckingham Palace in London, at the Portuguese Tomb of the Unknown Warrior at the Monastery of Batalha or outside the Greek Parliament building in Athens features often elaborate manoeuvres that, in the Greek example, amount to almost balletic movements. Taken out of context, these might seem caricatured, but they are expressing a particular logic, one that is separate from civilian logic.

Routines

We could multiply these examples of rituals for other logics, but there is something missing in this account, something that I wish to indicate by means of a comparative account of the practices of communion in the Christian churches of Scotland and England. The example used to illustrate these points is the Christian ritual of communion as practiced in eighteenth-century Scotland and England. The key point of contrast here is between open and closed communion. In the former, there is no qualification for the receipt of communion, which is often taken frequently. The church aspires to be a universal one, only excluding from the ritual those who have been found guilty of breaking core tenets of the faith. The consequence is that only minimal routines are necessary to prepare the conditions for exercise of the ritual, such as purchase of the necessary materials. Such was the system that obtained in the Church of England, a Protestant religious polity characterised as Episcopalianism – that is, a form of hierarchical organisation marked by the formal authority of the bishop (Boulton, 1984). Matters are very different in closed communion. Here, the sacrament is restricted to those who have met entry qualifications, whether these are membership or knowledge. In the Reformed Protestant tradition represented by the Presbyterian Church of Scotland access to communion was restricted to those who could demonstrate their awareness of the basics of the belief system. Communion was to be strictly limited both in the times when it was offered and those to whom it was offered (Holmes, 2006). As practice evolved, communion was often held once a year, as preparation for participation was stressed. In turn, this related to the emphasis placed on the understanding of the Biblical foundations that were held to be fundamental to faith. Accordingly, the catechisms that we met earlier were used as the basis for education and examination. Ministers held special sessions in which they expounded the catechism, and they conducted annual examinations of the faithful to test their knowledge and hence their suitability for communion. This challenging and time-consuming task necessarily meant that communion was a rare event; it was generally only celebrated once a year in most parishes in the eighteenth century. A desire to streamline the process meant the introduction of rolls of those deemed fit to participate. Detailed examination was then limited to those, generally the young, who sought admission to communion for the first time. This, however, did not mean that the routine of examination faded, rather that it shifted to the scrutiny of rolls to make sure that all on it were in good standing. Over time, this evolved into the production of printed templates on which to enter the information, templates that also evolved in order to record attendance (Mutch, 2015).

At this point, it is important to note who was doing this examination. In Presbyterianism, local parishes were administered by the minister together with a 'session' comprised of a number of 'elders'. From the promulgation of church's 'procedure manual', the *First Book of Discipline* in 1561, a key role was reserved for the Elders in their support of the minister:

> For such as be so dull and so ignorant that they can neither try themselves nor know the dignitie and mysterie of that action cannot eate and drink of that Table worthily. And therefore of necessity we judge that everie yeare at the least, publick examination be had by the Ministers and Elders of the knowledge of every person within the kirk.
>
> (Cameron, 1972: 186)

Selected by the existing session and ordained for life (and so strictly speaking not 'lay') these elders assisted the minister in maintaining discipline in the parish, acting, as it were, as his eyes and ears amongst the congregation. It was this collective body that ran the routines that made the ritual of closed communion possible. Once those who were fit to participate had been identified, some means of ensuring that they, and only they, had access to the communion venue was necessary. In one typical parish, Rayne in Aberdeenshire, the minutes for 21 June 1772 record that it was 'Appointed the people of the Western side of the Parish to attend Thursday after the sermon to receive their Tokens'.[1] This introduces a very concrete symbol of the importance of membership in Presbyterian practice, the communion token. The session at Rayne possessed 'A Box filled with Tokens, with a stamp for striking tokens'.[2] Such tokens, generally of lead, bearing the year of communion and the parish name, were distributed to each communicant. Access to the communion venue was guarded by members of the session, who collected these tokens. They also served the tables, making sure that communion materials were present and order maintained. These duties could be onerous; as communion was only taken once a year it became a focus for mass participation, often involving significant numbers necessitating a series of consecutive sittings. After the event was over, sessions could count the communion tokens they had collected and so get a sense of how many had participated. Over time, the printed communion rolls became a means of recording this information, so that the participation of each individual in the congregation could be tracked (Mutch, 2015). It should be clear that one concomitant of a belief in closed communion, which flowed from a particular interpretation of Biblical injunctions, was a range of routines that, in particular, demanded comprehensive record keeping.

Towards the end of his life, Foucault recognised that he had underplayed the importance of Weber's work. There is, of course, a seeming incompatibility here. While Foucault laid stress on the importance of practices as shaped by and being the key to understanding broader discourses, Weber tended to dismiss the everyday. As Hennis points out for Weber 'in all social phenomena it is the non-everyday that interests him, that which bursts through everyday life' (Hennis, 1988: 181). While Foucault can be criticised by theologians for abstracting practices from broader systems of belief, it is just those broader belief systems that form the main thrust of Weber's work. In the context of religion, of course, this is best known through the enduring debate stimulated by Weber's (1976) thesis about the Protestant ethic. That work centres on the implications for secular activity of the Protestant emphasis on predestination. This is the theological argument that salvation comes about not through the performance of good works, but through the receipt of God's grace. It is God alone who decides who is to be saved. That decision is in his hands, and believers have been marked out to be either amongst the elect who are to enjoy eternal life, or the damned, condemned to eternal agony in the fires of Hell. This rather bleak set of beliefs caused considerable anxiety to the faithful, who sought evidence that they had received grace through certain marks. Amongst these could be worldly success, giving rise, argued Weber, to a focus on success in worldly activities as a good in its own right. There has been, of course, much debate about the link between such matters of religious belief and shifts in economic activity (Ghosh, 2014). In his response to critics of *The Protestant Ethic* Weber insisted that 'what interested me centrally was not what nurtured the expanding capitalism but the developing type of human being that was created out of the confluence of the religious and economic components' (Chalcraft and Harrington, 2001: 106).

Historians of Protestantism have suggested that the impact of predestination as a theological doctrine might have been overemphasised in the ensuing debate (Kadane, 2013). Even theological adepts recognised that the doctrine was a complex and difficult one. Not least was the concern that if somebody felt that they had the marks of saving grace and so were a member of the elect that they could then engage in any form of conduct secure in the knowledge that they were saved. This was not just an abstract matter: in 1723, Lieutenant Colonel J. Blackader of Stirling recorded the investigation of a claim of adultery on the part of an apparently devout member of the congregation. '[N]otwithstanding of these horrid scandals of adultery and perjury', he noted with horror, 'he is enjoying a peace of conscience, that surpasses not only all natural, but all spiritual understanding'. This was because of his belief that 'God sees not their sins as the sins of others, and is not angry with them as with others; and their views being only on free grace and pardoning grace, they do not entertain those frightful ideas of sin which they call a legal spirit: so that when they fall into even gross sins and scandals they are not uneasy' (Crichton, 1824: 529). Because of these dangers, the mysteries of predestination were, argued the devout elder Walter Steuart of Pardovan, in his widely used book of guidance for church procedure, to be reserved for the schooling of theological adepts rather than being preached to the averagely faithful (Steuart, 1709: 106). Such considerations mean that Mathew Kadane, in his study of the diary of the English Nonconformist clothier Joseph Ryder suggests that providence, the belief in an interventionist supreme being who provided evidence through particular events, was far more significant. The problem, Kadane suggests is that Weber (just like Foucault) 'paid overwhelming attention to prescriptive literature and official culture' (Kadane, 2013: 90).

However, it is possible to find some hints in Weber that point to the importance of examining practices, especially the practices that lay behind rituals, in more detail. These are to be found in some relatively little used passages in his work on religious sects. For Chalcraft (1994), this work is an essential complement to *The Protestant Ethic*. In it, Weber relates membership of sects to business success because of the certification of moral quality that membership tests provide. Two important facets here are the existence of membership and the denial of sacraments to any other than fully qualified members. So Weber notes that

> The tremendous social significance of admission to full enjoyment of the rights of the sectarian congregation, especially the privilege

of being admitted to the Lord's Supper, worked among the sects in the direction of breeding that ascetist professional ethic which was adequate to modern capitalism during the period of its origin.

(Weber, 1948: 312)

Weber goes on to note, although only in passing, some organisational concomitants of this restriction of sacraments, such as the circulation of certificates amongst congregations. This presupposed, as we have seen, further organisational practices such as the recording of membership. It also required specific roles to maintain discipline, and the importance of lay elders is stressed. However, he continued even here to return to the central importance of the internalisation of ascetic values:

The church discipline of the Puritans and of the sects was vested, first, at least in part and often wholly, in the hands of laymen. Secondly, it worked through the necessity of one's having to hold one's own; and, thirdly, it bred or, if one wishes, selected qualities. The last point is the most important one.

(Weber, 1948: 316)

As Bruno Dyck and his collaborators have argued, 'surprisingly little of that research [on Weber] has specifically examined the relationship between the values evident in different religions and the practices of those religious organizations' (Dyck et al., 2005: 52). Gorski, in his stimulating account of the origins of 'the disciplinary revolution', which he examines in the context of the Calvinism of Dutch Reformed Protestantism, notes Weber's comments on sects and observes of Foucault, 'one would expect a brief overview of the various disciplinary mechanisms invented by Protestant and Catholic religious reformers and of the ways in which territorial rulers utilized them as part of their strategies of domination'. However, he continues, Foucault moves on to an extensive discussion of treatises on governance. 'On the concrete social mechanisms through which this power operated', notes Gorski, 'the central concern of so much of his work, Foucault is strangely silent' (Gorski, 2003: 24)'. Gorski locates such concrete mechanisms in the disciplinary practices that emerged from putting Calvinist beliefs into effect. Those practices often involve matters of governance. Other writers, although not drawing on Weber, have pointed to such mechanisms in historical work on religious denominations. Leonard Arrington and Davis Bitton (1979) analyse the 'ward' structure of nineteenth-century Mormonism, pointing to the involvement of (male) lay members, all of whom who were deemed worthy being ordained to a lay priesthood. Each ward was under the control of a bishop, but 'This bishop was not elected by the people of his congregation. He was appointed by higher church authorities, a reflection of the tight central control and hierarchical nature of the church' (Arrington and Bitton, 1979: 207). Andrew Holmes (2006) examines the similarity of the practices of Ulster Presbyterianism to the Scottish practices that were their model, as discussed above. But often we lack this level of detail.[3] And further, the focus often tends to be on the rituals themselves and not on the practices that make them possible. In order to bring these practices out of the shadowy world they have been consigned to, I draw on the debates in organisation theory on the nature and status of routines.

Organisational Routines

Routines have been an important part of evolutionary approaches to economics, associated in particular with the work of Nelson and Winter (1982). Here routines were seen as the building blocks of organisations, although in a way that regards them as 'black boxes'. In influential work, Martha Feldman (2000) has argued that such an approach neglects the variation that can be found if we examine the performance of the routine. Subtle changes in the performance of a routine over time can lead to endogenous change. Routines, that is, can be conceptualised as 'generative systems', the source of organisational change. Feldman's perspective, developed with Brian Pentland, has stressed the performance of routines. Routines are defined as, 'repetitive, recocognizable patterns of interdependent actions, carried out by multiple actors' (Feldman and Pentland, 2003: 950). A key focus in their various articles is the stress on agency. Routines are not just abstract sets of instructions; they are performed. This means that they are, 'not only effortful but also emergent accomplishments. They are often works in progress rather than finished products' (Feldman, 2000: 613). Given this perspective, those who perform the routines, it is argued, are not blind rule followers but active selectors from a menu of possibilities, 'from which organizational members enact particular performances' (Feldman, 2000: 612). While work in this tradition has produced interesting empirical work, it raises a number of concerns. It seems a fairly fundamental critique that we lose a sense of the 'routineness' of routines (Birnholtz et al., 2009). That is, an everyday use, as expressed in dictionary definitions, would stress the rote aspects of routines. Thus, the *Oxford English Dictionary* (2011) has as its primary usage the following: 'A regularly followed procedure; an established or prescribed way of doing something; a more or less mechanical or unvarying way of performing certain actions or duties'. In the accounts given in the Feldman and Pentland tradition, the focus has been on how routines emerge from performance, placing stress on the uniqueness of each instantiation of the routine. Sometimes the examples given seem far from 'routine' in the dictionary sense of the term. The practices of moving students into university accommodation that form the basis of Feldman's (2000) initial formulations, for example, occurred once a year. A related concern is that this focus on performance collapses ideas about the routine into the performance of the routine. While individual performances will have to respond to the vagaries of unique instances, this does not necessarily mean that the overall structure of the routine, as laid down by organisation procedures will be challenged.

This is problematic in two senses. One is that we lose the connection with the wider organisation. The second is that the way in which participants might draw upon broader resources in framing their actions is even less clear. The first problem has received some attention, albeit somewhat muted, in the literature. In a study of conflict over a pricing routine, for example, Mark Zbaracki and Mark Bergen (2010) show how the marketing function were able to deploy ideas drawn from formal pricing theory as a powerful counter to the more experiential arguments of the sales function. It was not that the formal pricing theories were used, but that, '...whereas the sales force tended to focus on concrete pricing terms, the marketing group offered a more abstract language rooted in economics' (Zbaracki and Bergen, 2010: 968). As they note, 'jurisdictional battles reflect political, institutional and cognitive forces drawn from macrosocial battles' (Zbaracki and Bergen, 2010: 968). In similar fashion, Anna Essén (2008), in a study of Swedish homecare routines, points to the way in which routines are put into practice through the deployment of cultural norms that exceed and come from outside the genesis of formal rules.

Zbaracki and Bergen point to struggles over the nature of routines between particular organisational groups, groups that obtain their standing from organisational arrangements. A similar clash is reported by Luciana D'Adderio (2008) in her study of the impact of software in a manufacturing company. Her language here is that of 'occupational community', but this points to the differences engendered by the particular forms of organisational structuring of expertise. D'Adderio speaks of management as a particular form of community, which rather tends to underplay the significance of hierarchical position in conditioning the nature of routines. This aspect of power in organisations is better addressed, albeit briefly, by Jennifer Howard-Grenville's study of the use of a particular decision technique in a computer hardware fabrication company. She notes here that

> ...in all cases the individuals with greater command over the resources will be better able to change embedded routines over time. Changing routines that are strongly embedded in cultural structures may rely heavily on the use of authoritative and relational resources because they can be used to frame and negotiate, over time, shared meaning, shared norms, and collective identity.
>
> (Howard-Grenville, 2005: 634)

In a study of waste management organisations, Scott Turner and Violina Rindova (2012) show how particular artefacts, such as scheduling techniques, were used to prepare detailed guides for action, such as collection routes. Not only were everyday routines tightly conceived and executed, but routines for managing exceptions, although by necessity looser, were in place. Such artefacts, 'are largely introduced by the organization and reflect the management's view of how the routine should function' (Turner and Rindova, 2012: 42). These examples suggest that organisational routines are not just emergent from action but are shaped by organisational structures. As Marc Ventresca and Bill Kaghan argue

> We draw particular attention to the importance of bureaucratic processes, managerial work, and their relation to organizational stability and change. We underscore the importance of resisting efforts to separate analytically (whether by initial assumption or by research design) the performance of routine activity from the supporting social structures and meanings.
>
> (Ventresca and Kaghan, 2008, 55–56)

However, their advice is generally ignored in the mainstream of work on organisational routines, with the broader context, extending to the existence of rules, bracketed out. Of course, those rules can never provide an exhaustive guide to performance and, as Essén (2008) shows, actors draw upon their own experience and broader cultural norms to produce an effective performance. However, she also shows how participants often welcome rules as a framework for action. Regardless of the response of participants, there is a powerful incentive, Ingvaldsen (2015) argues, for managers to seek to codify practices in the name of consistency and transferability. That such efforts are bound to be only partially successful does not mean that the efforts are insignificant in their impacts (Reynaud, 2005). As D'Adderio points out

> formal procedures and rules can always – in theory – be worked around and dismissed, in practice they often play a role. Especially when embedded in artefacts such as software, and/or entangled into thick organisational interrelationships, they become visible, pervasive, difficult to change or avoid, easier to enforce.
>
> (D'Adderio, 2008: 784)

An alternative formulation has been developed by Geoff Hodgson as a way of avoiding these concerns. Routines are conceived as 'organizational dispositions to energize conditional patterns of behaviour within an organized group of individuals, involving sequential responses to cues' (Hodgson, 2008: 21). While patterns of behaviour are still embedded in this formulation, the attention is now placed on routines as organisational dispositions. Routines in organisations are not just, therefore, the creative response to particular situations (although they involve that), but they are the organisationally sanctioned response to specific cues. They may be performed slightly differently every time that they are invoked, but that performance is generally within specific parameters. It is important, as well, to consider the relative degree of involvement of particular participants and their ability to shape the ongoing performance of the routine. A historical approach can be valuable in not only locating routines in a specific context, showing the organisational, cultural and social factors that shape it and give particular direction to performance, but also in showing that routines themselves have a history. We can illustrate this by outlining the history of one routine in Christian practice, that of the visitation.

Routines in History: The Visitation

Gorski (2003) notes household visitations in the work of Schilling on Reformation Germany as one means of discipline, a means of discipline not covered by Foucault. In his history of the emergence of the research university in Germany, William Clark (2006) observes how the routine of visitation of educational establishments became an instrument of state control in the eighteenth century. From its origins in the control of ecclesiastical organisations, such visitations carried forward the tradition of detailed questionnaires as a guide to those conducting the visitation. While Clark notes that Oxbridge managed to claim exemption from state visitations, he does not consider the continuing nature of visitations by the church to educational establishments in Scotland until the end of the eighteenth century. We have noted the practice of examination of the faithful by the Scottish Presbyterian minister, but the minister was also subject to disciplinary practices, most notably in the form of the visitation (Mutch, 2015). The visitation of a parish by a committee of the higher administrative unit, the presbytery, was a distinctive feature of Scottish church governance in the eighteenth century, but the routine of visitation was not one limited to Scotland or to Presbyterianism. There are problems in giving a comprehensive account of the practice of visitation, simply because we are dependent on incomplete historical work. However, from this work we can both suggest the evolution of the practice of visitation, especially the difference that lay participation made, and the different content of a similarly named routine in different contexts.

In 1910, Walter Frere not only published a series of transcripts of documents relating to visitations in England but also provided a general introduction to the practice. He saw this as originating in organisational developments in the early church, as the church moved from initial enthusiasm to settled organisational form. The key figure was the bishop, who controlled a diocese, an area of land featuring a number of administrative units. Much then depended on the way such units were specified, which impacted on who carried out visitations. As he noted

> The dioceses in Italy remained small; naturally the bishop only undertook such a district as he found that he could visit effectively. The effect of this policy survives even to the present day. Still the Italian dioceses are small; the bishop has only such an area as he can personally supervise; and in Italy there has never been much done in the way of devolution by the bishops of their duty of visitation to other persons — archdeacons or the like.
>
> (Frere, 1910: 17)

Thus, the account provided by Bigoni, Gallardo and Funnell (2013) on visitations in the diocese of Ferrara in the fifteenth century notes the direct role of the bishop. By contrast, in other countries such as France, Germany and England, the office of archdeacon came to assume the role of deputy for the bishop, who ruled over far bigger dioceses.

In all these instances, however, the bishop retained some control through the formulation of lists of questions to be posed at visitations. While there were questions about the church building and its contents, most of the early questions were about the conduct of and the nature of the beliefs held and expounded by the priest. 'Truly', concludes Frere (1910: 30), 'a visitation was a serious ordeal where this was carefully carried out'. As we will see, there was a trade-off between the comprehensiveness of the questions to be posed and the practicality of inquiring about them. Echoes of these concerns are to be found in the twenty-six questions used by the bishop of Ferrara in the fourteenth century. As Bigoni, Gallardo and Funnell report

> The Bishop was expected to investigate the morality of each cleric, verifying if he "lives honestly" or "allows games or dances in the sacred areas". Furthermore, he was to assess the discharge of the cleric's pastoral duty, checking if the priest "administers sacraments" or if the believers "assiduously attend religious services."
>
> Bigoni, Gallardo and Funnell (2013: 577)

What is noticeable, therefore, in these documents is the persistent emphasis on the conduct of the priest and his conformity to the requirements of the hierarchy, with a minor note concerned with the resources of the local church and how they were deployed.

An exception to this focus can be seen in the visitation articles of the reforming Bishop of Lincoln, Grosseteste, in 1233. His sixty-six articles begin with seven questions about lay conduct, beginning with a question about whether any in the parish are living together out of wedlock.

Altogether, there are fourteen questions about lay conduct, with a further six about the support the church received from the laity. By far the greatest number of questions, 36 are to do with the conduct of the priest, with just two questions about the fabric of the church. These were the questions of a reforming bishop who, unusually, conducted his own visitations, so the balance of questions were to do with the preparations that had been made. We will note the connection between visitations and movements of reform below, but Frere notes in the 'fourteenth and fifteenth centuries visitation proceeded on lines of routine and documents are fewer and formal. This is especially the case with diocesan visitation, where bishop and archdeacon followed a constant course of inquiry and had normal means of correction' (Frere, 1910: 117). However, the consideration of lay conduct directly remained a minor note until the Reformation, at which point there was a divergence in practice between England and Scotland. In England, Frere notes the increasing use of visitations to pursue a political agenda, one connected with the monarchical control of the Church of England. From 1535, political interventions are prominent, paralleling the situation in France 'where the Parlement of Paris had recently been exercising a close supervision over church affairs of every sort, and had sent its commissaries to visit Religious Houses' (Frere, 1910: 119). By contrast, the Scottish reformers rejected any conflation of church and state. They initially envisaged a repurposing of the role of the bishop, renaming these as superintendents who 'shall not only preach, but also shall examine the life, diligence, and behaviour of the ministers, the order of their churches, and the manners of the people' (Cameron, 1972: 123). Over time this disciplinary oversight mutated into being the responsibility of the presbytery, a body which covered a small number of parishes. These bodies in their turn evolved new versions of the questions that shaped the visitation, with more emphasis now on the conduct of the population. The attention paid to the conduct of the minster continued, now with remarkable and somewhat terrifying specificity, as in the following extract from the suggested question in the widely used handbook authored by Walter Steuart of Pardovan:

> Hath your minister a gospel walk and conversation before the people? And doth he keep family worship? And is he own who rules well his own house? Is he a haunter of ale-houses and taverns? Is he a dancer, carder or dicer? Is he proud or vain-glorious? Is he greedy, or wordly, or an ursurer? Is he contentious, a brawler, fighter or striker? Is he a swearer of small or minced oaths? Useth he to say, Before God it is so; or in his common conference, I protest, or, I protest before God. Or says he, lord, what is that? All of which are more than yea or nay? Is he a filthy speaker or jester? Bears he familiar company with disaffected, profane or scandalous persons? Is he dissolute, prodigal, light or loose in his carriage, apparel, or

> words? How spends he the Sabbath after sermon? Saw ye him ever
> drink healths?
>
> (Steuart, 1709: 60)

What had changed were the people to whom these questions were posed. Whereas in the visitation articles that we have reviewed (and as remained the case in England), the questions were a guide to the archdeacons who carried out the visitations, in Scotland, the questions were to be posed to the elders and heads of households. In turn, the minister was questioned about the conduct of his elders and the moral and spiritual health of his congregation. What changed was thus the involvement of the lay in the conduct of visitations (Mutch, 2015).

In the Catholic system, considerable attention might be paid to laying down routines, but these were often operated by members of the hierarchy. In another example, Quattrone (2004) gives us details of routines within the Jesuit order that involved accountability practices, but those involved were all internal to the order. Jesuit educational organisations, Clark (2006) notes, continued to be subject to visitations to ensure that strict adherence to the organisation's procedural logic was being maintained. In the diocese of Ferrara, the proceedings were recorded by a notary and by some related routines. If one had not already been supplied, the notary compiled an inventory of church assets. The visitation also inspected the accounts of income and expenditure that were to be kept by a 'massoro' or layman. These 'massari', selected from the wealthiest inhabitants were, say Bigoni, Gallardo and Funnell (2013), a key link in the process. They were appointed by the bishop at the end of the visitation and were 'in charge of helping the priest in taking care of the Church's properties and managing his benefice. They were also to report to the Bishop that the changes required were implemented after the visit. They were in effect the eyes and ears of the Bishops, reporting on the priest's failure to comply with his orders' (Bigoni, Gallardo and Funnell, 2013: 581). From the evidence presented, the involvement of the lay was partial and had no organisational form. In the Church of England there was a little more provision for lay involvement. Each parish had (usually) two churchwardens, generally elected annually but sometimes serving for longer periods of office (Tate, 1983). They were to respond to the questions asked of them and to 'present' those who had offended against church discipline. Several writers on the church in the eighteenth century have commented on the ineffectiveness of church discipline as expressed in the annual archdeacon's visitations. They note the frequent recording of 'omnia bene' ['all is well'] in churchwardens' returns to the questions posed by archdeacons before their visitations (Gregory and Chamberlain, 2003: 160, 183, 232; Spaeth, 2000: 64–72). There was a little more organisational structure in the English case, but it was again heavily subject to the influences of custom. In particular, involvement was episodic rather than enduring. The distinctive feature of the Scottish context was the enduring, corporate, nature of church bodies, which enabled the evolution of processes of detailed record keeping.

Again, there are interesting differences in the use of records to facilitate visitations. The growth of literacy and improvements in the production of paper, so making record keeping more cost-effective, facilitated greater keeping of records, but those records varied considerably between denominations. In the Italian case, the written record was compiled outside the local situation by a specialised actor. Local records are inferred, but their failure to survive outside urban contexts might suggest something about the thoroughness with which they were kept. In England, the record was held centrally and took a standard form that lent itself to ritual completion. Any locally held records were fragmented in nature and heavily conditioned by custom. In Scotland, records were kept in considerable detail at several levels of the organisation, and checks were put in place to ensure that this happened. Those carrying out visitations were expected to have received the parish's records of discipline and accounts in advance and, as we saw in Chapter 3, to have 'revised' them in detail. Over the course of the eighteenth century, physical visitations of parishes died away, to be replaced by the inspection of church records. In similar vein, Clark (2006: 371) notes the 'traditional visitation of universities came to an end around 1789. In Prussia, for example, ministerial visitations of the old sort became rare, then ceased. A university sent yearly tables (Jahrestabellen) on itself instead. The long night of the early modern police state had disembodied academics and transformed the university into a self-registering machine, no longer in need of visible ministerial hands.'

The failure to sustain visitations in their originally conceived form in Scotland after the 1740s points to the episodic nature of the routine of visitation and the need to connect it to wider social trends. In particular, visitations were associated with bursts of reforming activity. John Tillotson (1994) associates visitations of nunneries in fourteenth-century Yorkshire with the reforms of Pope Boniface VII, just as the visitations in Ferrara were prompted by the reforms of Pope Eugenius IV. We have seen that the thorough-going visitations of Grosseteste were associated with the reforming vigour of that energetic prelate. In similar vein, although in a very different ecclesiological context, the Scottish revival of the visitation gained momentum after the consolidation of the Presbyterian system of church governance in 1690. Such bouts of reforming zeal tended to fade away in the face of the practical difficulties associated with the extensive rounds of questioning envisaged by the reformers. Put simply, it was too demanding on resources of time and effort to carry out comprehensive visitations. Perhaps, too, visitations became less salient once they had achieved their purpose of instilling a sense of order and discipline. In Scotland, once the first flush of enthusiasm and disciplinary labour was over, the less expensive means of monitoring by the examination of written records, in terms of the time of the presbytery, won favour. The framers of the initial guidance simply failed to take into account the sheer press of business, imagining a system without recalcitrant laymen and ministers with human failings. This reminds us that examination of routines has to involve the reciprocal relationship between formal guidance and embodied practice.

What this brief outline of the routine called 'visitation' does is remind us of two features of practices. One is that practices, even if they have the same name, vary in terms of the particular conjunction of time and place. The involvement of the lay, related in turn to the ecclesiological commitments of the different denominations, was a particular differentiator in giving new content to a practice that otherwise appeared to have similar form. But the second is that practices themselves have a history. They do not simply emerge from performance. They are, of course, adjusted to meet the demands of that performance, as the framers of formal guidance cannot envisage all the combinations of circumstances that performance will confront. But that performance is often guided by explicit formulations that in their turn draw on historically shaped understandings. The practice, for example, of framing visitation visits through the issuing of centrally determined questionnaires, has a long historical pedigree, even if the content evolved. Those performing routines, that is, draw on the to-hand resources that they find.

For the theologian Jeremy Carrette (2000: 110) Foucault 'assumes that aspects of religion can be explored by isolating the social manifestations of religion without considering how theological ideas have informed the social context'. The other side of the coin might be found in much of Weber's work, where the focus is on bodies of formal beliefs. The challenge is to combine the two approaches, to look, as Gorski (2003) suggests, for the 'concrete mechanisms' by which logics operate. The problems of not doing so can be found in those works that draw conclusions about, for example, the impact of theological debates on economic activity without specifying the practices, which made those debates concrete. Such, for example, is the thrust of Friedland's critique of the work of Dotan Leshem. Leshem (2016) seeks to explain *The Origins of Neoliberalism* by a detailed examination of the works of the early Church Fathers. Doing so, he argues, bolsters the argument of Foucault that governmentality had its origins in the East. He then, in brief comments, moves to the Reformation as an engine of economic development, but in an extremely compressed way in which it is difficult to see the connections between the complex debates he covers and the formulations of, for example, Jean Calvin. In particular, there is no consideration of the ways in which theological debates might be converted into practices, practices that might then inform secular activity. It is practices, the next chapter will argue, rather than logics, that actors seize hold of. The unintended consequence might be, in time, the changing character of those logics.

Summary

Practices are a central part of Friedland's formulations. A closer examination of practices as emergent from human activity but, once emergent, solidified into rituals and routines, enables the investigation of the historical development of such practices. Developments in organisational theory have brought routines out the shadows, foregrounding their potential to act as generative systems. However, much of this work fails to take account of the historical shaping of such routines, not only in their own internal development but also in the variable historical contexts in which they have been practised. A key dimension that is revealed by historical comparisons is the differential involvement of actors in their operation. It is practices that actors engage in, but those practices can, in their turn, entangle actors in the wider ramifications of logics.

Notes

1 National Records of Scotland, Edinburgh. Records of the Church of Scotland, Parish of Rayne, session minutes, CH2/310/6 1772–1800, 21 June 1772.
2 CH2/310/6 1772–1800, 3 February 1772.
3 Unfortunately, the interesting work of Niels Vinding and collaborators (Hashas, de Ruiter and Vinding, 2018) on the organisational structures of Islam in Western Europe came to my notice too late for consideration but it exemplifies just the sort of research on other religious denominations that is required.

References

Archer, M. (1995) *Realist Social Theory: The Morphogenetic Approach*, Cambridge: Cambridge University Press.
Archer, M. (1996) *Culture and Agency: The Place of Culture in Social Theory*, Cambridge: Cambridge University Press.
Archer, M. (2000) *Being Human: The Problem of Agency*, Cambridge: Cambridge University Press.
Arrington, L. and Bitton, D. (1979) *The Mormon Experience: A History of the Latter-day Saints*, London: George Allen & Unwin.
Asad, T. (1993) *Genealogies of Religion: Discipline and Reasons of Power in Christianity and Islam*, Baltimore: John Hopkins University Press.
Baltzell, E. (1979) *Puritan Boston and Quaker Philadelphia: Two Protestant Ethics and the Spirit of Class Authority and Leadership*, New York: Free Press.
Bhaskar, R. (1979) *The Possibility of Naturalism*, Hemel Hempstead: Harvester.
Bigoni, M., Gallardo, E., and Funnell, W. (2013) 'Rethinking the sacred and secular divide: accounting and accountability practices in the Diocese of Ferrara (1431–1457)', *Accounting, Auditing and Accountability Journal*, 26(4), 567–594.

Birnholtz, J., Cohen, M. and Hoch, S. (2009) 'Is it the "same"? observing the regeneration of organizational character at Camp Poplar Grove', in Becker, M. and Lazaric, N. (eds.) *Organizational Routines: Advancing Empirical Research*, Cheltenham: Edward Elgar, 2009, 131–158.

Boulton, J. (1984) 'The limits of formal religion: the administration of holy communion in late Elizabethan and early Stuart London', *London Journal*, 10(2), 134–154.

Bourdieu, P. (1990) *The Logic of Practice*, Cambridge: Polity.

Cameron, J. (1972) *The First Book of Discipline*, Edinburgh: Saint Andrew Press.

Carrette, J. (2000) *Foucault and Religion: Spiritual Corporality and Political Spirituality*, London: Routledge.

Chalcraft, D. (1994) 'Bringing the text back in: on ways of reading the iron cage metaphor in the two editions of The Protestant Ethic', in Reed, M. and Ray, L. (eds.) *Organizing Modernity: New Weberian Perspectives on Work, Organization and Society*, London: Routledge, 1994, 16–45.

Chalcraft, D. and Harrington, A. (2001) *The Protestant Ethic Debate: Max Weber's Replies to His Critics, 1907–1910*, Liverpool: Liverpool University Press.

Clark, A. (2004) 'Testing the two modes theory: Christian practice in the later Middle Ages', in Whitehouse, H. and Martin, L. (eds.) *Theorizing Religions Past: Archaeology, History, and Cognition*, Walnut Creek, CA: AltaMira Press, 2004, 125–142.

Clark, W. (2006) *Academic Charisma and the Origins of the Research University*, Chicago, IL: University of Chicago Press.

Crichton, A. (1824) *Life and Diary of Lieutenant Colonel J. Blackader*, Edinburgh: H. S. Baynes.

D'Adderio, L. (2008) 'The performativity of routines: theorising the influence of artefacts and distributed agencies on routines dynamics', *Research Policy*, 37, 769–789.

Donati, P. and Archer, M. (2015) *The Relational Subject*, Cambridge: Cambridge University Press.

Dyck, B., Starke, F., Harder, H. and Hecht, T. (2005) 'Do the organizational structures of religious places of worship reflect their statements of faith? An exploratory study', *Review of Religious Research*, 47(1), 51–69.

Essen, A. (2008) 'Variability as a source of stability: studying routines in the elderly home care setting', *Human Relations*, 61(11), 1617–1644.

Feldman, M. (2000) 'Organizational routines as a source of continuous change', *Organization Science*, 11(6), 611–629.

Feldman, M. and Pentland, B. (2003) 'Reconceptualizing Organizational Routines as a Source of Flexibility and Change', *Administrative Science Quarterly*, 48, 94–118.

Foucault, M. (1999) *Abnormal: Lectures at the Collège de France 1974–1975*, New York: Picador.

Foucault, M. (2009) *Security, Territory, Population: Lectures at the Collège de France 1977–1978*, Basingstoke: Palgrave Macmillan.

Fox, K. (2005) *Watching the English: The Hidden Rules of English Behaviour*, London: Hodder & Stoughton.

Frere, W. (1910) *Visitation Articles and Injunctions of the Period of the Reformation, Volume I, Historical Introduction and Index*, London: Longmans, Green & Co.

Friedland, R. (2009) 'Institution, practice and ontology: towards a religious sociology', *Research in the Sociology of Organizations*, 27, 45–83.

Ghosh, P. (2014) *Max Weber and the Protestant Ethic: Twin Histories*, Oxford: Oxford University Press.

Gorski, P. (2003) *The Disciplinary Revolution: Calvinism and the Rise of the State in Early Modern Europe*, Chicago, IL: University of Chicago Press.

Gregory, J. and Chamberlain, J. (2003) *The National Church in Local Perspective: The Church of England and the Regions, 1660–1800*, Woodbridge: Boydell.

Hashas, M., de Ruiter, J. and Vinding, N. (eds.) (2018) *Imams in Western Europe: Developments, Transformations, and Institutional Challenges*, Amsterdam: Amsterdam University Press.

Hennis, W. (1988) *Max Weber, Essays in Reconstruction*, London: Allen & Unwin.

Hodgson, G. (2008) 'The concept of a routine', in Becker, M. (ed.) *Handbook of Organizational Routines*, Cheltenham: Edward Elgar 15–28.

Holmes, A. (2006) *The Shaping of Ulster Presbyterian Belief and Practice 1770–1840*, Oxford: Oxford University Press.

Howard-Grenville, J. (2005) 'The persistence of flexible organizational routines: the role of agency and organizational context', *Organization Science*, 16(6), 618–636.

Ingvaldsen, J. (2015) 'Organizational learning: bringing the forces of production back in', *Organization Studies*, 36(4), 423–444.

Kadane, M. (2013) *The Watchful Clothier: The Life of an Eighteenth-Century Protestant Capitalist*, New Haven, CT: Yale University Press.

Leshem, D. (2016) *The Origins of Neoliberalism: Modeling the Economy from Jesus to Foucault*, New York: Columbia University Press.

Lukes, S. (1974) *Power: A Radical View*, London: Macmillan.

Mutch, A. (2015) *Religion and National Identity: Governing Scottish Presbyterianism in the Eighteenth Century*, Edinburgh: Edinburgh University Press.

Nelson, R. and Winter, S. (1982) *An Evolutionary Theory of Economic Change*, Cambridge, MA: Harvard University Press.

Oxford English Dictionary (2011) 'Routine', http://www.oed.com/, [accessed 17 March 2015]

Petterson, C. (2014) *The Missionary, the Catechist and the Hunter: Foucault, Protestantism and Colonialism*, Leiden: Brill.

Porpora, D. (2015) *Reconstructing Sociology: The Critical Realist Approach*, Cambridge: Cambridge University Press.

Quattrone, P. (2004) 'Accounting for God: accounting and accountability practices in the Society of Jesus (Italy, XVI–XVII centuries)', *Accounting, Organizations and Society*, 29, 647–683.

Reynaud, B. (2005) 'The void at the heart of rules: routines in the context of rule-following. The case of the Paris Metro Workshop', *Industrial and Corporate Change*, 14(5), 847–871.

Schmidt, L. (2001) *Holy Fairs: Scotland and the Making of American Revivalism*, Grand Rapids, MI: Eerdmans Publishing Co.

Sennett, R. (2002) *The Fall of Public Man*, London: Penguin.

Spaeth, D. (2000) *The Church in an Age Of Danger: Parsons And Parishioners, 1660–1740*, Cambridge: Cambridge University Press.

Steuart, W. (1709) *Collections and Observations Methodised, Concerning the Worship, Discipline and Government of the Church of Scotland*, Edinburgh: Andrew Anderson.

Tate, W. (1983) *The Parish Chest: A Study of the Records of Parochial Administration in England*, Chichester: Phillimore.

Tillotson, J. (1994) 'Visitation and reform of the Yorkshire nunneries in the fourteenth century', *Northern History*, 30, 1–21.

Torrance, I. (2014) 'A particular Reformed piety: John Knox and the posture at communion', *Scottish Journal of Theology*, 67(4), 400–413.

Turner, S. and Rindova, V. (2012) 'A balancing act: how organizations pursue consistency in routine functioning in the face of ongoing change', *Organization Science*, 23(1), 24–46.

Ventresca, M. and Kaghan, W. (2008) 'Routines, 'going concerns' and innovation: towards an evolutionary economic sociology', in Becker, M. (ed.) *Handbook of Organizational Routines*, Cheltenham: Edward Elgar, 2008, 52–86.

Weber, M. (1948) 'The Protestant sects and the spirit of capitalism', in Gerth, H. and Wright Mills, C. (eds) *From Max Weber*, London: Routledge & Kegan Paul, 1948, 302–322.

Weber, M. (1976) *The Protestant Ethic and the Spirit of Capitalism*, London: Allen and Unwin.

Whitehouse, H. (2004) *Modes of Religiosity: A Cognitive Theory of Religious Transmission*, Walnut Creek CA: AltaMira Press.

Winchester, D. (2008) 'Embodying the faith: religious practice and the making of a Muslim moral habitus', *Social Forces*, 86(4), 1753–1780.

Zbaracki, M. and Bergen, M. (2010) 'When truces collapse: a longitudinal study of price-adjustment routines', *Organization Science*, 21(50), 955–972.

6   Logics

Introduction

> Nations stumble upon establishments, which are indeed the result of
> human action, but not the execution of any human design.
>
> (Ferguson, 1767: 119)

A prime criticism of much work in new institutionalism is that it drifts
towards an actor-centred approach, in which actors can combine and
blend different logics to meet their interests and needs. Approaches like
that under the heading of 'institutional entrepreneurship', with its focus
on the social skills of individual actors, run the risk of smuggling the
rational actor in through the back door. Such an approach is encouraged
by viewing logics as decomposable bundles of elements. By contrast, I am
going to argue that actors do not select logics, but practices. In doing so,
they import into their specific context not only the practice itself but also
the logic that is immanent in it. Over time, that practice might change
the logic that operates within an organizational field; but, I contend, not
necessarily the institutional logic. Moreover, that process is a long and
complex one, often involving multiple actors, sometimes acting in concert, at other times building on the prior actions of others. Thus it is, as
in the aphorism cited from Ferguson, often hailed as a founding figure of
modern sociology, that changes in broader social arrangements emerge
as the unintended consequences of shorter term actions. I illustrate this
process by an extended case study of the emergence of a specific practice
in one economic field, the employment of salaried mangers in UK brewing. I examine how the practice originated in a specific context and met
with resistance as it travelled, showing how changes in one field can be
linked to broader logics. Drawing on this case, I then discuss how we
need to operate with multiple temporalities when considering institutional change. Logics, as well, exist in relationships of complementarity
and contradiction to other logics. In addition, sometimes practices that
emerge and develop within one institution burst its bounds to such a
degree that new logics emerge.

Developing the 'Managerial System'

The practice to be explored in this section was actually a bundle of practices characterised by contemporaries as 'the managerial system'. Within the organisational field structured around the production and sale of alcoholic drinks for consumption within premises licensed by the state in England and Wales, there emerged, starting in Liverpool in the 1840s, a system featuring the employment of salaried managers to run public houses. That system involved routines for monitoring and controlling the activities of managers. At the micro level, this meant the strict enforcement of rules laid down for the conduct of the pub. The example given below, pasted into a blank house takings register, indicates in detail that a company was prepared to go to to control what happened in the pub, a level of detail that differed significantly from other contemporary practice.

RULES
**For the observance of the Law and Good Order on all the Licensed Premises belonging to Peter Walker & Son Warrington and Burton Limited.
SPECIAL. - All Beers on Draught must be measured**

---

1. No Credit shall be given to any person under any pretence whatever.
2. No Wages shall be paid on the premises except to those employed in the house.
3. No person on duty shall treat or be treated by a customer or other person.
4. No smoking allowed while on duty.
5. No money, watch, parcel, or other thing shall be taken in charge from any customer or other person.
6. No foreign money shall be exchanged, nor any banknotes unless the parties are well-known to be responsible and respectable householders.
7. No Army Certificate, Advance Notes, Sailors' monthly money notes, Pawnbroker's duplicate ticket, or any other document, article or thing shall be received, purchased or taken as security from a customer or other person.
8. No raffle shall be allowed to take place, nor shall Betting or Gaming of any kind be permitted.
9. No person shall be supplied who is disorderly or apparently under the influence of drink, or (if for consumption on the premises) who is under 18 years of age.
10. No young person shall be supplied with liquor for consumption off the premises who is under 14 years of age, except in corked or sealed bottles of not less than one reputed pint. The expression "Sealed" means secured with any substance without the destruction of which the cork, plug or stopper cannot be withdrawn.
11. No Police Officer shall be served or harboured while on duty, and any complaint against the police to be reported at once to the out-door Manager.
12. Should a Police Officer or other person, at any time, point out any matter in the course of business as being in his opinion an infringement of the Law, whether he intends to report the same to the authorities or not, the Manager or his Assistant shall forthwith procure the names and addresses of any witness who may be present.

13. Should any person be charged with being intoxicated on the premises, the Manager or his Assistant must endeavour to at once procure the opinion of a Doctor as to the said person's condition.
14. No persons except those employed in the house shall be allowed to remain on the premises during closed hours.
15. Should any Police Officers or Constables in the execution of their duty demand admittance during closing hours, it is the duty of the Licensee, or those in charge, to immediately admit them, and give every facility to examine the premises.
16. A full and true account of each day's takings, and also a faithful account of all stock sold in, out of, or upon the premises shall be kept and rendered by the Manager, and no false entry shall be made in any such Account or in the day book.
17. The Manager is responsible for the house being in every respect well conducted, and shall report at once any irregularity or any misconduct of the assistants under his charge.
18. The House to be opened and closed in accordance with the Law prevailing at the time.
19. Penalty for the breach of any of the above Rules, Dismissal.

To enforce these rules, there was staff of house inspectors or 'out-door managers' under the control of a specialised department. A key device for controlling the activities of house managers was the collection and analysis of detailed information on transactions, as emphasised in rule 16.

The distinctiveness of these arrangements in the context of the mid-nineteenth century can be seen by placing them against the conventional practices involved in running pubs (Mutch, 2003). Emerging from the brewing of beer on the premises, the traditional way of running pubs from their emergence in the seventeenth century onwards was as 'free houses'. This was where an independent business person owned the premises and brewed their own beer for resale. The eighteenth century saw the rise of the 'common brewer', commercial brewing concerns who brewed at scale and supplied free houses. Frequently, owners of free houses became indebted to brewers and, in return for financial support, became 'tied' to take only the products of the brewery. Breweries started to take possession of properties and to install tenants to sell their beer. Such tenants were charged a low property rent but were obliged to take beer and other supplies from the brewery, which made money by charging a premium on these supplies (the so-called 'wet rent'). In both free and tied houses, the breweries were concerned with the production of beer, not with what happened in the pubs. In this 'production logic', the pubs were seen simply as distribution outlets. As we will see, the practice of direct management was an important part of inverting this logic, of adopting a retailing logic.

In the 1840s, however, the use of salaried managers to run public houses was a novelty, one which can be traced back to the activities of the Liverpool brewers Peter Walker & Son (Mutch, 2006c). Peter Walker was an innovative Scottish brewer, credited with inventing a brewing process that brought new efficiencies and was widely adopted. His son, Andrew Barclay Walker, was granted a licence for a public house on Brownlow Hill in Liverpool in 1846. By 1851, he was brewing with his father in Warrington and the name of Peter Walker & Son became a familiar one in Liverpool. It was Andrew who appears to have been the force behind the business, and particularly behind the retailing side in Liverpool. In 1851, he took over the management of the Coperas Hill Vaults for his uncles David and Robert. David and Robert were colliery managers in St Helens, with David managing Andrew's colliery interests there. The direct management of public houses may have arisen from this reciprocal family arrangement. In the following year, Andrew acquired vaults at Byrom Street, in 1854 in Fox Street, in 1855 in London Road and in 1856 in Soho Street. All these properties were rented and run as managed houses. They sold beer from Peter Walker & Son, brewed at Warrington, and wines and spirits from Andrew Barclay Walker & Co. It would seem that the running of these houses under direct management might have been partly as a result of Andrew drawing on family experience in the coal business, partly as a contingent response to his uncles' trust in his competence and partly a response to conditions in the town.

Liverpool had developed in the early nineteenth century as a great world port, particularly in the import of cotton to feed the expanding Lancashire cotton mills (Milne, 2000). Because of the large volume of transient custom for its pubs, often from customers who favoured spirits over beer, the town's pubs bore a different character to those elsewhere in the country. The high value of the spirit trade and the need for capital to develop and expand properties made tight control over their running desirable. Huge numbers of sailors arrived in the port at favourable states of the tide, with money to spend and a short time in which to do so. In such conditions, being able to respond to short-term shifts in demand by moving labour made the running of a collection of pubs as a unified estate more desirable. However, these factors applied to all the town's pubs, but it was Walker who saw the possibilities of direct management. He used the transaction records generated by direct management to measure the profitability of his pubs, devising accounting schemes to collect and measure financial performance. As we have noted, he had family experience in the coal business to draw upon, but there may have been wider influences from his Scottish background (Mutch, 2005). The rapid development of the Scottish economy in the late eighteenth century saw one of the most rapid bouts of industrialisation and urbanisation in the world. The sheer pace of change and the need for external capital saw many enterprises being managed on behalf of investors, rather than being run by owner managers as was more typical in England. Cooke (2010), for example, notes the widespread use of managers or managing partners in the Scottish cotton industry. As he points out, one 'significant difference between firms in England and Scotland was the prevalence of multiple partnerships in Scotland. This enabled Scottish entrepreneurs to spread risks and to recruit partners with different skills and assets' (Cooke, 2010: 176). In similar vein, Perchard (2007) notes a higher proportion of Scottish collieries being run by professional managers. In turn, the widespread use of multiple partnerships derived from differences in the Scottish and English legal systems. While the English system was a common law one, which restricted the development of partnerships, the Scottish legal system, which had retained its independence following the Treaty of Union between the two countries to create Britain in 1707, was based on Roman civil law. Under common law, any partner had the right to dissolve the partnership in order to realise their capital; Scottish law allowed for transferable shares. Scottish banks, for example, 'had relatively large memberships, arising from the fact that they were able to separate ownership from control' (Acheson et al. 2011: 505). Such separation also fostered the development of management as distinct from ownership (although some stake in the business was often expected). It would seem that Walker was drawing on this familiarity with and acceptance of direct management in responding to the particular trading conditions that he was faced with.

There does appear to be a connection between the practices adopted by Walker to manage his pubs and wider institutional logics. It is not that Walker mobilised the resources of the Scottish legal tradition to adopt direct management but that aspects of that tradition facilitated particular modes of economic action that then shaped to-hand practices. It is also not the case that Walker appeared to proselytize on behalf of direct management. It is true that after his death the company that was then run by his sons produced a triumphalist account of their first fifty years in business (Walker, 1896). Influenced no doubt by the abrasive nature of debates over licensing in the city, it contained a forthright defence of the 'managerial system'. This was placed firmly in the context of the growth of multiple retail operations, arguing that it 'offers the prospect of order evolved from chaos' (Walker, 1896: 80). In this it was 'a product of the natural evolution of our commercial system, and has its precise equivalent in other trades in that process which has reduced small traders to the position of managers of large establishments' (Walker, 1896: 81). This process, based on 'system and principle' had at its heart the discipline and control that could be applied to managers and, through them, to customers (Walker, 1896: 82). Managers were subject to 'a rigorous system of official inspection' that checked their adherence to a set of rules, the rules reproduced above. But this was after Walker's death in 1893 and, while he was twice the mayor of Liverpool, his role in both local and trade politics seems to have been a largely passive one. His concerns were more with the management of his business affairs, both in brewing and in the South Wales coal industry.

The fortunes of the managerial system pioneered by Peter Walker & Son diverged in ways which are instructive about the relationship of economic practices to wider logics. By 1891, over half of the public houses in Liverpool were owned by companies, and direct management was the preferred means of operating them. In 1912, the chairman of the licensing bench proclaimed that 'houses managed for brewers are conducted more in conformity with the wishes of the bench than tenanted houses' (cited in Mutch, 2006c: 13). However, elsewhere in the country, with the exception of the city of Birmingham, tenancy remained the preferred model. The resistance to the managerial system had a number of roots, which can be illustrated by the company's problems with its managed houses in Crewe (Mutch, 2006c: 12). The railway town was the first site for expansion out of Liverpool, with two houses being acquired in 1866. By 1893, the company had seven houses in the town, all managed. In that year, the magistrates insisted that the houses be converted to tenancies. The company refused but decided to comply in the following year. However, in 1908, allegations were made by the chairman of the licensing justices that the tenancy agreements were bogus. A slander case ensued, won by the company, but the case illustrates some of the restrictions on the export of the Liverpool model at a time when there was considerable debate over the status of licensing law.

These problems were seen most clearly in the company's attempts to break into the London market (Mutch, 2006c: 13). That the company was still capable of innovation was seen by the launch of lager brewing at Burton in 1909. At about the same time, it opened a London office on St Pancras Road that was to handle its entry into both London and the export trade. The purchase of the De Beauvoir Arms followed in 1911, and by the end of 1912, the company had eight houses in the London area. It began an extensive advertising campaign and sought the support of the licensed trade through its sponsorship of trade events. However, these efforts were to little avail, for the magistrates, with the support of the London trade, set their faces firmly against the direct management of houses. The company appeared before Tower Hamlets magistrates in 1912 asking for a transfer of the licence to its manager, Alfred Burford. Opposed by the East London Licensed Victuallers and Beersellers' Protection Society, it was unsuccessful, the magistrates concluding that Burford 'is not, and would not, have any personal interest in the licence or in the premises, or in the profits of the trade, but is, and would be, a salaried servant of the brewery company, for whose benefit the retail trade would be carried on'.[1] In this stance, the magistrates echoed both the concerns of the Crewe magistrates and opinion on other London benches. Despite a case contesting the status of managers in Liverpool being settled in favour of house management, the London magistrates in particular continued to oppose their employment.

That opposition by magistrates indicated some of the impact of the legal system, especially the fragmented form that a common law system took, one which relied both on cases being brought to court and on decisions made in one part of a system being noticed and honoured elsewhere. In turn, much rested on two broader cultural practices: the status accorded to tenancy and the characterisation of the law of employment in the phrase 'master and servant'. Both owed a good deal to the practices associated with the political and social control exercised by a landed aristocracy, an aristocracy that provided both the models and on many occasions the personnel to stock legal benches. In a society dominated by those who drew their wealth and prestige from agricultural land, the tripartite model of aristocratic owner, independent tenant and dependant labourer was a powerful material practice and cultural symbol. Many brewers owed their origins to farming and deployed the wealth they accumulated to buy their way into the 'landed interest'. Socially distant from those who use their pubs, they preferred to run them at arm's length using a tenancy model familiar to them from their farming pursuits. In turn, the tenant was seen as an independent person, more likely to adhere to licensing regulations because they had a stake in the success of the business and more to lose than an employee. So in Leeds the magistrates 'have always declined to transfer a licence to a mere manager or servant, with a few exceptions which could be explained as to railway companies and limited liability companies'.[2] The phrase 'mere servant' is a recurrent one in opposition to the employment of managers. So in Sheffield they were regarded as '... mere servants, who have no interest whatever in the management and success of the house'.[3] The accuracy of such statements could be (and was) contested, but their impact was to restrain the spread of direct management.

There are echoes here of the discussion of the impact of political and other logics on the development of the railways in three different contexts – Britain, France and the United States – in the nineteenth century. In Britain, Frank Dobbin (1994: 159) argues, 'English [sic] political traditions gave sovereignty to elite individuals rather than to autonomous communities, as in the United States, or to the central state, as in France'. He stresses some particular features of the British political system, with its emphasis on the holding of political authority by elite individuals in a dispersed system bolstered by a common law legal system. 'In each country', he argued 'traditional state institutions had supported certain social practices as constitutive of order and others as inimical to order. When faced with rapid change in the economy, policymakers applied these principles of political order to the industrial realm. Thus, the logic of political organization became the logic of industrial organization' (Dobbin, 1994: 214). It is interesting in this context to note that Captain Harry Boldero, a Tory Member of Parliament who Dobbin cites as a key player in resisting government incursions on the running of railways, was also an opponent of the professionalisation of the army officer corps, arguing that this was incompatible with the gentlemanly ideal (Harries-Jenkins, 1977: 278). In turn, Mussachio and Turner (2013) note the conservatism of English judges operating in a common law system that privileged partnership and resisted claims of limited liability. This conservatism was reflected in wider debates where opposition to limited liability drew on the wider ideas about personal responsibility embedded in practices such as tenancy (Djelic, 2013). There was, thus, a powerful nexus of ideas and practices that resulted in resistance to public house managers and it meant that the next phase in the diffusion of the practice came from an unexpected source.

The activities of brewers like Walker, with their financial incentive to supply ever larger quantities of alcoholic drink with all the concomitant social evils, were opposed by a vigorous temperance movement (Harrison, 1994). Within the movement there were clear differences between those who advocated complete abstention and those who sought some form of rapprochement with the industry, seeking to ameliorate its worst effects (Greenaway, 1998). For the latter, the influence of the 'Gothenburg system' was of particular significance. In the Swedish system, public houses were taken into municipal ownership and run by salaried managers under strict instructions about what could and could not be sold. At the heart of this was the notion of 'disinterested management'. This referred to the person of the manager themselves as having no financial stake in the success of the pub. There were a number of initiatives under the broad heading of disinterested management, but the most successful was the Trust House Movement (Gutzke, 2006). This was an umbrella movement where local trusts were set up to purchase and operate public houses, with the aim being to make a profit that could be ploughed back into more outlets. Outlets were designed to be alternative attractions, modelled on the traditional pub but selling food and hot beverages as well as beer. Salaried managers were to be encouraged to sell food: 'The resident licensed Managers are paid a fixed salary, and obtain no profit on alcoholic sales.... Managers are given a substantial interest in the sale of food and non-intoxicants, and are bound by their Agreement to supply these when asked for' [Peoples Refreshment House Association (PRHA), 1912: 5]. By 1912, there were some 300 pubs being run on trust lines, with a Central Public House Trust Association for information and guidance.

The composition of the governing body of the Peoples Refreshment House Association, one of the most successful of the constituent bodies, gives a good flavour of its social standing. Under the presidency of the Bishop of Chester were seven vice presidents, including another bishop, a cardinal, two earls, two lords and a knight. Their pubs were heavily concentrated in rural areas. The first pub at Sparkford, Somerset, acquired in 1897 was 'exactly the type of house contemplated by the founders of the Association as best fitted for the initial experiment; i.e., a country inn, supplying the wants of the local farmers and labourers, with no competitor in the village' (PRHA, 1912: 15). One advocate, Earl Grey, argued

> The experience of our public-house trust movement has proved that, when a public-house is conducted as a refreshment room and not as a mere drinking bar, when food and non-intoxicants are served as readily as beer and spirits, when food and drink of the best quality only are served, when managers are paid a fixed salary and have no interest whatsoever in pressing the sale of alcoholic liquors, when they are encouraged to promote the sale of non-intoxicants, when you have a system of management under which no man is obliged to drink for the good of the house, when men feel that they can enjoy the society of a public-house without being called upon to buy alcoholic liquors, the result is a considerable diminution in the sale of alcoholic drink.[4]

While it remained a minority movement, largely confined to rural areas, the success of direct management as patronised by the rural elite challenged the hegemony of the tenancy model. Direct management acquired new respectability as a model, one that was given further impetus by the war that Britain entered into with Germany in 1914. As the war progressed, concerns were raised about the impact of drinking on the production of the munitions that were being used in huge numbers. The Carlisle district was a major centre of munitions work and so central to the British war effort. The perceived adverse impact of drinking on productivity led to the government taking the breweries and pubs of the area into public ownership in January 1916. William Waters Butler of the Birmingham brewers Mitchells and Butlers (one of the prime users of direct house management) and Sydney Nevile of the London brewery Whitbread joined the Control Board. The pubs in the district were converted to direct management. Large numbers were shut down and the remaining outlets were radically revamped. Under direct management there was an emphasis on food and on curbing drinking. The impact of this on drinking habits was contested, but what was important was the demonstration effect that the scheme had. It meant that in the years following the war, a number of companies took up the notion that pubs needed to change. They needed to offer a greater range of beverages and to improve their food, and to do so in surroundings that would make the pub respectable (Gutzke, 2006).

The experience of Carlisle and other centres where pubs were converted to direct management, coupled with the experience of the Trust House Movement, helped to make management of pubs an acceptable practice. It was one that gained momentum in the inter-war years with the so-called 'improved public house movement' (Mutch, 2010). This was a new strategy on the part of a number of brewers, who accepted in part the critique of traditional public houses emanating from the moderate wing of the temperance movement. Rather than simply ignoring conditions in their houses, leaving their running to the discretion of their tenants, these brewers built new pubs, often in the suburban housing estates that were replacing urban slums, which featured a much-improved environment and, significantly, the provision of food alongside the traditional range of alcoholic drinks. Many of the pubs were of considerable size, which were beyond the capital resources of all but the most substantial of tenants and so fostered a move towards direct management and its associated systems. In London, where several companies sought to build very large managed pubs, their efforts ran up against the conservatism of the magistrates. In 1924, for example, the brewers Whitbread sought the transfer of the licence of the Lord High Admiral in Marylebone to a manager, but this was opposed by the local Licensed Victuallers' Association and turned down by the magistrates. On appeal to the quarter sessions the transfer was upheld, leading the *Brewers' Journal* to speculate that London magistrates might now allow managers in 'improved' houses, if not in the normal run of London pubs. However, the next month they reported on yet another appeal by Barclay Perkins, this time from the Newington justices. The argument of the justices was that the manager was so tied by his agreement as to be not properly in control of the pub. Again, this appeal was upheld, but the licensing magistrates were a major stumbling block to changes in the pub (Mutch, 2010). Not all brewers were enthusiastic adopters either; Peter Walker & Son (by now merged with the rival Liverpool firm of Robert Cain & Sons to form Walker Cain, but still trading under its old name) was decidedly lukewarm. However, the movement succeeded in detaching a portion of temperance opinion away from opposition to the pub and as such helped secure the continuing legitimacy of the trade. It also furthered the agenda of more progressive sections of the trade of shifting the emphasis towards retailing and customer service.

Following the Second World War, in which beer and pubs were seen as vital to the maintenance of morale, the opposition of both magistrates and the temperance movement were no longer factors. Now the challenge was to respond to changing social conditions, such as the increasing privatisation of leisure time with the diffusion of television and the demand for leisure facilities that would appeal to women customers. Companies such as Ind Coope and Whitbread had begun to explore new types of retail outlet and to engage in market research (Mutch, 2006a). Direct management meant a commitment to heavy overhead costs, but gave tighter control of activities in the pub, as well as both the wholesale and the retail profit. The practice gained a boost in the 1950s because of the desire of many pub owning brewers to offer a wider range of products, notably food. Not only did this require capital investment to provide the necessary facilities, but it also needed selling and other skills on the part of those running the pubs. The result was the widespread adoption of management and a shift to a retailing logic on the part of most, if not all, the major players in the industry. In 1960, Walker Cain merged with the Leeds-based brewer Joshua Tetley & Son. In the following year, the new company joined with Ind Coope and Ansells to form Allied Breweries. Although a key constituent of the new organization was the originator of the practice of house management, its experience was swallowed up by the production focus of the new entity, and Allied Breweries lagged behind the rest of the sector in its adoption of the retailing logic that conversion to management supported (Mutch, 2006b).

It thus took just over 100 years for the practice of house management to become a legitimate business practice in this particular field of economic activity. From the outline provided we can take a number of conclusions. One is that throughout it was not logics that were adopted, but practices. Andrew Barclay Walker, it would appear, drew upon models that he found to-hand in his background (Mutch, 2007). His innovation was to apply such models in a consistent manner in a different context. However, the response to that innovation was sharply divergent. In Liverpool, the specific combination of social and market conditions, which gave rise to a perceived major problem with drunkenness, meant that both political and legal authorities saw much merit in relying on the control exercised over salaried managers to address broader concerns. Opposition in the fraught conditions of rapid urbanisation and widespread casual labour was fragmented and could not draw upon the predominantly rural imagery that sustained opposition elsewhere. Indeed, the very success of the initiative in Liverpool linked it with the social problems associated with the city, and so hardened resistance elsewhere. So it was that, with a few exceptions, licensing magistrates refused to countenance the practice of direct management until support came from an unexpected quarter, the rural elite associated with moderate temperance. Over the course of a century, therefore, the practice of management gained adherents until it became respectable and legitimate. In the process, the logic of retailing became strengthened, both at the level of the field constituted by the sale of alcoholic drink and, in turn, at the broader societal level, but this could not be claimed to be the intentions of the originators and adopters of the practice. Rather, they had sought to address more immediate concerns and, in the process, provided to-hand templates for others.

A second conclusion is that the successful diffusion and adoption of the practice of the direct management of pubs was not the outcome of the efforts of a single 'institutional entrepreneur'. Indeed, the outline provided suggests the limits of that term. Historical narratives cause us to question the account of institutional change embedded in actor-centred conceptions such as the institutional entrepreneur. In her discussion of the evolution of the Paris Opera since its inception in the seventeenth century, Victoria Johnson (2007: 119) shows how 'the recombination of models that led to the founding form of the Opera emerged not through the efforts of a single actor, but instead through the interactions of that actor with influential others in his environment'. In the case of the direct management of public houses, Walker was indeed an entrepreneur, but one who sought to make money, not shift an institution. Provided that he could operate successfully, he was content to develop his business interests. His successors, it is true, did seek to make the case for management more strongly, but even here this was more in the mode of a defence of company practice. Their success was made visible in the physical form of their magnificent pubs but, perhaps even more importantly, symbolically in the form of the Walker Art Gallery that Andrew Barclay Walker donated to the city. The respectability of art and the elevation of its donor to the ranks of a knighthood eased the way for his model of direct management to be adopted by members of the rural elite, anxious to provide a working model of temperance that could counter both drunkenness and the alarming political consequences of militant teetotalism, strongly associated in England with popular nonconformism. In turn, the success in operational terms of the Trust House Movement provided members of the brewing industry with the ammunition they needed to pursue an agenda that saw a decided turn away from pubs as mere outlets for the sale of alcohol towards a more retailing orientation. While that turn was not entirely successful, it not only brought respectability to the industry but also provided a training ground for the experimentation with practices that would prove to be central to the field in the years following the Second World War. This was thus collective 'entrepreneurship' that succeeded over time in legitimising a practice and enhancing the prospects of a retailing logic that, by the 1990s, had trumped the hitherto dominant production logic. But this was not the collective action of a social movement. Rather, it was an unfolding process that needs attention to temporality to appreciate.

The adoption of practices also has to be seen in the context of enabling conditions, conditions that a historical account reveals. Thus, argue Jensen et al. (2018), the success of dairy cooperatives in Denmark, something that has been seen as central to the fortunes of the country's agricultural economy, was not just a result of distinctive patterns of social life. Rather, it rested on technical innovations, such as field rotations and crop selection, which were pioneered by the estate administrators on the home farms of large country estates. They imported the so-called 'Holstein' system from German-speaking areas, often together with skilled Dutch cowkeepers, in the eighteenth century, thereby adapting the system to Danish conditions and proving its technical superiority over other practices. The establishment of dairy cooperatives to process the resulting products thus drew on these examples, something that was then consolidated by the folk high schools that combined study of technical processes with an emphasis on participatory democracy. As Jensen et al. note, this process unfolded over well over a century. As they suggest, efforts to translate cooperative agricultural practices to other contexts were often a relative failure, as they failed to take into account these enabling conditions.

Finally, the story of the adoption of direct management suggests the importance of relationships between different forms of logic. That relationship could in some conjunctures of time and place be complementary, at others contradictory. So, at the same point in time, the different balance of the logics in particular places could either support or oppose the adoption of practices. The disparity was in part because of the existence of devolved legal and political systems, meaning that in Liverpool licensing magistrates could bow to particular local pressures. More than that, during the course of the nineteenth century, they became advocates, together with the police, of a practice that their fellows elsewhere set their faces firmly against. In most of the rest of the country, the combination of adherence to the model of tenancy derived from agricultural practice and the gentlemanly ideal associated with the dominant political practice of the ruling elite meant that direct management was not able to achieve legitimate status.

Practices Change; Logics Endure

Friedland's (2009) discussions of logics tend to focus on the relationship between practice and substance at a particular point in time. Although his work with Alford did argue that institutional logics 'have specific historical limits', what those limits were was not pursued in any detail (Friedland and Alford, 1991: 248). In addition, as we have seen with both visitation routines and management systems, practices have their own historical trajectory. The study of history, with its focus on multiple temporalities, suggests that, once emergent from particular practices, logics can endure while the detail of the practices they influence can change. An example of this in organizational analysis is provided by the careful tracing of change in legal practice in Anglo-German law firms undertaken by Michael Smets, Tim Morris and Royston Greenwood (2012). They show that practices reflected assumptions built into the different legal logics provided by, on the one hand, English common law and, on the other, German civil law. It was when these practices were brought together that tensions ensued, tensions that were eventually resolved by hybrid practices. That such practices might, over time, become adopted as organizational practice is where their account leaves us. We can imagine that, once adopted by particular organizations, such practices might, in time, change similar practices in the field demarcated by commercial law as shaped by the needs of cross-national finance. However, whether such developments might change the particular nature of the law in each country, given its basis in very different and enduring conceptualisations of the law, is open to considerable doubt.

The specific difference that Smets, Morris and Greenwood draw our attention to is the construction of contracts. Contracts drawn up by German lawyers were sparse in form, resting on the specification of standard terms in legal codes. By contrast, English lawyers produced dense contracts with many clauses. This difference reflected the assumptions embedded in different legal systems, suggesting a more enduring logic. As we saw in Chapter 4, grievance procedures in US companies were modelled on perceptions of legal practice. 'Grievance procedures appear rational', argue Edelman et al. (1999: 416), 'because they look like the system of appeals available in the public legal process'. These same grievance procedures came to be accepted over time as evidence of best practice by the courts and so changed the substance of the law. On their account, this process took place over a period of some thirty years. However, what did not change (although they do not discuss this) was the underlying logic of a common law system, in which the interpretation of laws by judges depends in turn on cases being brought, results being published and precedents drawn on. This is a quite different logic from the emphasis on codification in civil law systems, a logic that could be found in the royal academies of seventeenth-century France that Johnson (2007) examined. Here, royal academies, 'an organizational form sponsored by the king and traditionally devoted to private discussion among academy members', were seen as the to-hand template for the organization of the Paris Opera (Johnson, 2007: 104). In turn, those academies promoted a logic of centralized political control, in which the 'main goal was codification of guidelines for production in an academy's given area of cultural or scientific specialization' (Johnson, 2007: 108). These examples suggest that we need to exercise caution in talking of institutional change. In the case of the law, for example, there is no doubt that the shift towards legislation as the source of much law has influenced both civil and common law, leading some scholars to point to the emergence of mixed systems. It is rare, however, for there to be a shift from one distinctive legal logic to another. In Cyprus, a country with a civil law tradition, British colonial influence led to the formal adoption of the tenets of English common law in 1935 (Hatzimihail, 2013). This externally imposed shift from a civil law tradition was the culmination of a fifty-year process and still left traces of previous logics in place, such as aspects of an inquisitorial approach. Practices may change readily, organizations more slowly but, history suggests, logics endure. That is not to say that they do not change, but these examples of contrasting legal systems mean that we need to be careful to contextualize institutions to particular conjunctures of time and place.

The change we examined in the case of the management of pubs involved change in practices within one field, changes that gradually effected change in broader logics, such that a retailing logic became a legitimate part of economic logic. These changes were not the product of specific events but happened gradually and with cumulative effect. The thinkers of the Scottish Enlightenment such as Adam Ferguson had a particular concern with history and the ways in which changes in institutions happened gradually. As Berry (2013: 51) suggests in his account of their theory of history, thinkers such as Ferguson, William Robertson and David Hume held 'that "events" unfold gradually and imperceptibly, beneath the radar (so to speak) of individuals with their intentions and deliberative purposes'. Their account of historical change was, Berry argues, an institutional one, in which changes in practices gradually signal a change from one stage of history to another. In arguing for this, they were in part drawing on very real experience of the juxtaposition of two forms of society in the same country. The land of economic development and enlightenment thought characterised by the environs of Edinburgh was contrasted with the very different social and economic conditions of the Highlands. Writing in the 1760s, these thinkers had the memory of a bitter civil war to draw upon. They also drew on the initial stirring of anthropological investigation engendered by contact with the indigenous peoples of North America. They were particularly concerned with the preconditions for the emergence of commercial society, which they theorised in terms of stages of development. Typically, four stages are often attributed to this group of thinkers: hunters, herders, farmers and commercial society. For Berry, stadial theory is used as an ordering device for a history of institutions. For the Scots, says Berry (2013: 204), 'social institutions are the locus of societal differences, and their social scientific account of social or moral causation made them aware that behaviour and values are largely a product of institutions. There is no road-block to institutional change'.

Berry demonstrates how sophisticated much of this discussion was. Representing early work in the fields of sociology and historical sociology, it had a considerable on later thinkers, notably Marx. However, the stages theory was taken up not as an analytical device but as a description of the inevitable stages that societies had to go through in order to achieve progress. In the hands of vulgar Marxists, it became a crude and inflexible account. In such an account, politics had to ensure the completion of a stage of development, often drawing on the prototypical template of England, before proceeding to the next stage. For Massimiliano Tomba (2013), this was to ignore Marx's engagement with the example of Russia. Here, centres of advanced industrial production with their accompanying industrial working class coexisted with older forms of economic development, notably peasant agriculture. Because of the possibility of learning from more advanced centres of economic development, intermediate stages of development could be jumped. Such experiences called into question the value of a stages theory of development. Instead, argues Tomba, a geological metaphor is more pertinent. Such a metaphor, he suggests

> expresses a stratification of geological layers, and not a succession of stages. The secondary is superimposed on the primary without deleting it. The historical materialist, dealing with periods of history as if they were geological epochs, simultaneously ensures the visibility of the different layers. The historical forms do not follow a linear model of past and present, but they become 'geological formations' in which the already-been coexists with the now, allowing us to think the co-presence of temporalities on a surface and not according to a linear vector.
>
> (Tomba, 2013: 175)

As he points out, 'archaic' economic practices, such as slavery, can coexist with more 'advanced' forms of economic development: indeed, sometimes the latter can depend on the former. Tomba's argument here is to do with economic development, in which he argues that devices such as the world market act to synchronise phenomena that operate with differing temporalities. However, we are interested in the layering of institutional logics. Although the metaphors of strata and sedimentation have limits, because they do not account for dynamic connections across logics, they do point to different paces of change in logics. Economic practices, for example, may change with considerable rapidity, while religious practices are more enduring. It is this concern with multiple temporalities that characterizes much historiographical debate (Osborne, 2015). This is not time as a variable, but history as irreversible.

An influential scheme that also grows out of Marxist concerns with historical development is that associated with the French Annales school (Tosh, 2000). Developed from the work of the historian Marc Bloch, this focuses in particular on the 'long durée' – the slow unfolding of structures of productive forces and demographics that conditioned human activity at shorter scales of action. Particular attention is paid in this tradition to the investigation of 'mentalities', that is, the habits of thought that are associated with particular historical conjunctures. The focus of such work is, as Tosh (2000: 98) puts it, 'those gradual transformations in mental and social experience which were reflected on the surface of events in only the most oblique manner'. By contrast, critics of this approach have tended to focus on the importance of significant events, events that reveal the contradictions that have been generated over time. For Arendt (1958: 273), for example, it is 'not ideas but events [that] change the world – the heliocentric system as an idea is as old as Pythagorean speculation and as persistent in our history as Neo-Platonic traditions, without, for that matter, ever having changed the world or the human mind – and the author of the decisive event of the modern age is Galileo rather than Descartes'. There are echoes here of the argument that Archer (1996) makes about cultural contradictions. Ideas, she argues, can exist in manifest contradiction without disturbing the surface of social affairs until the emergence of a new collective force that can seize upon such contradictions and mobilize them in the pursuit of a collective endeavour. Thus, it is not to a purely intellectual history nor an account of practices divorced from the development of ideas but the relationship between the two that we need to explore.

For the historian William Sewell

> events should be conceived of as sequences of occurrences that result in the transformation of structures. Such sequences begin with a rupture of some kind — that is, a surprising break with routine practice. Such breaks actually occur every day — as a consequence of exogenous causes, of contradictions between structures, of sheer human inventiveness or perversity, or of simple mistakes in enacting routines. But most ruptures are neutralized and reabsorbed into the preexisting structures in one way or another — they may, for example, be forcefully repressed, pointedly ignored, or explained away as exceptions.
>
> (Sewell, 2005: 227)

The example given above of the changes in legal practice in Anglo-German legal firms is a good illustration of both routine practices being challenged by changing circumstances and the change that ensued as occurring at different temporalities on different scales of action. Initially, both sets of lawyers resisted change, resting on their own legal traditions. Gradually, however, hybrid forms emerged to deal with contradictions that could not be wished away but had to be addressed in new practices of writing contracts. Such changes in practice might then migrate to the organizational level and from there might influence practice at the level of the field of multinational commercial law, resulting in blended systems. However, as argued above, change in the basic contours of the contrasting civil and common law system, established as they have been over centuries of development with the concomitant vehicles for education and socialization, is unlikely to happen unless victim to exogenous shock.

Historically Specific Forms of Logics and Their Relationships

We have seen in the above example that the law as a societal institution takes very different forms in England and Germany. We could point to other areas of social life where it is important to see institutions as differentiated, while still adhering to a central form of logic. If, for example, we take religion in terms of the definition we have previously encountered, that is, 'any mythically sustained concern for ultimate meanings coupled with a ritually reinforced sense of social belonging' (Demerath and Schmitt, 1998: 382), then the logic inherent in that statement can be instantiated in a variety of forms. To take Western Christianity as a starting point, there was a time when, in broad terms, the institutional logic was consistent with an undifferentiated institution, in which the Catholic Church provided both the authorized belief system and the approved practices, as well as the only legitimate organizational form. However, the Reformation saw the emergence of competing formulations in all these dimensions (MacCulloch, 2004). At least three major competing formations, each with their own formal statements of belief, their own distinctive practices and their own organizational form, came into existence: the Lutheranism that characterized much of Germany and northern Europe; the Calvinism of the Netherlands and Scotland; and the Episcopalianism of England. From this time, any consideration of 'religion' as an institution within Christianity has to consider the particular form that is under consideration.

This specific form then comes into relationship with the other institutions that constitute society. In some cases, this forms a complementary relationship. In Scotland, for example, one can trace a mutually supportive relationship between religion, law and education (Mutch, 2015). Scots law drew heavily on a Roman law tradition, in which there was, by European standards, an early attempt to codify legal rules and promulgate these in written form. This in turn rested on widespread literacy in an educational system that featured the same focus on starting from first principles that characterized both the law and the particular religious form of the Church of Scotland. In turn, that church both monitored and encouraged the growth of a basic education system and a higher education system (Sher, 2015). This distinctive complex of institutional forms can be seen in sharper focus when contrasted with the position in England, where a common law tradition and a state church featuring both a nominal hierarchy and a strong element of devolved authority fostered the enduring influence of custom and tradition. This was reinforced by an ad hoc and fragmented educational system, whose pinnacles in the form of the universities of Oxford and Cambridge remained profoundly shaped by and limited to particular religious traditions (Carter, 1990). The implications for economic activity are that the distinctive complex of logics in Scotland gave rise to a particular focus on accounting and accountability (Mutch, 2016). This sheds light on the significant contribution of Scots to the development of the accounting profession, indicating the value of setting organizational developments in their broader historical context (Previs and Merino, 1997).

One response to the 'paradox of embedded agency' that has prompted much debate amongst institutional theorists is to introduce the notion of contradictions between institutions and their associated logics as a source of change (Seo and Creed, 2002). Embedded agency refers to the argument that, if all actors are shaped by the same institutional environment, which provides shared norms to guide action, then how can change occur? However, such an argument presupposes one overarching and closely integrated institutional system. That such systems, leading to prolonged periods of stasis, can exist is indicated by Archer's example of India. However, as she notes, such integration is rare, and it is more likely to find contending institutional orders. As she notes, 'all agents are not involved in all of them, whilst some are involved in several' (Archer, 1995: 228). As a consequence, actors are exposed to different practices and the assumptions inherent in them, exposure that is open to transfer. Institutional theorists have pointed to the field as the place where contending logics come into play and potentially open up possibilities for change. Smets et al. (2015), in a fascinating ethnographic account of traders in the Lloyds of London insurance market, point to the creative and ongoing work that actors engage in to reconcile the contending logics of community and market. They examine the micro practices involving the creative use of space and dress as methods of segmenting, bridging and demarcating contending logics. However, from our earlier discussion, we might cast some doubt on whether these are contending institutional logics, or rather whether they are intra-institutional logics. That is, the deployment of the term community is, as we have seen, of a different order to institutions like religion. I have argued that it should rather be seen as a rhetorical device that points to forms of organising. In the case of Lloyds of London, it points to an occupational community with its distinctive norms. In other words, the contending logics here are contained within an overarching market logic.

As we have already seen, this points to the existence of subsidiary logics within an overarching logic, just as within the UK brewing industry, there was contention between production and retailing logics. The same could be said for the US academic publishing market examined by Thornton. Within domains other than the economic, we find a similar delineation of subsidiary orders, whether these be denominations in religion or legal systems in the legal order. Often such subsidiary logics are relatively self-contained, but their logics are revealed when changing states of the world bring their practices into contact with those from another subsidiary order. Thus, as we saw in the example of Anglo-German contracts, the very different practices of writing contracts in common and civil law jurisdictions are revealed when broader economic shifts mean that cross-jurisdictional contracts are required. Comparative lawyers point to the impact of the harmonisation of international accounting standards on commercial law, where the assumptions in contending legal systems on, for example, fairness in contracts, are brought into stark relief (Grossfeld, 2013; Kwon, 2004).

Such contacts happen in specific historical contexts. In their exploration of the emergence of what they term a 'corporate' logic in the United States in the second half of the nineteenth century, William Occasio, Michael Mauskapf and Christopher Steel (2016: 677) have argued that in 'contrast to the ideal-typical approach, we propose that societal logics are historically constituted cultural structures'. They see the existing work on institutional logics (in this case in the tradition of Thornton et al, not Friedland) as insufficiently historical, proposing implicitly transhistorical ideal types. They suggest by contrast that societal logics are emergent over time and are constituted by representations and archives that serve to fix collective memories. While, however, the thrust of this book has been clearly to situate institutional logics both at the level of society and in particular conjunctures of time and place, this is not to eschew efforts at abstract conceptualization. Rather we need both. We need the abstraction of features from historical examples and then the sensitive reinsertion of those concepts into concrete historical conjunctures. In addition, the argument of Occasio et al. that 'the constitution and configuration of societal logics are contingent on the historical processes outlined in our model such that the accumulation and metanarration of historical events can give rise to new societal logics while erasing others' (Occasio et al. 2017: 686) does not give sufficient attention to the enduring nature, while changing, of societal institutions. We have seen that not only are practices linked at specific times to particular logics but also that those practices have a history, a history that casts a good deal of doubt on accounts that place overmuch stress on contingency and change.

Emergent Institutions

It is true, however, that the historical record indicates that, over time, practices can burst the bounds of their formative institutional order and come to constitute a new institutional order with its own logic. The classic case of this is the emergence of what I have termed the institution of knowledge from the formative institution of religion. Ways of knowing the world, and their associated educational arrangements, start with control by a priesthood (Bourdieu and Passeron, 1977). As Weber notes

> The priesthood, as the only agents capable of conserving tradition, took over the training of youth in the law and often in purely administrative technologies, and, above all, in writing and calculus. The more religion became book-religion and doctrine, the more literary it became and the more efficacious it was in provoking rational lay-thinking, freed of priestly control.
>
> (Weber, 1948: 351)

That process could, indeed, be facilitated by the imperatives of the religious logic without the knowing or desiring of its adherents. In that subsidiary logic represented by Reformed Protestantism in Scotland, there was an early emphasis on the desirability of widespread elementary education. The ambition to provide a school in every parish was not to provide learning for its own sake but to equip the faithful with the ability to read the sacred word. It was also to provide a mechanism for those with the facility to learn classical languages with a route to the universities at the pinnacle of the system to bolster the ministerial cadre. That this was effective, at least in the lowland parts of the country, can be seen in the observation of the Reverend Thomas Boston of his congregation in the early eighteenth century that 'I had never seen in a country-kirk more Bibles than appeared in ours' (Morrison, 1899: 215). Of course, the skills of reading could also be applied to secular activities. In addition, the church set much store by the teaching of basic arithmetic in its schools, with a view to supporting the accountability for resources that was a central part of its governance. As an unintended consequence of these actions, which were designed to foster religious, not secular, activities, the church facilitated the development of not only individual capabilities but also an educational system that developed a logic of its own.

It took time for educational systems to escape the control of religious bodies and, even where that was ultimately possible, the traces of religious origins lived on. For the Jesuit seminaries, despite their considerable educational innovations, such as detailed curricula, the core focus was on the instilling of discipline. Educational activities remained subordinate to the claims of religious authority, reinforced by strict visitation practices and extensive reporting and control systems. Other educational systems, such as those in Scotland, managed to wriggle free of religious visitation over time, and Oxbridge managed to avoid it altogether. In Germany, by contrast, 'Protestant princes ... did two things: they took over the clerical apparatus in their lands and, in the matter of the visitation, they subsumed their academics under it' (Clark, 2006: 342). However, state control meant the development of the university system to meet secular needs, especially of the provision of skilled administrators to staff state bureaucracies. From the early nineteenth century onwards, this saw the growth of specialized academic departments and roles such as the research professor, with the logic of academic excellence, privileging novel research and the publication of results. In turn, this example had a considerable impact, argues Clark, on the research universities of the United States. However, even here, given a market system with the absence of central regulation, religious bodies continued to found their own educational organizations, in part to provide training for the clerical incumbents of their various denominations. Other systems continued to provide such religious training, although now shrinking to faculties of theology or divinity. However, the existence of such centres within the university, although now subject to the academic imperatives of status, continued to mould the wider provision. Oxbridge, for example, given the dominance of the Church of England (other denominations being unable to attend until the nineteenth century) maintained a focus on classical knowledge as the key to the formation of character. This saw the neglect of more vocational forms of education, such as medicine. Adam Smith was scathing of his time at Oxford. He won an Exhibition to support attendance at Balliol College in 1740 but found it full of 'exploded systems and obsolete prejudices' (Buchan, 2003: 123). Still more intemperate was the self-taught mason and geologist Hugh Miller in his dismissal of the continuing influence of religion on the development of scientific inquiry in England in the mid-nineteenth century. 'The mediaeval miasma,' he thundered, 'originated in the bogs and fens of Oxford, has been blown aslant over the face of the country: and not only religious but scientific truth is to experience, it would seem, the influence of its poisonous blights and rotting mildews' (Miller, 1853: 248). This continuing dominance of Anglican ideas meant that vocational education in science and medicine was to be more readily found north of the border. As the economic historian Ashton (1968: 14) observed of the early nineteenth century, if 'the Scottish system of primary education was in advance of that of any other European country at this time, the same was true of the Scottish universities. It was not from Oxford or Cambridge, where the torch burnt dim, but from Glasgow and Edinburgh, that the impulse to scientific inquiry and its practical application came'. So it was that Edinburgh in particular trained most of the university-educated doctors in the United Kingdom in the eighteenth and early nineteenth centuries (Allan, 2015). Accordingly, it took centuries for the institutional order of knowledge to shape its own distinctive organizations, practices and roles. Even here, the enduring marks of its origins in religious systems left their traces, traces that might be more evident in taken-for-granted ways of operating, rather than in content. As Bourdieu and Passeron point out for the French context,

> Endowed by the Jesuits with particularly effective means of imposing the academic cult of hierarchy and inculcating an autarkic culture cut off from life, the French educational system was able to develop its generic tendency towards autonomization to the point of subordinating its whole functioning to the demands of self-perpetuation.
> (Bourdieu and Passeron, 1977: 149)

Summary

History is not just about locating institutional logics at particular times and places but also about showing the slow emergence of new combinations of substance and practices. Understanding this is the key to why Pierson (2004: 133) argues for the use of the term 'institutional development' rather than 'institutional change'. The latter term cedes too much ground to notions that institutions can be changed by individual actors exercising choice and not enough to the idea that such choices are them-selves profoundly shaped by the logics in which actors find themselves. Development allows for the idea that institutions change slowly over time, often as the unintended consequences of actors who, rather than seeking institutional change, have innovated in practices that are seen to meet the needs that are to-hand.

Notes

1 'Manager v. tenant', *Brewers' Journal*, 15 Oct. 1911, 545.
2 British Parliamentary Papers, Royal Commission on Licensing, C. 8523, Second volume of evidence XXXV, 1897, 73.
3 RC Licensing, 258.
4 The Parliamentary Debates (Hansard) Vol 136, Forth series, 14–28 June 1904, 223.

References

Acheson, G., Hickson, C., and Turner, J. (2011) 'Organisational flexibility and governance in a civil-law regime: Scottish partnership banks during the Industrial Revolution', *Business History*, 53(4), 505–529.

Allan, D. (2015) 'The universities and the Scottish enlightenment', in Anderson, R., Freeman, M. and Patterson, L. (eds.), *The Edinburgh History of Education in Scotland*, Edinburgh: Edinburgh University Press, 2015, 97–113.

Archer, M. (1995) *Realist Social Theory: The Morphogenetic Approach*, Cambridge: Cambridge University Press.

Archer, M. (1996) *Culture and Agency: The Place of Culture in Social Theory*, Cambridge: Cambridge University Press.

Arendt, H. (1958) *The Human Condition*, Chicago: University of Chicago Press.

Ashton, T. (1968) *The Industrial Revolution 1760–1830*, Oxford: Oxford University Press.

Berry, C. (2013) *The Idea of Commercial Society in the Scottish Enlightenment*, Edinburgh: Edinburgh University Press.

Bourdieu, P. and Passeron, J. (1977) *Reproduction in Education, Society and Culture*, London: Sage.

Buchan, J. (2003) *Capital of the Mind: How Edinburgh Changed the World*, London: John Murray.

Carter, I. (1990) *Ancient Cultures of Conceit: British University Fiction in the Post-War Years*, London: Routledge.

Clark, W. (2006) *Academic Charisma and the Origins of the Research University*, Chicago: University of Chicago Press.

Cooke, A. (2010) *The Rise and Fall of the Scottish Cotton Industry 1778–1914: The Secret Spring*, Manchester: Manchester University Press.

Demerath, N. and Schmitt, T. (1998) 'Transcending sacred and secular: mutual benefits in analyzing religious and nonreligious organizations', in Demerath, N., Hall, P., Schmitt, T. and Williams, R. (eds.), *Sacred Companies*, New York: Oxford University Press, 1998, 381–392.

Djelic, M.-L. (2013) 'When limited liability was (still) an issue: Mobilization and politics of signification in 19th-century England', *Organization Studies*, 34, 595–621.

Dobbin, F. (1994) *Forging Industrial Policy: The United States, Britain, and France in the Railway Age,* Cambridge: Cambridge University Press.

Edelman, L., Uggen, C., and Erlanger, H. (1999) 'The endogeneity of legal regulation: grievance procedures as rational myth', *American Journal of Sociology,* 105, 406–454.

Ferguson, A. (1767) *An Essay on the History of Civil Society,* Cambridge: Cambridge University Press.

Friedland, R. (2009) 'Institution, practice and ontology: towards a religious sociology', *Research in the Sociology of Organizations,* 27, 45–83.

Friedland, R. and Alford, R. (1991) 'Bringing society back in: symbols, practices, and institutional contradictions', in Powell W. and DiMaggio P. (eds.) *The New Institutionalism in Organizational Analysis,* Chicago: University of Chicago Press, 1991, 232–266.

Greenaway, J. (1998) 'The "improved" public house, 1870–1950: the key to civilized drinking or the primrose path to drunkenness?', *Addiction,* 93(2), 173–181.

Grossfeld, B. (2013) 'Comparatists and languages', in Legrand, P. and Munday, R. (eds.), *Comparative Legal Studies: Traditions and Transitions,* Cambridge: Cambridge University Press, 2013, 154–194.

Gutzke, D. (2006) *Pubs and Progressives: Reinventing the Public House in England 1896–1960,* DeKalb, IL: Northern Illinois University Press.

Harries-Jenkins, G. (1977) *The Army in Victorian Society,* London: Routledge and Kegan Paul.

Harrison, B. (1994) *Drink and the Victorians: The Temperance Question in England 1815–1872,* Keele: Keele University Press.

Hatzimihail, N. (2013) 'Cyprus as a mixed legal system', *Journal of Civil Law Studies,* 6(1), 37–96.

Jensen, P., Lampe, M., Sharp, P. and Skovsgaard, C. (2018) 'Getting to Denmark: the role of elites for development', Carlos III University of Madrid. Figuerola Institute of Social Sciences, History, Working Papers in Economic History, 18–03.

Johnson, V. (2007) 'What is organizational imprinting? Cultural entrepreneurship in the founding of the Paris opera', *American Journal of Sociology,* 113, 97–127.

Kwon, H. (2004) *Fairness and Division of Labor in Market Societies: A Comparison of the U.S. and German Automotive Industries,* New York: Berghahn.

MacCulloch, D. (2004) *Reformation: Europe's House Divided 1490–1700,* London: Penguin.

Miller, H. (1853) *First Impressions of England and its People,* Edinburgh: Johnstone and Hunter.

Milne, G. (2000) *Trade and Traders In Mid-Victorian Liverpool: Mercantile Business and the Making of a World Port,* Liverpool: Liverpool University Press.

Morrison, G. (1899) *Memoirs of the Life, Time and Writings of the Reverend and Learned Thomas Boston,* Edinburgh: Oliphant, Anderson & Ferrier.

Musacchio, A. and Turner, J., (2013) 'Does the law and finance hypothesis pass the test of history?', *Business History,* 55(4), 524–542.

Mutch, A. (2003) 'Magistrates and public house managers, 1840–1914: another case of Liverpool exceptionalism?', *Northern History,* 40(2), 325–342.

Mutch, A. (2005) 'Management practice and kirk sessions: an exploration of the Scottish contribution to management', *Journal of Scottish Historical Studies*, 24(1), 1–19.

Mutch, A. (2006a) 'Allied Breweries and the development of the area manager, 1950–1984', *Enterprise and Society*, 7(2), 353–379.

Mutch, A. (2006b) *Strategic and Organizational Change: From Production to Retailing in UK Brewing 1950–1990*, London: Routledge.

Mutch, A. (2006c) 'Public houses as multiple retailing: Peter Walker & Son 1846–1914', *Business History*, 48(1), 1–19.

Mutch, A. (2007) 'Reflexivity and the institutional entrepreneur: a historical exploration', *Organization Studies*, 28(7), 1123–1140.

Mutch, A. (2010) 'Improving the public house in Britain 1920–1940: Sir Sydney Nevile and 'social work'', *Business History*, 52(4), 517–535.

Mutch, A. (2015) *Religion and National Identity: Governing Scottish Presbyterianism in the Eighteenth Century*, Edinburgh: Edinburgh University Press.

Mutch, A. (2016) 'Religion and accounting texts in eighteenth century Scotland: organizational practices and a culture of accountability', *Accounting, Auditing & Accountability Journal*, 29(6), 926–946.

Occasio, W., Mauskapf, M. and Steele, C. (2016) 'History, society, and institutions: the role of collective memory in the emergence and evolution of societal logics', *Academy of Management Review*, 41(4), 676–699.

Osborne, P. (2015) 'Out of sync: Tomba's Marx and the problem of a multilayered temporal dialectic', *Historical Materialism*, 23(4), 39–48.

Peoples Refreshment House Association. (1912) *Public House Reform*, Westminster: PRHA.

Perchard, A. (2007) *The Mine Management Professions in the Twentieth Century Scottish Coal Mining Industry*, Lewiston, NY: Edwin Mellen Press.

Pierson, P. (2004) *Politics in Time: History, Institutions, and Social Analysis*, Princeton: Princeton University Press.

Previs, G. and Merino, B. (1997) *A History of Accountancy in the United States*, Columbus, OH: Ohio State University Press.

Seo, M. and Creed, D. (2002) 'Institutional contradictions, praxis and institutional change: a dialectical perspective', *Academy of Management Review*, 27(2), 222–247.

Sewell, W. (2005) *Logics of History: Social Theory and Social Transformation*, Chicago: University of Chicago Press.

Sher, R. (2015) *Church and University in the Scottish Enlightenment: The Moderate Literati of Edinburgh*, Edinburgh: Edinburgh University Press.

Smets, M., Morris, T. and Greenwood, R. (2012) 'From practice to field: a multilevel model of practice-driven institutional change', *Academy of Management Journal*, 55(4), 877–904.

Smets, M., Jarzabkowski, P., Burke, G. and Spee, P. (2015) 'Reinsurance trading in Lloyds of London: balancing conflicting-yet-complementary logics in practice', *Academy of Management Journal*, 58(3), 932–970.

Tomba, M. (2012) *Marx's Temporalities*, Leiden: Brill.

Tosh, J. (2000) *The Pursuit of History*, Harlow: Longman.

Walker, P. (1896) *Walker's Warrington Ales*, Warrington: Peter Walker & Son.

Weber, M. (1948) 'Religious rejections of the world and their directions', in Gerth, H. and Wright Mills, C. (eds.), *From Max Weber*, London: Routledge & Kegan Paul, 1948, 323–359.

7 Materiality and Identity

Introduction

In the summer of 2017, the Welsh village cricket club from Carew had the unusual distinction of being crowned as champions of the Pembrokeshire Cricket League and relegated in the same season. They were relegated for manipulating the scoring system. Cricket is an unusual game in that a team can comprehensively outplay another, but the match can still end in a draw, thanks to either the dogged resistance of the poorer team or, highly likely in Britain, the intervention of the weather. Accordingly, the scoring system that awards points tries to adjust for such outcomes by awarding bonus points for batting and bowling performances, as well as points for a win or a draw. In Carew's case, they started the final match of the season twenty-one points ahead of their nearest rival, Cresselly, who were also that day's opponents. A win would give Cresselly twenty points; further bonus points available for how well they batted or bowled would give them the potential of topping the table. Accordingly, Carew declared after scoring eighteen runs for the loss of one wicket. Because of this, Cresselly were certain to win, but could not pick up any bonus points, thus making Carew champions (BBC, 2017).

Outrage greeted this course of action; a disciplinary committee decided that Carew's actions were against the spirit of the game and so they would start the next season in the lower division as punishment. Clearly, the disciplinary committee were drawing on a sporting logic, founded in ideas about fair play to arrive at their decision. The logic had given the teams an identity as cricketers, in which actions that might be appropriate in other logics were ruled as lacking legitimacy. Part of the discussion in this chapter is the way in which logics bestow identities, discussion that draws on the logic of play in particular. But there is also the question of the performative impact of the material practice that is embedded in the drawing up of tables of performance. Such practices, that is, do not just mirror action in the world, but also shape it. League tables that have their origin in a competitive sporting logic can transfer to influence action in other domains, carried by particular objects. Such material practices are often facilitated by technological artefacts.

Institutional theory has been criticised for its lack of attention to materiality, so this chapter draws on debates in the information systems literature to point to how we might bring materiality into our analyses. It does so through a discussion of both objects and spaces.

Materiality

As a domain in which technological artefacts loom large, it is understandable that those working in information systems have been exercised by the nature of material properties. It is particularly the case for those interested in the implications of ICT for organisational life. Some of the debates can be illustrated in the changing work of the influential author Wanda Orlikowski. In her earlier work, a distinction was made between the *scope* and the *role* of technology (Orlikowski, 1992). Scope referred to the designed artefact and its intended uses, role to the ways in which that scope was perceived in a concrete setting (perceptions that might diverge considerably from the intentions of designers). In practice, much of her work was concerned with the *role* of technology, with a particular focus, drawn from Giddens, on the knowledgeability of actors faced with flexible forms of technology. The tendency to focus on the malleability of technological artefacts was then developed in order to be aligned with the notion of structures on memory traces that we have seen in the formulation by Giddens of his structuration theory (Orlikowski, 2000). Any notion that organisational structures and policies might be made concrete in material form was thus rejected.

So far, then, material properties were banished from our consideration, but they make a dramatic comeback in Orlikowski's (2007) later work. Strongly influenced by the work of the feminist physicist Karen Barad (2003), Orlikowski has formulated the notion of 'sociomateriality'. Now,

> materiality is integral to organizing, positing that the social and the material are *constitutively entangled* in everyday life. A position of constitutive entanglement does not privilege either humans or technology (in one-way interactions), nor does it link them through a form of mutual reciprocation (in two-way interactions). Instead, the social and the material are considered to be inextricably related – there is no social that is not also material, and no material that is not also social.
>
> (Orlikowski, 2007: 1437)

From material properties having been relegated to the background, simply being the raw materials subject to the infinite possibilities of agential interpretation, they have become, through a considerable *volte face*, the constitutive elements of social activity. While at one level one could hardly disagree, given the embodied nature of human action, that all action is shot through with materiality, sociomateriality gives us no analytical purchase on those aspects of social life that privilege certain aspects of materiality, drawing on it to shape organisational life. An alternative approach that draws on the resources of critical realism is one that recognises first of all that the material properties of particular arrangements matter in limiting what can be achieved and secondly that such properties allow particular arrangements to be inscribed into artefacts that then form the taken-for-granted context for action. Given that a morphogenetic approach stresses the importance of the material properties of particular forms of technology, further discussion of what we take 'materiality' to mean is helpful. As Ian Hutchby (2001: 3) points out

> materiality here need not be thought of only in physical terms. We may, for instance, be able to conceive of the telephone as having a materiality affecting the distribution of interactional space through the promotion of what I will call conversational 'intimacy at a distance'... Likewise, we can conceive of the interfaces of expert systems or internet conferencing software as having a materiality affecting navigation through a technically bounded interactional space as people attempt to orient themselves in the sequential order of a particular interaction.

This consideration of materiality as involving more than the concrete physicality of particular technological artefacts parallels the focus of John Clark, Ian Mcloughlin and Howard Rose (1988) on architecture in their consideration of engineering systems. That is, the same hardware and software could be configured in different ways to produce very different implications for organisational arrangements. Clark et al stress the need to take a systemic approach, in which the crucial system properties are those that emerge from particular forms of organisation of technology. In considering such material properties, we will also wish to remember that users are not faced by 'technology' as an abstraction but by concrete instantiations (D'Adderio, 2004). That is, some of the discussion in social constructivist accounts (Edwards, Ashmore and Potter, 1995; Grint and Woolgar, 1997) is posed at a hypothetical level, which pushes the discussion beyond the practical constraints faced by both users and organisations (Hutchby, 2001). Whilst these constraints are ultimately social and economic, the material constraints posed by technology can not all be released or changed at the same pace.

When considering the interpretive flexibility of some forms of ICT artefact, Orlikowski may have had in mind applications like spreadsheets. The combination of columns and rows to form matrices of cells into which data can be input and manipulated opens the way to a wide range of applications, some often pushing the boundaries of what original designers might have imagined. There comes a practical point, however, at which such uses, while technically possible, become infeasible in an organisational context. Spreadsheets, that is, can be used to mimic the functionality of databases but will be unable to match the latter's practical performance, simply because their underlying design premises are different. There is a limit, that is, to flexibility and in practical terms material properties, such as processing power and speed, matter. This can be illustrated in the case of the widely used Enterprise Resource Planning systems, which use database architecture to attempt to provide organisations with a single point of entry for data. The practical consequences of such systems are to limit organisational flexibility of use and design in a number of stages. One is with the selection process, which Neil Pollock and Robin Williams (2009) demonstrate is inherently complex and uncertain. This is because existing systems that might be used as reference points are already embedded in organisational contexts that have shaped their use. Once chosen, that is, the specific features of the selected system point to particular routes for action. Such routes can be resisted through the customisation of the software, but such customisation in itself has resource consequences, not least that it may hinder the subsequent uptake of updates to the software. Such considerations often mean that organisations take the route of least resistance, adopting the practices, and so the assumptions, built into the software. Indeed, argue Jos Benders, Ronald Batenburg and Heico van der Blonk (2006), much of the attraction for many senior decision makers is that such systems seem an ideal way of enforcing 'best practice'. In this way there is a process of 'technological isomorphism' at work, in which organisations come to adopt similar practices because of their inscription into the technology they have bought. The penalties then for ignoring what the software presents can be severe. In 2004, the UK furniture retailer MFI hit the headlines when major problems were reported with its implementation of an ERP system. The system was designed to automate its supply chain, but the new system in practice meant that customer orders were not being fulfilled. The problems in MFI appeared to be ones of data quality, with the system depending on the disciplined entry of data at source (Mutch, 2008a). The material properties of the system were not the subject of agential interpretive flexibility but rather, once set constrained agential action, demanding that roles be carried out according to the precise specifications inscribed into the system.

At the level of the organisation, these broader influences become contextualised in dominant logics that shape what counts as information in organisations. Whilst drawing on broader resources, these logics are also the product of contending interpretations associated with groupings within the organisation, of which the strongest remain functional or occupational groups (Sackmann, 1991). Such groups use contending ideas about information to seek to consolidate their own position in organisations. In doing so, a particularly powerful way is if they can inscribe their values into the ICT-enabled systems that the organisation uses. Such inscription often occurs at the level of the rules, especially those to do with data definition, which form the basis of such systems (Bowker, 2000). Definitions that accord with what is perceived as the 'natural' form of such technologies are particularly powerful. The technology does not in this sense determine such information use, but it suggests particular logics, reinforced by broader images, which are difficult to resist. These factors then form the taken-for-granted conditions in which organisational members use information. Such conditions are particularly powerful when built into regularly used artefacts, such as reports and blueprints, which suggest ways of using information that seem 'obvious' and 'natural'. As such, their limitations are only revealed in conditions of breakdown, when the taken-for-granted aspects of practical knowledge are revealed.

Work in the information systems domain, therefore, suggests that material properties are important in carrying the logics that condition action. Such logics can be carried in objects, which can take on a particular form because of the demands of a particular logic and then transmit that logic. The case of poor boxes in a range of Christian settings can be used to illustrate this point. But, as we have seen, materiality does not just apply to physical objects. The arrangement of spaces can also be important in providing to-hand containers for action, which instantiate particular logics. The shifting nature of the spaces encapsulated by Christian church buildings (in which the poor box also features) shows how spaces instantiate logics.

Material Objects: The Poor Box in Historical Context

The market square in the Belgian city of Bruges is dominated by its medieval Belfort or belfry. On its second floor are two sets of wrought iron gates, behind which sit massive charter chests. Fabricated in about 1290, the gates feature ten locks. Eight of the keys were held by the deacons of the town's trade guilds. The remaining two were held by the mayor and the head of a district known as Sint-Janszestendeel. All had to be present for the documents that related to the privileges of the town to be consulted. In this case, the primary security was applied to the gates that protected the chest (although these also feature locks). By contrast, in the Discovery Museum in Newcastle upon Tyne in the UK is a large wooden cabinet known as the 'Town Hutch'. Made of oak and banded with iron for additional strength, one end is semi-circular and has a lid that lifts up. Round the edge of this substantial piece of furniture are nine locks, the keys to which were held by eight town councillors and the mayor. The strongbox, medieval in origin, held the documents and treasure of the town's governing body and sat in the Guildhall, the centre of local administration. The hutch and its contents were a prime target in times of political unrest. The different forms of these material objects, both designed to preserve the documents on which the towns' prosperity rested, suggest not only a particular state of technological development in the provision of objects designed to protect valuable resources but also their positioning in a broader social and political context. In both cases, a collective form of accountability is suggested, in which all have to be present, rather than the later delegation of tasks to specified officials. As the caption to the Bruges artefacts suggests, because of this, 'the doors were only rarely opened and such an occasion always involved a certain measure of pomp and circumstance'. An examination of the place of such chests in the context of different religious polities over time suggests the combination of both technological advances and broader logics in both shaping the nature of objects and the role of those objects in embodying specific logics.

In 1199 Pope Innocent III, in order to collect funds for a Christian crusade against the Muslims of the Holy Land, ordered that 'there should be placed in every church a hollow trunk, fastened with three keys, the latter to be kept severally by the bishop, the priest of the church, and some religious layman' (Roe, 1929: 108). The formulation suggests two things. One is the state of technological development, such that chests were rather crude in construction and designed to be used *in situ*. The other was the provision for three locks, something that was to persist even in the face of changing social organisation. Advances in craft skills meant that later chests have the possibility of being portable, raising the possibility of detaching them from their original spatial location. In addition, as technological capacity developed, there arose the possibility of acquiring chests with a sophisticated level of security from producers located in Germany. In the restored church of Laurenskerk in Rotterdam is an impressive display of several iron strong boxes. Such strong boxes were produced in large numbers in Germany and Austria and are often known as Nuremberg or Augsburg chests, from the towns most closely associated with their manufacture. In the words of Roe (1929: 37), discussing an example in the church at Watford,

> These coffers are invariably constructed on the same plan. The actual keyhole is in the lid, concealed by a small plate, which springs up when a knife is inserted beneath one of the reinforcing straps. The lock, a complicated piece of mechanism, is attached to the inner surface of the lid, and the bolts are multiple, sometimes amounting to as many as a dozen or sixteen in number. In the Watford example there are five bolts only. Often the mechanism of the lock is covered with a plate of pierced steel, engraved with devices. A false keyhole is placed somewhat ostentatiously on the front.

Their presence in large numbers in the Reformed Protestant churches of the Netherlands is testament to not only the wealth of local parishes and their trade connections to Germany but also of a shift in the contents of the chest.

In pre-Reformation Catholic churches, chests were used for the storage of the vestments and other objects needed for the celebration of specific rites. As Whiting (2010) notes for England, the move to Protestant forms of worship rendered many of these receptacles surplus to requirements. No longer needed, either, were the offertory boxes attached to the shrines of particular saints dedicated to their upkeep. In their place was an injunction to put in place boxes to receive alms for the poor. Each parish was to

> provide a strong chest with a hole in the upper part thereof, having three keys, which chest you shall set and fasten near the High Altar, to the intent that the parishioners should put into it their oblations and alms for the poor neighbours.
>
> (Roe, 1929: 33–34)

The three keys were continued, but now these were to be shared between the cleric and two churchwardens. A number of shifts were signalled by this subtle change in the material artefact. Behind it lays the ruthless expropriation of the monasteries and other bodies that had often provided relief facilities for the infirm and socially disadvantaged. The hopes of many pious reformers that the riches of the church would be directed towards better provision for health and education were dashed as the unscrupulous purloined them for personal gain. However, there was a further shift in that the logic of religion shifted from salvation through good works to salvation by grace. This shifted the focus from acts of personal charity to the emergence of a more structured approach to social problems in the Reformed polities of England, Scotland and the Netherlands. In 1549, notes Whiting (2010: 111), 'the new prayer book expected layfolk at communion services to offer alms "unto the poor men's box, each one according to his ability and charitable mind"'.

While both England and Scotland adopted forms of Reformed Protestantism as their national churches, there were, however significant differences, differences that were manifested in and embodied by the material object that was the poor box. It is significant that in many cases the medieval chests that English parishes possessed were repurposed to hold the alms given for the poor. Such chests were often not intended to be moved: 'There is no evidence that lifting-rings were ever attached to this coffer,' observes Roe (1929: 14) of a medieval chest in Aldenham, Hertfordshire, 'and the omission is significant. In old parlance, the piece was intended to remain in its abode "for ever"'. As we will see in considering the material arrangement of space, this had consequences where activities in connection with poor relief took place. However, responsibility for that poor relief gradually shifted to the local state.

Often the lines were blurred, but over time the churchwardens became responsible for raising money for the maintenance of the church fabric. They were selected on an annual basis so, not only were the sums that they dealt with relatively small, but their limited term of office meant that income was often raised when needed on an episodic basis. Such factors mean that the need for specialist repositories was reduced and the old artefacts could continue in service. By contrast, lay involvement in the Presbyterian Church of Scotland was far more thoroughgoing. A body of elders, the kirk session, supported the minister in his spiritual duties. They also, crucially, retained responsibility for poor relief and so needed to find ways of accounting for and safeguarding often substantial sums of money. The poor box was therefore a significant and important artefact, but the available evidence suggests that it diverged in significant ways from its equivalents in England.

A first observation is that there was often not one box, but two (Mutch, 2015). One functional split was between a little box as a repository for collections and a larger box as the home for the capital stock of the session. The money in the little box could be used to meet immediate demands, with that in the larger box only being dipped into at times of particular exigency. The larger box contained the documents and other valuables held by the church. That at Fraserburgh in 1742 had three compartments, 'one for holding the Communion Cups, linen and Basins, another for registers, bonds, bills or other papers of value, and the third with several drawers for holding the differently species of money' (McPherson, 1945: 30). What is significant here is that mention of bonds and bills. It reminds us that the session not only collected large sums of money, but, in the absence of a secure banking network, also lent out the money it possessed at interest. The documents it stored in its larger chest were vital evidence of what was owing to it. Bonds were secured on property; bills were evidence of more short-term lending (Mutch, 2017).

In general, these boxes had two keys, so a departure from practice south of the border. Keys were held, usually, by the treasurer and one of the other elders. This was often the session clerk, who was usually the parish schoolmaster but could be any member of the session. The box and its keys, therefore, were symbolic of the greater role of lay involvement in the governance of the church. At this point, we can contrast practice in the Church of Scotland to that recorded by Paulo Quattrone for the Jesuit order in Italy in the sixteenth and seventeenth century, where he notes

> the padlock for the College cash box ... required two keys, one to be kept by the Procurator, who was in charge of economic affairs, and one by the Rector, who was responsible for the College and its overall missionary, pedagogical, and economic activities.
>
> (Quattrone, 2004: 666)

While Quattrone's key actors were officials of the Society of Jesus, the key holders in the Church of Scotland represented both the inside and outside of the world in which the church sat. The inside was represented by the minister whose presence was essential for financial transactions to take place. Closely linked to him was the session clerk, who often shared a common educational background. This enabled the completion of the records that formed such an important part of the accountability system of the local church. But this also relied on the participation of the elders, especially the treasurer. Increasingly literate themselves as the century wore on, being drawn from the ranks of the 'middling sort' in the locality, these men were thus exposed to the operation of systems of accountability. So the outward appearance of the box, and the means of access to it, might be superficially similar, but the broader context in which it sat gave a different symbolic resonance to the possession of keys.

As we have noted, material objects do not have to be physical ones. The appearance of a spreadsheet on a computer screen may mimic the layout of accounting analysis sheets, but its appearance is governed by code that produces the appearance of a material object. Increasingly it is such artefacts that facilitate certain forms of action, such as the compilation of league tables that leach from the sporting domain to rank all sorts of aspects of social life. Just as the filing cabinets that Jo-Anne Yates (1989) examines led to shifts in the construction of internal company communications (single subject memoranda, for example) and so embedded a particular logic of organisation, so the organisational capabilities of ICT may be powerful organising devices that in turn shape the conduct of work. This is particularly the case when access to the properties embedded in software is tightly tied to particular roles in the organisation, such as when only those with a particular role profile can access nominated areas of an ERP (Hinings, Gegenhuber, and Greenwood, 2018). In this way, the association of practices with positions that Bhaskar outlined is made 'concrete'. The embedding of logics into material artefacts makes them more likely to be adopted. Once inscribed in software, such combinations are difficult to amend. However, Marion Fourcade (2011), in her study of the practices of assigning a value to nature suggests some limits to the thesis, associated with Donald Mackenzie, that economic theories, embedded in particular practices, are an engine rather than a camera. That is, theories, facilitated by, in this case, the power of computer models are performative. They do not simply mirror existing arrangements but bring them into being. Something similar can be said about the visual devices that the software consultancies studied by Pollock and Williams (2009) use to rank market offerings. Presented in the form of 'magic quadrants' in which the existing functionality offered by a product is mapped against the potential for future development, these devices shape the direction of those developments by encouraging developers to produce functions that will allow them to move into the most desirable part of the quadrant. While these are persuasive arguments, Fourcade (2011) sounds an important note of caution. She studied practices of valuing nature following oil spills in the USA and France. Noting that awards for compensation were far greater in the US than France, she suggests that material practices have to be considered in the context of the wider institutional logics in which they are embedded.

In the USA, not only was the idea of 'wilderness' one with powerful symbolic resonance, but it was one mirrored in the possession by the state of significant tracts of land. By contrast, in France the history of a densely populated agricultural society based on peasant holdings meant that the notion of ascribing a value to nature was not widely shared. As she notes

> a cultural understanding of nature as a *lieu de vie*, a lived-in practical reality where man occupies *de facto* a central place, dominates the political projects of French ecologists—in sharp contrast with the more radical approaches to conservation found in the United States, where untouched nature is afforded a special moral ground.
> (Fourcade, 2011: 1739)

In addition, although she does not explore the place of experts in civil law systems, she observes that it is 'a well-established pattern in common law systems, [that] the culture of "discovery" and expert evidence generally favors the incorporation of all forms of outside knowledge in a competitive effort to present "facts" under a particular light' (Fourcade, 2011: 1734). A combination of factors thus led to a much higher value being placed on abstract nature in the USA than in France. The specific method in the USA was to attribute a value to nature on the grounds of the subjective value to individuals in the population as a whole (determined by survey methods). By contrast, the French method was to assess the actual damage caused to localities and their residents, thus producing much lower claims for compensation. The consequence was that the large, punitive, damages awarded in the USA were devoted to conservation efforts, whereas the much smaller sums in France were largely spent on specific local infrastructure. That the focus on specific damages in French civil law was not an isolated instance limited to environmental damage but reflected a more general practice can be seen in the law relating to compensation for medical accidents. The scales adopted, which refer to specific harms, 'cannot adequately reflect', argues Genevieve Helleringer (2011: 1136), 'the richness of human life from a spiritual, intellectual, sensorial, emotional, or professional perspective'. 'Though it is merely indicatory', she continues, 'it is part of French legal culture'. The conclusion Fourcade (2011: 1724) draws is that

> the mere availability of certain economic technologies does not guarantee their performative effects for the simple reasons that these technologies may not muster enough institutional and political support or that they may not resonate enough with the cultural claims they are supposed to represent.

Material objects, that is, as with the poor box, have to be seen in historical and comparative context. Something similar can be claimed for the organisation of space.

Space and Logics: Churches and Liturgies

The royal injunction about the provision of collection boxes for the poor in the parish churches of the Church of England carried with it implications for the spatial organisation of those churches. The provision for the box to be fastened in place near the High Altar located it at the east end of the church. The fact that it was to take dues following the administration of the sacrament of communion also meant that this key ritual was to take place near the altar (Addleshaw and Etchells, 1948: 25). Embedded in the positioning of the poor box were assumptions that had serious consequences for the spatial organisation of churches, consequences that reflected the different logics embedded in Catholic and Protestant liturgies. What happened was a change in use of space, from one where space was divided by role, as in the clergy/lay split, to one marked by liturgical function, where the nave was used for those elements of the liturgy that privileged the reading and hearing of the word, the chancel being reserved for communion. Such a functional division was not just an Anglican preserve but was also characteristic of Lutheranism (Addleshaw and Etchells, 1948: 45). As such the division marked something of an uncomfortable compromise between the spaces that had been handed down in built form and the new logic of a Protestant liturgy. In many cases that discomfort was a real bodily experience, as chancels were inadequate to accommodate the numbers of people wishing to take communion.

Quite often, the downgrading of the sacred nature of the chancel meant that it had, in the eighteenth century, been given over to secular activities, such as hosting the school. The vicar of Wymeswold, Leicestershire, who masterminded the nineteenth century restoration of the parish church recalled in horror that the 'chancel was devoted to the girls' Sunday school: the space within the rails to parish meetings. In that area, connected in every Christian's mind with the most holy rite of his religion, sounded the obscene brawls and blasphemous oaths of the village farmers: and at those rails was the weekly mockery called paying the poor enacted' (Alford, 1846: 8). As we noted above, many chests were never designed to be moved and so it made sense to take the meetings that decided on the disposition of its contents to its location. The organisation of space carried with it not only religious but broader logics, particularly with the allocation of space by occupation. In many churches, specific areas, demarcated by elaborate screens, often bearing heraldic emblems, marked off the private pews of the wealthy and powerful. In the main body of the church, pews were often allocated by family, with the more prosperous inhabitants having pride of place. In the church of Fulbeck, Lincolnshire, the north aisle was reserved for the servants of the dominant landholders, the Fanes. Not only were these servants surrounded by memorials to the ancestors of their employers, but they were faced by the exhortation, drawn from the Book of Proverbs, 'My son, fear thou the LORD and the king and meddle not with them that are given to change', a warning that could clearly be generalised to conditions in the village. Meanwhile, the south aisle was reserved for the village poor, so that the practice of religion performed the secular divisions of everyday life. Of course, spaces such as churches, just like sports stadiums or law courts laid out the logic that they rendered in spatial form in a fairly direct fashion.

In his account of the rise of the research university, Clark pays a good deal of attention to the presence of material objects and their disposition. He notes the connection between the chair from which the medieval professor read his text and the cathedra or seat that the bishop occupied when present at services in his cathedral (Clark, 2006: 72). From this physical object is derived the metonymic term for those assuming the role of professor, their chair. But this is not just a symbolic survival. The focus that Clark places on the importance of the position from which the lecturer addresses students is also to be found in the work of Bourdieu and Jean-Claude Passeron on higher education in France in the 1960s. For them 'physically elevated and enclosed within the magisterial chair which consecrates him, he [the professor] is separated from his audience by a few empty rows' (Bourdieu and Passeron, 1994: 11). The organisation of physical space reproduces a hierarchical logic, one which Bourdieu and Passeron see as ultimately dedicated to the reproduction and preservation of a professorial elite. The logic at operation is, they argue, one that is internal to the pedagogical process, one which has emerged from ultimately religious models and has secularised the authority of the priest in the form of the teacher (Bourdieu and Passeron, 1977: 64). While in other forms of the educational logic, such spatial relations have been abandoned, it remains the case that elevated positions for teachers and fixed rows for students continue to characterise many teaching spaces in continental Europe, contributing to the continuing reproduction of a hierarchical and didactic educational logic.

Other spatial consequences of logics could be rather less evident, but nonetheless provided a taken-for-granted context in which practices were carried out. Biernacki (1995), for example, points out the ways in which the different layout of British and German woollen textile mills could be traced back to different conceptions of the value of labour. Yorkshire mills looked like small fortresses, enclosing a world of master and servant with tight access controls but relatively free movement of labour within the mill walls. By contrast, what Biernacki terms the 'cellular' layout of German mills meant tight constraints on worker movement within the factory. To give another example, the distinctively Scottish form of housing known as the tenement flat, that is, tall buildings containing individual apartments grouped round a common stair, is a material consequence of the development of Scottish land law, with its long retention of feudal elements (Craig, 2011). Although subsequent reforms have removed these features, the material evidence remains in the shape of a built environment that has become 'natural' and taken-for-granted. It only ceases to be 'natural' when contrasted, for example, with the terraced houses that constitute distinctive working-class housing in England (Hoskins, 1963; McCrone, 2017). Thus, the disposition of material objects in particular spaces embodies a logic that is more powerful in its operation by fading into the background.

Identity

At the 77th minute of a football match in 2016 between Liverpool and Sunderland at Liverpool's Anfield Stadium, something never seen in the grounds 132-year history occurred: up to 10,000 of the crowd of some 44,000 got up and walked out of the stadium (Press Association, 2016). They chose the moment as a symbolic protest against the decision by the club's owners to raise ticket prices for some seats from £59 to £77 a match. The protest was prefigured by banners in the crowd proclaiming 'supporters not customers'. These sprang out of a declaration on the website of the club's owners, Fenway Sports Group (FSG), that they sought to turn 'fans into customers'. Here was a clash between identities supplied by two competing logics, a sporting logic derived, ultimately, from the logic of play and an economic logic. The example also indicates a clash between logics derived from different parts of the world; in this case a collision between North American ownership of sports 'franchises' and British notions of sports 'clubs' in which notions of support are tightly interwoven with the historical conditions of development (Markovits and Hellerman, 2001). As Biernacki (1995) points out, although positions (in his case, those of the overlooker) can occupy similar places in organisational structures, they can be infused with deeper meaning because of their mobilisation of wider logics. In his case, differences in the valuation of labour emphasised the technical functions of British overlookers and the supervisory functions of their German counterparts, despite both carrying out broadly similar functional roles. A consideration of the logic of play as manifest in both sports and popular music can help our understanding of how logics shape and manifest in particular identities, bringing out powerfully the roles of belief and desire in adherence to particular logics.

Huizinga, writing in the 1940s, would be sceptical about any connection between play and what he would see as mere entertainment. The codification of the informal rules of play and the growth of formal organisations seen in many sports meant that they were now too serious to be regarded as play. 'This view will probably run counter', he recognised, 'to the popular feeling of to-day, according to which sport is the apotheosis of the play-element in our civilization. Nevertheless, popular feeling is wrong' (Huizinga, 1949: 198). This comment, together with others such as it 'would seem as if the mentality and conduct of the adolescent now reigned supreme over large areas of civilized life which had formerly been the province of responsible adults' give an indication of the rather Olympian judgments from on high that dismiss consideration of popular culture in the work of some social theorists (Huizinga, 1948: 205). Arendt, Walsh (2015: 133) notes, for example, as observing 'mass culture which, strictly speaking, does not exist, but mass entertainment, feeding on the cultural objects of the world'. There is an echo here of the dismissive approach taken to popular music by Theodore Adorno or other members of the Frankfurt School. A similar note might be found in Sennett's mention of the insights to be gained by 'serious, real, genuine art' in a book that, as we have noted, uses Huizinga's work to suggest the importance of play in establishing the conventions that regulate social life (Sennett, 2002: 38). However, as Ken McLeod argues, '[g]iven the near universal exposure to both sports and popular music, it would seem that all our identities are, at least in some small way, influenced by the confluence of these cultural forms' (2016: 227). A focus on practices as explored in work on both popular music and sports can indicate that taking play seriously as a logic has important consequences for identities.

'Some people', the legendary manager of Liverpool Football Club Bill Shankly is alleged to have said, 'believe football is a matter of life and death, I am very disappointed with that attitude. I can assure you it is much, much more important than that' (cited in McCrone, 2017: 525). A supporters' group at the club that is named 'Spirit of Shankly' draws on this sense of passionate identification with the football club that they support. There is a strong steak of romantic nostalgia in such attachments, which can be problematic in some ways, but which suggests the strongly enduring nature of such attachments in the face of globalising trends. In order to explore such attachments further, we need to distinguish between the divergent logics of participation and spectatorship. Markovits and Hellerman (2001) cast this as a distinction between activity and culture, noting that the widespread participation in soccer in the United States does not necessarily translate into what they term a 'hegemonic sports culture'. The latter is manifest in media coverage and the everyday talk of followers that, they argue, remains dominated by the 'Big Three' sports of baseball, American football and basketball. Soccer here can at best achieve marginal status, crowded out by existing loyalties, whereas the situation in the rest of the world is that it is football that dominates the sports space. While their discussion and that which follows here concentrates on the followers, it is worth briefly considering the logic at work in participation in sports in particular because it raises important questions about a further distinction, that between professionalism and amateurism.

The professions are a key logic in the account provided by Thornton, Occasio and Lounsbury (2012), drawing on the extensive work in the organisational literature. But an examination of the literature on sports raises some complexities about the notion of professionalism that might cast some doubt on erecting it as a central institutional logic of society (as opposed to an important logic of organisation). For in the sports arena, it does not connote a specialised area of knowledge with restrictive entry qualifications and self-regulation, but rather of a distinction between those who carry out an activity for reward, as opposed to those who engage in the activity for pleasure. Lincoln Allison's (2001) partisan account suggests some of the complexities that have been found in defining the boundary between professionalism and amateurism. He sees the latter to have been at the heart of the origin of organised sports. Here it was coupled with a distinctive notion of voluntary service in English civil society, coupled with the notion of the 'gentleman' (masculinity, as he argues, also being at the core of the emergence of modern sports). It was only in the United States that the full force of commercialisation was let loose on sports provision. As Markovits and Hellerman (2001: 62–63) note, early baseball teams were

> run by and for the players with oversight and financial subsidies by trustees whose involvement usually derived from "sporting" and or civic interest. However, Chicago's William Hulbert engendered the idea of exploiting baseball's institutional team charisma for the profit of businessmen through the revolutionary concept of harnessing the joint stock company as an essential instrument in the commodification of a sport.

In other sports and other parts of the world, the organisation of sports by voluntary clubs with a degree of attachment to values engendered by the amateur ethos, something exemplified by our opening story of the violation of the spirit of the game by Carew Cricket Club, persisted. For Allison it was commercialism, the power of the market, that was a greater threat to the values of amateurism than professionalism. After all, he points to the importance of the voluntary sector in providing services that elsewhere were provided by the state. In the UK, lifesaving services at sea are provided by the Royal National Lifeboat Institution, a voluntary organisation supported by charitable donations. While the men and women who crew lifeboats are overwhelmingly 'amateur' in the sense of having other jobs and giving of their time voluntarily, their training and expertise are in no doubt 'professional' in quality. A similar distinction might be found in popular music, where the focus for those who carry out the activity as a paid experience is likely to be on expertise in performance, whereas in amateur activities participation is more for the satisfaction engendered by involvement. However, in both cases it is arguable that the major impact in society is to be found in those who follow.

There is no doubt that in some cases the gap between sport as played at elite level and that played by amateurs has, under the pressures of commercialism, rendered the former as closer to entertainment, as in the case of, especially, American football. Voices internal to the ranks of sports followers also recognise and critique such tendencies. In English football, sharply rising ticket prices and the spread of all-seater stadia have led to significant changes in how participants perceive games. In the words of one supporter, 'the difference between seats and terraces is the difference between a form of entertainment and a form of culture... We've lost the culture' (cited in Tempany, 2016: 171). Often such claims are articulated through the lens of community. 'Everywhere', argue Markowits and Hellerman (2001: 31),

> the gradual weakening of working-class culture and the concomitant lessening of traditional communities centered around the old ball park, the home pitch, the team pub, or the neighborhood bar is associated with a loss of authenticity and a commercialization that any true fan of the respective sport decries.

However, as well as such concerns articulating a very bounded concept of 'community', they are also most applicable to the very elite and heavily commercialised levels of sports. At the more grassroots level the traditional attachments remain, as revealed by an intriguing examination of the crossover between popular music and sports in the practice of singing at British football matches. Here, crowds adapt current songs to comment on players and teams in a process that Colin Irwin (2006: 13), drawing on the folk singer Martin Carthy, investigates as representing

> the one true surviving embodiment of an organic living folk tradition; i.e. a network of songs which evolved out of existing songs, sung by the people, adapted to meet the specific needs of geographical identity and seemingly created by spontaneous combustion, the unheralded originators remaining anonymous.

For Irwin,

> ask anyone – anyone – what it was about going to their first match that got them hooked, and they will tell you the atmosphere. And by atmosphere they mean the fans. And by the fans they mean the singing. There is an extraordinary tribal spirit that binds fans together as one solid, fiercely united representation of a community and creates an almost irresistible intensity.
>
> (Irwin, 2006: 13)

From his visits to many football clubs, he concluded that 'that the true quality football lies in the Premiership; the quality but not necessarily the fun, and definitely not the heart or soul' (Irwin, 2006: 275). Once again, the essence is that of fun, fun that is often obscured by the demands of commercialism, which animates, together with the demands of community, a form of passionate attachment to a team that in turn shapes the nature of the identity conferred by support.

It is interesting to contrast this form of commitment to that expressed by followers of popular music, although studies of fandom tend not to do this. In part this is because of the very nature of sports followership, which seen as more tribal in nature (Duffett, 2013: 3). The notion of community articulated in sports is often heavily male in character and restricted to members of particular ethnic groups. The rapid growth in participation in football/soccer by women is often not reflected in either the composition of crowds for elite games or in the hegemonic sports cultures. In addition, popular music has often given new possibilities for identities and attachments to men who were turned off by aspects of the masculinity performed by elite sports. 'The rise of rock 'n' roll', McLeod (2016: 32) has argued,

> saw the advent of a glamorous career choice that, particularly for young men, promised a life of pleasure, adulation, power, and satisfaction previously bestowed only on star athletes. The arrival of the Beatles in America and their effeminizing hair length and attention to fashion began to challenge a notion of physical integrity that had previously underpinned both sports and music.

While these distinctions are important, there are parallels in the distinctions that observers have drawn between forms of attachment to both domains. For Duffett (2013: 31), 'fans are more than consumers because they have especially strong emotional attachments to their objects and they use them to create relationships with both their heroes and with each other'. He stresses the non-commercial nature of fan culture, a point that is made strongly in a rare and exemplary ethnographic study of the fans of one particular icon of popular music, Bruce Springsteen. Daniel Cavicchi (1998: 8) argues that rather than thinking about music fandom as pathology or as resistance, to me it might be more interesting to think about music fandom as the creation of much needed meaning in the daily lives of otherwise ordinary people, a way in which members of this modern media-driven society make sense of their selves and their relations to others.

From this, he suggests that a focus on the work that fans put into their attachment and what this does for them is revealing. So, for example, he notes different levels of participation in concerts by fans and other audience members. Fans have distinctive practices that they enact at key junctures of performance that make them active rather than passive participants in these events. Fans, he says

> define their difference from ordinary audience members in terms of different kinds of musical participation. Everyone may attend the same concert, but fans and nonfan audience members come to that concert with different expectations, have different experiences, and leave with different feelings. Ordinary audience members are people who assume a temporary role before a stage to take a break from the hustle and bustle of their everyday lives and be entertained. Fans, however, are people whose role before a stage never ends; a concert is not a break from, but a continuing reaffirmation of, their everyday lives. In fact, being a fan is a lot like being a musician in that both live a lifestyle based on musical activity. Just as musicians are practicing, composing, and traveling between concerts or recording sessions, fans are collecting, writing fanzines, and making pilgrimages between concerts or listening to CDs. And as a professional musician might interpret a performance a bit differently than an infrequent performer – seeing it as only one part of a job rather than a uniquely exhilarating event, for instance – fans interpret a performance differently than ordinary audience members, seeing it as a ritual rather than as entertainment.
>
> (Cavicchi, 1998: 95)

(It might be noted that these are distinctively *American* practices of audience participation. Ian Anderson of the British rock band Jethro Tull, who achieved considerable success in the USA, complains that, when touring the country

> the audience will have a meaningful proportion of people who are rock fans, and maybe only know us for a couple of songs that fit the genre that they like. They can be quite noisy, and maybe enthusiastic, but very noisy, and if you're trying to play some gentle acoustic moment, that occurs in many of Jethro Tull's rock songs, moments

of big contrast and dynamic change, where it's just a voice and an
electric guitar, then there is a tendency for those people whose lives
are steeped in meat and potatoes, they don't have the patience or the
tolerance for those changes in mood.

(eFestivals, 2011))

Once again, the importance of ritual in sustaining logics that are derived
from ultimate values is stressed. The consequence for the group of fans
that Cavicchi studies is not so much resistance to commercial pressures,
but a turning of their back on them. Springsteen fans, argues Cavicchi
(1998: 63),

constantly work to devalue the role of the music business in their
fandom: first, by creating a specific, shared understanding of Springsteen as a "common man," who has a life apart from the one promoted by industry marketing; second, by developing a number of
complex tape-trading and ticket searching methods which decrease
the significance of record company products and services. Both activities help make the music business more of an absence than a
presence in daily life.

The logic of play, as mediated through a particular form of performance,
provides an alternative, enduring and powerful value system embodied
and enacted through distinctive practices.

However, participation in popular music can go beyond attending concerts. At concerts, however, there might be active audience participation,
but it is still secondary to the primary performance on the stage. Participation, though, can be far more than this, as can be seen in the example
of the Northern soul movement in the United Kingdom. 'Northern soul',
according to aficionado and commentator Stuart Cosgrove (2016: 7),
'is a scene founded on obscure music from the African-American society and works according to codes of behaviour that baffle outsiders'.
Emergent in the United Kingdom in the 1960s but at its most vigorous
in the 1970s, this was a music scene that was heavily working class in
character. It featured all-night dancing sessions, notably at the legendary
Wigan Casino from 1973 to 1981. The codes of behaviour that Cosgrove
refers to included styles of dress and dancing. The latter was vigorous
and physical, featuring acrobatic moves and so favouring music with a
distinctive rhythm. The lyrics of the songs danced to were not of great
import (indeed, Cosgrove only mentions their content towards the end of
a 266-page account); what did matter was the obscurity of the records.
As Cosgrove (2016: 40) notes 'obscure black American labels from the
sixties became the holy grail, and original copies as opposed to reis-
sues, or the vilified bootleg copies, came to define the scene'. In addition,
other practices were an important part of the bundle that manifested the

commitment. 'Lists', claims Cosgrove (2016: 48), 'are an essential part of the culture of northern soul: play lists, wants lists and discographies of the rare labels that populate and give shape to the scene'. As one reviewer of Cosgrove's book observed 'it's hard to talk about musical obsession without laying your hands a little on the concepts of religion. There were catechisms, initiation rituals and publications that served the same purpose as the Gospels' (McKillop, 2016: 28). Here is an example of how adherence to one genre of popular music could develop distinct practices of involvement that were thoroughly creative and participatory, even if from the outside they might appear to be simply practices of consumption.

The fans Cavicchi studied distinguished between different categories of commitment to the cause they espoused, something that makes fandom difficult to study. In distinguishing between followers, supporters and fans, McLeod (2016) is articulating these distinctions that are also found in the expressions of fans themselves. Here followers are those who have a passing interest in, say, a particular sports team, watching out for its results but not engaging routinely in activities. The supporters who rejected the role of customer in the case of Liverpool Football Club were regular attenders at matches who would view their active participation as distinguished from those who attended to view a match as entertainment. The fan, then, is somebody who takes their support to higher levels, bordering in some cases on obsession. The title of one collection of responses to popular music, *Starlust*, suggests the heights of erotic desire to which fandom can propel adherents (Vermorel and Vermorel, 1985). This depth of adherence has led some analysts to trace the parallels between religious commitment and such levels of support for sports and popular music stars. Anja Lobert (2012), for example, uses the concept of ritual to examine the practices that fans engage in which develop and sustain intense commitment. This is not to argue that fandom is a form of religious commitment, rather that it is important to examine rituals, especially those experienced collectively, as a key means of articulating commitment. As the British political activist David Widgery recalled of his work with Rock against Racism in the 1970s, his 'experiences had taught us a golden political rule: how people find their pleasure, entertainment and celebration is also how they find their sexual identity, their political courage and their strength to change' (cited in Rachel, 2016: 233).

Summary

Material objects are a powerful means of articulating logics, especially when they become to-hand and taken-for-granted. The configuration of objects into spaces that organise the performance of logics provides a stage for the playing out of identities that gain their force from the substance that animates attachment to the logic. However, such logics also play out both in relation to other logics and through the lens provided by other forms of collective organisation and identity. These limits on the operation of logics are the starting point for the following, and concluding, chapter.

References

Addleshaw, G. and Etchells, F. (1948) *The Architectural Setting of Anglican Worship,* London: Faber and Faber.

Alford, H. (1846) *A History and Description of the Restored Parish Church of Saint Mary, Wymeswold, Leicestershire,* London: J. Burns.

Allison, L. (2001) *Amateurism in Sport: An Analysis and a Defence,* Abingdon: Routledge.

Barad, K. (2003) 'Posthumanist performativity: toward an understanding of how matter comes to matter', *Signs,* 28(3), 801–831.

BBC. (2017) 'Carew Cricket Club relegated after 'unfair' win over title rivals', BBC, http://www.bbc.co.uk/news/uk-wales-south-west-wales-41404646 [9 October 2017].

Benders, J., Batenburg, R. and Van der Blonk, H. (2006) 'Sticking to standards; technical and other isomorphic pressures in deploying ERP-systems', *Information and Management,* 43(2), 194–203.

Biernacki, R. (1995) *The Fabrication of Labor: Germany and Britain, 1640–1914,* Berkeley, CA: University of California Press.

Bourdieu, P. and Passeron, J. (1977) *Reproduction in Education, Society and Culture,* London: Sage.

Bourdieu, P. and Passeron, J. (1994) 'Language and relationship to language in the teaching situation', in Bourdieu, P., Passeron, J-C. and de Saint Martin, M. (eds.), *Academic Discourse,* Cambridge: Polity, 1994, 1–34.

Bowker, G. (2000) 'Biodiversity, datadiversity', *Social Studies of Science,* 30(5), 643–683.

Cavicchi, D. (1998) *Tramps Like Us: Music and Meaning Among Springsteen Fans,* New York: Oxford University Press.

Clark, J., McLoughlin, I., Rose, H. and King, R. (1988) *The Process of Technological Change: New Technology and Social Choice in the Workplace,* Cambridge: Cambridge University Press.

Clark, W. (2006) *Academic Charisma and the Origins of the Research University,* Chicago: University of Chicago Press.

Cosgrave, S. (2016) *Young Soul Rebels: A Personal History of Northern Soul,* Edinburgh: Birlinn.

Craig, C. (2011) *The Scots' Crisis of Confidence,* Glendurael: Argyll Publishing.

D'Adderio, L. (2004) *Inside the Virtual Product: How Organizations Create Knowledge Through Software,* Cheltenham: Edward Elgar.

Duffett, M. (2013) *Understanding Fandom: An Introduction to the Study of Media Fan Culture,* London: Bloomsbury.

Edwards, D., Ashmore, M. and Potter, J. (1995) 'Death and Furniture: the rhetoric, politics and theology of bottom line arguments against relativism', *History of the Human Sciences,* 8(2), 25–49.

eFestivals (2011) 'Ian Anderson interview: Wychwood's headliner speaks exclusively to eFestivals', http://www.efestivals.co.uk/festivals/wychwood/2011/interview-iananderson.shtml [9 October 2017].

Fourcade, M. (2011) 'Cents and sensibility: conomic valuation and the nature of "nature"', *American Journal of Sociology*, 116(6), 1721–77.

Grint, K. and Woolgar, S. (1997) *The Machine at Work: Technology, Work and Organization*, Cambridge: Polity.

Helleringer, G. (2011) 'Medical malpractice and compensation in France: part II: compensation based on national solidarity', *Chicago Law Review*, 86, 1125–1138.

Hinings, B., Gegenhuber, T. and Greenwood, R. (2018) 'Digital innovation and transformation: An institutional perspective', *Information and Organization*, 28(1), 52–61.

Hoskins, W. (1963) *The Making of the English Landscape*, Harmonsworth: Penguin.

Huizinga, J. (1949) *Homo Ludens: A Study of the Play-Element in Culture*, London: Routledge & Kegan Paul.

Hutchby, I. (2001) *Conversation and Technology : From the Telephone to the Internet*, Cambridge: Polity.

Irwin, C. (2006) *Sing when you're Winning: Football Fans, Terrace Songs and a Search for the Soul of Soccer*, London: Andre Deutsch.

Lobert, A. (2012) 'Fandom as a religious form: On the reception of pop music by Cliff Richard fans in Liverpool', *Popular Music*, 31(1), 125–141.

Markowits, A. and Hellerman, S. (2001) *Offside: Soccer and American Exceptionalism*, Princeton, NJ: Princeton University Press.

McCrone, D. (2017) *The New Sociology of Scotland*, London: Sage.

McKillop, A. (2016), 'Dancing to the Devil's Music', *Scottish Review of Books*, 11(4), 28–29.

McLeod, K. (2016) *We are the Champions: The Politics of Sports and Popular Music*, London: Routledge.

McPherson, J. (1945) *The Kirk's Care of the Poor, with Special Reference to the North-East of Scotland*, Aberdeen: John Avery.

Mutch, A. (2008a) *Managing Information and Knowledge in Organizations*, New York: Routledge.

Mutch, A. (2008b) 'Gaddesby: a Decorated church in its social and cultural context', *Transactions of the Leicestershire Archaeological and Historical Society*, 82, 171–188.

Mutch, A. (2015) 'In search of the poor box in the eighteenth-century Church of Scotland', *Review of Scottish Culture*, 27, 62–75.

Mutch, A. (2017) 'The business of religion: lending and the Church of Scotland in the eighteenth century', *Journal of Scottish Historical Studies*, 37(2), 136–154.

Orlikowski, W. (1992) 'The duality of technology: rethinking the concept of technology in organizations', *Organization Science*, 3(3), 398–427.

Orlikowski, W. (2000) 'Using technology and constituting structures: a practice lens for studying technology in organizations', *Organization Science*, 11(4), 404–428.

Orlikowski, W. (2007) 'Sociomaterial practices: exploring technology at work', *Organization Studies*, 28(9), 1435–1448.

Pollock, N. and Williams, R. (2009) *Software and Organisations: The Biography of the Enterprise-Wide System or How SAP Conquered the World*, London: Routledge.

Press Association. (2016) 'Liverpool fans' walkout protest: around 10,000 leave in 77th minute over ticket prices', *The Gurdian* 6 February, https://www.theguardian.com/football/2016/feb/06/liverpool-fans-walkout-thousands-ticket-price-protest [9 October 2017].

Quattrone, P. (2004) 'Accounting for God: accounting and accountability practices in the Society of Jesus (Italy, XVI–XVII centuries)', *Accounting, Organizations and Society*, 29, 647–683.

Rachel, D. (2016) *Walls Come Tumbling Down: The Music and Politics of Rock Against Racism, 2 Tone and Red Wedge*, London: Picador.

Roe, F. (1929) *Ancient Church Chests and Chairs in the Home Counties Round Greater London, Being the Tour of an Antiquary with Pencil and Camera Through the Churches of Middlesex, Hertfordshire, Essex, Kent and Surrey*, London: B. T. Basford.

Sackmann, S. (1991) *Cultural Knowledge in Organizations: Exploring the Collective Mind*, Newbury Park, CA: Sage.

Sennett, R. (2002) *The Fall of Public Man*, London: Penguin.

Tempany, A. (2016) *And the Sun Shines Now: How Hillsborough and the Premier League Changed Britain*, London: Faber & Faber.

Thornton, P., Occasio, W. and Lounsbury, M. (2012) *The Institutional Logics Perspective: A New Approach to Culture, Structure, and Process*, Oxford: Oxford University Press.

Vermorel, F. and Vermorel, J. (1985) *Starlust: The Secret Fantasies of Fans*, London: W. H. Allen.

Walsh, P. (2015) *Arendt Contra Sociology: Theory, Society and its Science*, London: Ashgate.

Whiting, R. (2010) *The Reformation of the English Parish Church*, Cambridge: Cambridge University Press.

Yates, J. (1989) *Control Through Communication: The Rise of System in American Management*, Baltimore: Johns Hopkins University Press.

8   The Limits of Logics

Introduction

Institutional logics provide a powerful analytical tool for examining the relationship between organisations in society. Conceptualising that society as a set of institutional orders, each emergent from an aspect of the embodied relationship of human beings with each other and the natural world provides a way of accounting for the range of forces shaping organisations and their zones of manoeuvre. Conceiving of institutional orders that are put in motion by internal logics motivated by belief in a core substance that is immanent in practices avoids the reduction of all activity to just one dimension of human existence. It explains the persistence of approaches to the world that, on some accounts, ought not to continue to exist. However, institutional logics are to be seen in conjunction with the other analytical tools that have been honed over the years to characterise social action, notably those of gender, class and ethnicity. Clearly, these concepts are themselves the subject of extensive literature; this chapter confines its attention to the interaction with logics.

Two preliminary reminders of Archer's work are in order before we move on to the detailed discussion. One is that, in her work on the relationship between *Culture and Agency* (Archer, 1996), she explores three sets of relationships – structure, agency and culture – that, she argues, contain the framing conditions for social activity and the take up of ideas. At the level of what she terms the cultural system, items can exist in relations of contradiction or complementarity. Where contradictions exist between items in the cultural system they might, as it were, slumber unnoticed unless there is a social group that seizes upon them and uses them for pursuing their own purpose. Likewise, social groups can also exist in relations of conflict or harmonious coexistence until developments push a social group to the fore that seeks to challenge existing arrangements. One such social group were merchants in the sixteenth century whose growing wealth and status entered into relationship with religious ideas. However, such tensions might exist without disturbing the cultural system. What is a particularly powerful motor of change, she argues, is when contradictions at the cultural level are seized upon in the course of conflict in the social system. Thus, she argues, the potential for change always exists, even if it is not realised. Even in cases of high levels of structural and cultural integration, potential fault lines existed that could be suppressed but not eliminated over the longer run of history. So, for example, she recognises that 'the entire matrix of ancient Indian institutions was internally related, and interconnecting lines could be drawn between caste/religion/kinship/economy/polity/law and education' (Archer, 1995: 219). Such a network of interconnections formed, she argued, a particular situational logic that, while it endured, provide sufficient benefits to each party to ensure its persistence. However, such constellations, she argues, are rare and limited to particular conjunctures of time and place. More usual is the potential for contradictions, either within an institutional order or, more likely, between them, to be seized upon by social groups.

A second reminder is the characterisation by Archer of agency as a collective capacity offered by cultural and structural positions. She presents a threefold model of people, distinguishing between persons, agents and actors. Persons, as we have seen in Smith's (2010: 61) work, are for critical realists 'a conscious, reflexive, embodied, self-transcending center of subjective experience, durable identity, moral commitment, and social communication'. Such persons are formed by not only the social contexts in which they find themselves involuntarily placed, but also by experiences during their long ontogenetic development with the natural world. Their capacities to engage in the social world are partly shaped by non-social forces but are crucially affected by their social location. So, argues Archer (1995:257), agents are '*collectivities* sharing the same *life chances*'. Drawing on the capacities and potentials developed by such social locations, actors enter into social relations, relations that are conditioned by the range of social categories – position-practices, organisations, fields – that we have examined. So, for Archer,

> The *conditional* influence of society works through the objective life chances which are dealt to us at birth. For the collectivities into which we are involuntaristically grouped affect the 'social actors' whom we are constrained or enabled to become voluntaristically. Yet someone has to do the becoming (which is neither fully random nor fully regular) and thus it was essential not to conflate 'human beings' and their capacities with social beings. Equally, it has to be allowed that it is the latter who, in combination, transform what it is socially possible for humans to become over time by their constantly elaborating on society's role array.
>
> (Archer, 1995: 293)

Gendering Logics

Archer says relatively little about gender in her work. In *Making Our Way Through the World*, she notes, although only in passing, the non-gendered nature of her respondents' attachment to family as an ultimate concern. She does note that the majority of autonomous reflexives in her qualitative sample were all male, but this is not pursued (Archer, 2007: 147, 193). In part this is because she is dealing with matters at a high level of abstraction. But it is also because her conception of persons and, especially, of their reflexive capacities, is built on an understanding of their emergence from biological phenomena that, for the capacities she is examining, are not differentiated by sex. The same holds true for Smith's (2010) extensive discussion of the features that constitute a person, in which the long list of distinctive traits relate to capacities for conscious action that are not biologically determined. Although neither writer draws upon it, one would suspect that they would concur with the defence of the sex/gender distinction that Caroline New (2005) makes. Such a distinction turns on the fact that typically persons can be assigned to a sex based on their possession of certain biological properties. As Cordelia Fine (2017: 85) notes,

> [a]bout 98–99 per cent of the population either have XY chromosomes and male genitals (testes, a prostate, seminal vesicles, and a penis) or they have XX chromosomes and female genitals (ovaries, fallopian tubes, a vagina, labia, and a clitoris).

However, while such biological differences give profoundly different reproductive roles, there is no reason, she argues, that this should give rise to behavioural roles. As Smith noted, while the conditions of human reproduction and development impose certain constraints that lead to versions of family life, there is a wide variation in time and space in the nature of those arrangements. Moreover, biological differences in reproductive capacity do not, Fine argues, based on the balance of scientific evidence, translate into differences elsewhere, notably in brain structure and activity. Such differences owe much more to what she terms the 'developmental system', a system consisting variously and non-exclusively of 'parents, peers, teachers, clothing, language, media, role models, organizations, schools, institutions, social inequalities' (Fine, 2017: 180).

That such a developmental system is profoundly gendered can be observed in the history of the institutional orders we have examined. While there have been historic barriers to the involvement in all these institutional orders to a greater or lesser degree, some of the orders have been seen as fundamentally gendered in their very nature. Such was clearly the view of Ferguson (1767) in his promotion of what he saw as the quintessentially masculine virtues of honour and courage as articulated in the military. These virtues were challenged by the rise of commercial society and the luxury that it brought in its train, luxury that was seen as effeminate (Berry, 2013; Neocleous, 2013). There is a link here to the growth of organised sports, especially in the United States. Allison (2001) notes the connection between organised sports and the English 'public' school system. The efforts put in to codify existing games was part of the project of 'muscular Christianity', the use of sporting activity to mould character. Such training was to equip boys with the character necessary to run a growing empire, for which reason and commerce were insufficient: 'required also [were] the ideas of prowess, loyalty and chivalry, reborn as modern sport and sportsmanship'. Thus, he argues, modern sport 'comes with the idea of masculinity built into it' (Allison, 2001: 5). Translated into an American context, where a ruling elite espoused similar ideals, the particular trajectory of American society produced a sports culture that valued violence and a militaristic sprit, most notably in the game that became known as 'American football'. 'The militarism of American society is openly reflected in its violent sports culture,' writes McLeod (2016: 137), arguing further that sports 'are more often aligned with the military, as both are stereotypically associated with masculine dominance and often patriarchal beliefs and institutional structures' (McLeod, 2016: 32).

As we have noted, the growth of popular music offered alternative models for male activity, involving practices such as the wearing of long hair that were traditionally associated with effeminacy. At the same time, Markovits and Hellerman (2001) note the eroding of the masculine nature of sports in the USA with the dramatic growth of football/soccer played by women. A dramatic growth in participation saw the USA become the most successful national team in the world on a stage in which the male equivalent was conspicuously absent (or notable for lack of competitive success). However, they also point to a crucial distinction between participation and followership. The latter, the propensity to attend and talk about sports, bolstered by media coverage, remains a masculine preserve. As they argue, a

> culture of sports following and affect—an overwhelmingly male preserve—has so far not been adopted by women for women's sport. For the most part, women do not immerse themselves in the culture of being fans and followers of a team and its sport as do many men.
>
> (Markovits and Hellerman, 2001: 180)

By contrast, popular music allows much more space for women to act as fans and, increasingly, as leading and central participants. Seeing play as a key part of social ontology thus offers opportunities for challenging the gendered nature of the other institutional orders, by providing role models and examples of successful practices.

Class

In his classic study of *The Making of the English Working Class*, E.P. Thompson (1968) examines the role of nonconformist religion, especially variants of Methodism, in shaping the working-class experience. Forced by economic, legal and social change to arduous work in dangerous conditions and to live in squalid housing, working people, from the tin miners of Cornwall to the coal miners of Durham, turned in their thousands to the consolations of religion. Emphasising the nature of Methodism in its popular forms as an emotional response, Thompson characterised it as the 'chiliasm of despair'. This was to emphasise the nature of belief and some characteristic religious practices, notably the great revivalist gatherings. However, as we have seen, religious activity also needs to be organised. While variants of English Methodism never fully implemented the complex organisational structure that we have met in Scottish Presbyterianism, it had of necessity, once the initial burst of enthusiasm was spent, to establish organisational routines. These, especially in the Primitive Methodist tradition, involved lay people in running the affairs of their chapels, and this exposure to organisational techniques became a training school for secular activities. Thus, it is a truism of English labour history that the ranks of early trade union organisers were dominated by those schooled in chapel organisation (Moore, 1974). This was as true for agricultural labourers as for Durham miners. Indeed, the former group often lived in villages dominated by conservative landowners whose world view was powerfully supported by Church of England vicars. In such a context, the chapel provided the only available venue for popular organising activities (Scotland, 1981). In a different context, Sewell (2005: 315) notes of Marseilles dockworkers' involvement in the political sphere that '[o]ne suspects that they were able to transpose the many of the skills, schemas, and routines developed in the daily life of the dockworkers' society onto the rather different organisational terrain of the political underground.'

As we have seen, the wider literacy associated with particular social groups can be seen as an unplanned consequence. For the 'middling sort' in seventeenth- and eighteenth-century Scotland, access to basic education in reading, writing and arithmetic arose from the concern of the church that believers should have direct access to sacred texts for themselves. In order to achieve this, basic schools were established, as far as material circumstances allowed, in a wide range of localities. As a consequence, capacities that could be turned to secular purposes, notably in the techniques of administration – the writing of letters and the keeping of accounts – were developed in a wide range of the population. These capacities were further developed by the possibility of practical engagement in the governance of the church, opportunities not available in other religious polities. In its turn, the country could not provide opportunities for the exercise of these capacities within its own boundaries, so producing a cadre of mobile experts available, in particular, for imperial service overseas. Of course, it is important to recognise that the widespread availability of such opportunities was not open to all. Many localities, either in remote rural areas or expanding urban slums, lacked the availability of basic education. And the need for basic material survival might curtail participation amongst the poorer sections of society. So class is an important determinant of how logics played out in practice.

For Bourdieu and Passeron, the relative autonomy of the education system had to be seen in the context of not only its relationship with other institutional orders, but also with the reigning structuring of class relations. As they argued,

> It is therefore necessary to construct the system of relations between the educational system and the other sub-systems, specifying those relations by reference to the structure of class relations, in order to perceive that the relative autonomy of the educational system is always the counterpart of a dependence hidden to a greater or lesser extent by the practices and ideology authorized by that autonomy. To put it another way, to a given degree and type of autonomy, i.e. to a determinate form of correspondence between the essential function and the external functions, there always correspond a determinate type and degree of dependence on the other systems, i.e. in the last analysis, on the structure of class relations.
>
> (Bourdieu and Passeron, 1977: 197)

The mechanism for ensuring that the education system played its (disguised) part in reproducing class relations was not the direct imposition of power so that educational relations in some way were a direct mirror of class relations, but through the more indirect route of the habitus. That is, a disposition to think and act formed by initial class positioning and fostered by the pedagogy of family and school could be transposed between institutional orders (their 'sub-systems'). However, we have already noted the problems with the concept of habitus. It follows from the argument presented in this book that we need to trace instead practices. It is practices that carry logics, and the crucial questions are to do with the power to select and define practices. While practices, such as routines, are performed differently in each unique encounter, this does not necessarily alter their overall specification. Increasingly important is the way that practices are solidified in technical form, with software having the capacity to inscribe rules in enduring fashion. Of particular importance is the way that assumptions are built into technical artefacts in the form of algorithms (Scott and Orlikowski, 2012). This gives power to those organisations and the individuals within them that set the parameters for such algorithms.

Ethnicity and Nation

In his exploration of the historical development of non-profit and voluntary organisations in the United States, Peter Dobkin Hall points out,

> Although I run the hazard of stereotyping ethnic groups, it does appear that "national" traditions (in the sense of familiarity with particular technologies of collective action) have a good deal to do with where particular groups locate themselves in the polity and, of course, with their propensity to occupy formal trusteeship roles. To say this is not to suggest that the political, church, and union activities evidently favored by Catholic immigrants are any less voluntaristic than the associational forms favored by the Germans and the WASPs. However, activities favored by Catholic immigrants were less likely to give rise to a recognizable trusteeship traditions, in part because the issue of moral oversight, so central to the stewardship dimension of traditional trusteeship, tended to be left to ecclesiastical authorities in Catholic communities. (However, it is interesting to contrast Jewish and Irish associational patterns: though the Jews were notably active in politics and trade-union activity, they also created a wide range of other kinds of voluntary bodies, whereas the Irish seldom did.)
>
> (Hall, 1992: 143)

Hall places this assertion in the context of the significant contribution of Presbyterian and Congregational churches in supplying a training ground in the skills needed to run other forms of organisation. It is not thus some form of 'essential' ethnic or national characteristic that produces these organisational capacities, but rather the distinctive practices that emanate from one or more institutional orders, in this case the particular flavours of religion that reflected the beliefs of migrants. It is important to note, once again, that while these organisational capacities were engendered by engagement with a particular religious tradition and were ultimately founded in the theological commitments of that branch of religion, they were not the purpose of those organisational arrangements. Rather, organisational arrangements became to-hand, the taken-for-granted and so 'obvious' ways of organising in different contexts.

Studies of conceptions of management in more recent times also point to persistent and patterned differences across nations. In a comparison of managers in Germany and the UK, for example, Ganter and Walgenbach (2002) note that in Germany managers are technical specialists whose authority is based on their knowledge, related in turn to an institutional context that places heavy stress on technical education. By contrast, management in the UK is seen as being about the leadership of people. In such a setting, managers are recruited on the basis of character traits rather than knowledge. As we have seen at a number of points, the British preference for character has deep-rooted origins in a number of institutional orders. Arising from religion were practices of governance that were founded on trust in the character of office holders, something generalised in the notion of the 'gentleman'. Fostered by the 'muscular Christianity' that we have observed in development of organised sports in the education system, this characterised a political logic based on the virtues of amateur leadership by an elite. The focus on a generalist approach to management meant, argued Lehrer, that British Airways was more able to adapt to radical innovation than its French and German comparators. Managerial background, argues Lehrer (2001: 373),

> explains why top managers in the three studied flag carriers coped with industry changes in the 1980s not by adopting convergent practices, but instead by following divergent paths of adaptation reflecting an almost instinctive reliance on the different endowments of institutional resources to be found in their macro environments.

In a similar fashion, we have also noted the work by Whittington and Mayer (2000) that suggests that models of organisation are conditioned by national institutional systems. In another example, it has been demonstrated that 'lean manufacturing systems' (that is, systems that devolve considerable autonomy to shop floor workers) that are successful in Germany do not work in the equivalent American manufacturing plants, even those where the technological base and the nature of the processes are similar. Freil (2005) argues that the differences are attributable to institutional factors, specifically the nature of labour laws and training systems. US labour laws encourage the use of temporary workers, whereas this is much more difficult in Germany. The consequence is that many temporary workers in the US plants are functionally illiterate, that is, unable to interpret the technical instructions on which lean processes depend. However, Freil argues that the problems are not only attributable to the nature of the workforce, but that workforce skills can be linked to broader training systems. The German focus on apprenticeships means that it was feasible to change training to emphasise problem-solving and team working. Freil concludes that,

> The nature of the countries' training systems seems to be the critical factor. If companies find it difficult to hire and retain workers with broad-based and analytical skills, lean production would prove difficult even if all other institutions were favorable.
>
> (Freil, 2005: 57)

History is invaluable in placing such differences in a deeper context. In thirteenth century France, argued Edwin Panofsky (1957), the builders of the great Gothic churches were following the logic that was embedded in the Scholasticism of theological writing and education. The focus in such writings on the clear exposition of terms and their logical connections, which, taken to extremes, became what Panofsky calls 'clarification for clarification's sake' was mirrored in the form and planning of architecture. 'It is not very probable,' thought Panofsky (1957: 23), 'that the builders of Gothic structures read Gilbert de la Porree or Thomas Aquinas in the original. But they were exposed to the Scholastic point of view in innumerable other ways'. The consequence was that architects and builders imbibed a way of proceeding that was to establish a clear and uniform set of relations between the different parts of a composition. So,

> [a]ccording to classic High Gothic standards the individual elements, while forming an indiscerptible whole, yet must proclaim their identity by remaining clearly separated from each other—the shafts from the wall or the core of the pier, the ribs from their neighbours, all vertical members from their arches; and there must be an unequivocal correlation between them.
>
> (Panofsky, 1957: 51)

The tendency towards systematisation and codification was, of course, already present in the civil law derived from Roman law precedents, and we have met the same tendency already in Johnson's account of the founding of the Paris Opera in the seventeenth century. As she notes, the proposers drew on existing models of organising, which in France were the royal academies connected to a strongly centralised state apparatus. The purpose of such academies was 'codification of guidelines for production in an academy's given area of cultural or scientific specialization' (Johnson, 2007: 108). A focus on codification and systematisation, what Bourdieu and Passeron (1977: 148) describe as 'the typically French religion of classification', thus seems to be an enduring organising principle that bound together the institutional orders that characterised French society.

In her discussion of the different fate of claims for compensation for the damage to the natural environment cased by oil spells in French civil law courts and American common law equivalents, Fourcade (2011) notes a key distinction being competing conceptions of wilderness. Alien to a French legal tradition that had emerged from a densely settled and intensively cultivated landscape over centuries, wilderness was a central concept to American considerations. In that historical evolution the market formed a central unifying force. As Markovits and Hellerman (2001: 46) observe, 'in their institutional presence and their culture, American sports are like American education and American religion: independent of the state, market driven, and ultimately subject to few, if any, regulating bodies outside those of their own creation.'

The impact on sports was to foster an emphasis on numbers and rules. Sports became subject to the detailed collection and analysis of statistics. In a society that anchors much of its legitimacy in meritocracy and achievement rather than in entitlement and ascription,' argue the authors (Markovits and Hellerman, 2001: 56), '"value free" numbers denote not only a sense of impersonal fairness but also a clarity of rank understood by everybody, regardless of cultural background and linguistic origins.' The focus on numbers is facilitated by an emphasis on detailed rules, with those rules being manipulated to alter the nature of play in a context where the existence of 'franchises' is guaranteed as money-making operations in closed leagues, as opposed to the potential for relegation facing clubs in football leagues elsewhere. The existence of such rules, as opposed to the taken-for-granted tacit rules of more flowing sports, engendered a distinctive focus on 'trick plays', ways of getting round rules without actually breaking them. 'Lastly,' suggest Markovits and Hellerman (2001: 79) '—as in politics—clearly stated, written, and universalistic rules had an equalizing effect on football by enhancing its attraction to otherwise disparate social groups. Rules thereby enhanced participation and contributed to the popularization—if, perhaps, less to the democratization—of this sport.' The application of these characteristics to other institutional orders lies behind a distinctive American exceptionalism, one that challenges the universal status of practices derived from that specific context (Billig, 1995: 54).

These considerations suggest some of the limits of institutional logics. That is, we cannot make an appeal to an abstract, timeless and universal logic of any of the institutional orders we have suggested as constitutive of society. Rather the impulse lying behind each logic, motivated by substance immanent in practices, has to be carefully contextualised to particular conjunctures of time and place. Place is important here in that it provides a boundary within which particular constellations of practices emerge over time, embodying taken-for-granted meanings that are rooted in enduring institutional orders.

Summary

This book, and the arguments in it, has been set in the context of debates within organisational institutionalism. So let us return to some of the key gains from the broad tradition of the so-called new institutionalism. One is to counter the claims of those who see social and organisational life as a matter of rational choice. In resisting the imperialistic claims of economics, both as a discipline and as a practical aspect of social life, institutionalism draws our attention to the central place of ideas and meanings. Not only do the claims of economics run up against the obdurate adherence of human beings to 'out-moded' and 'irrational' forms of being, be that religious or embodied in forms of play, but the very terms of economic activity are themselves shaped by ideas about what is legitimate and appropriate. A second important contribution of institutionalism is to draw our attention to the importance of taken-for-granted practices, practices that appear to be natural but have in fact been shaped by their conditions of production. In turn, such practices form a key part of the settings in which actors engage in social and or-ganisational activity. They become more powerful often to the degree in which they fade into the background, forming the common-sense con-ditions for action but subtly constraining the direction of that activity.

Given these advances, however, there remain problems within main-stream institutionalist approaches. The emphasis on practices often means that the broader context, both immediate and historical, fades from view. The focus is then on agential choice of practices, a focus that runs the risk of losing the initial insights into the shaping of practices and action. As one response to such concerns, the institutional logics approach has a number of values. One is that it reminds us forcibly that practices and organisations exist in societal contexts. A second is the attention to a multi-level operation of logics, in which societal logics are encountered in and mediated by field- and organisational-level contexts. Such distinc-tions, however, are routinely ignored in concrete analytical practice, with field-level logics being referred to as institutional logics. However, a more serious concern is with the method by which societal logics are derived. In the widely influential formulation of Thornton, Occasio and Lounsbury (2012), institutional logics are derived from the published reports of or-ganisational scholars. This restricts their scope and, importantly, tends to defeat the original ambition of Friedland and Alford (1991) to 'bring society back in'. The aim of this book has been to build on the Friedland and Alford tradition, especially as developed by Friedland, and, by using the resources of history, to suggest a social ontology.

That social ontology sees society as comprising a set of institutional orders, each composed of material practices and symbolic constructions and with a logic of their own. These orders arise from the embodied relationships of people with each other and with the natural world. Such a formulation rests in turn, as all social theories must do, on a set of anthropological assumptions about the capacities and limitations of human existence. In this book, such assumptions are derived from the work of those working in the critical realist tradition. Building on the central ideas of stratification and emergence, thinkers such as Archer (1995) and Smith (2010) have argued for the existence of embodied ca-pacities that distinguish the human condition. Although these capaci-ties emerge from biological attributes, they cannot, once emergent, be reduced to biological properties but rather form *sui generis* properties. Human beings are faced not just by the potential present in the capaci-ties for thought and reflexivity so generated but by the limitations that their needs for material survival pose. Such material needs, generated by and fulfilled by their engagement with the natural world, require the collective building of forms of existence. Once emergent, such forms of existence become institutionalised. Such institutions can take a range of forms depending on the contingencies of history. There is, that is, no 'natural' and one-to-one relationship between biological and psychological properties and the social world that human beings construct. Once emergent from human activity, this social world generates properties of its own that endure and form the conditions for future rounds of activity.

History provides a critical means of identifying the 'perennial problems' of human existence, to use Friedson's (2001) phrase, and how they have been addressed. Building on the contention by Friedland (2009) that institutional logics comprise a substance, something that through belief and commitment inspires actions, and practices that are animated by the substance and in which the substance is immanent, I have suggested a number of institutional orders that comprise a social ontology. Arising from the embodied interactions between people and their natural world, I have suggested three broad clusters. There are those social arrangements that tackle the meaning-making capacity of human beings: religion, play and knowledge. In order to build and maintain social life, human beings are by virtue of the human condition relational beings who need to find ways to tackle the strains of such relationships: through violence (the military), through formal agreements (the law) or through structured debate (politics). Human beings also have needs for material survival in their engagement with their bodily constitution and the world that they depend on: the family, the economy and medicine. I have suggested ways in which these logics play out in concrete historical contexts. While I have sought to abstract from such contexts in order to supply analytical concepts, it is important to recognise that logics play out in specific constellations of time and place. Historical forms of investigation provide a means of situating abstract contexts, of providing, in Archer's (1995) terms, analytical narratives of emergence.

I am going to recognise here that the treatment of these logics and their historical appearance has not been symmetrical. I have leaned, maybe too much, on examples from religion and from Scotland. This reflects the state of my own knowledge and the historical work I have undertaken. I am only too aware that I have drawn out only some key elements from orders of human activity that have a rich and complex apparatus of inquiry standing behind them. No doubt specialists in each of the areas will find much to object to in the ways in which I have characterised each order. However, I think it is important to focus on some of the key elements that seem to characterise each order and to draw out some commonalities. What a focus on practices often reveals is the extent to which taken-for-granted practices, such as rituals and routines, together with their associated material objects, have often been overlooked in much of the work on the individual orders. This is not true of all the work, as I have been able to draw on work that has brought to the surface taken-for-granted material arrangements of objects and spaces, but it remains the case that much historical work draws on either formal bodies of ideas or the development of formal organisations. There is, that is, an important research agenda, one that is facilitated by electronic access to archival material, to uncover the routine practices that shape social and organisational life.

Organisation theory has an important contribution to make to historical work here, in pointing to the importance of routines. In examining the place of practices in sustaining institutional logics, one important category is that of the ritual. The embodied performance of rituals can contribute to the felt 'rightness' of logics, creating a shared performance amongst adherents that can overcome different cognitive understandings. However, rituals entail routines, routines that are often concealed, as it were, back stage. At a very basic level, somebody has to prepare the stage for the performance of the ritual. But such preparations often involve questions of who is to participate in the ritual and how such participation is to be controlled. This leads to routines of governance, recording and accountability that are often vital parts of the maintenance and influence of logics. The literature on organisational routines, with its focus on the generative potential of routines, is significant here in pointing to items to be opened up and examined. However, in turn, the literature on routines often divorces them from their wider historical context. This is important in two regards. One is that, as I have sought to show, routines too have a history. They do not spring from performance unconditioned but are related to past performances that form to-hand templates. The second is that practices, such as routines, may only function successfully when the pre-conditions are right. Both these conditions suggest that it is not at all easy to take practices from one setting and transpose them into another. At the very least, models of self-sufficient dissemination or transmission are flawed, failing to recognise the substantial translation work that is required. But even a focus on translation can fail to register the degree to which elements of the logic within which practices have been created tend to adhere to the practice as it moves.

All these considerations suggest a degree of caution is needed when speaking of change. Here, a multi-level model that distinguishes between change at the level of practice, field logic and institutional logic is of considerable value. Actors, it has been argued, select practices rather than logics, being unaware of the wider ramifications as they seek answers to pressing problems. Operating as they do across institutional orders, they may select practices from one for implementation in another without realising the logical entailments that follow in the wake of such transfer. However, change at this level, constrained as it is, may still be much easier than change at the level of the field or, especially, the institution.

At these levels it makes more sense to join with Pierson (2004) in talking of 'development' rather than 'change'. Development emphasises not only the slower pace of change but also the involvement of multiple actors.

Practices have been rather neglected in the critical realist tradition of social theory that underlies much of the argument that informs this book, but there is no reason why they cannot be accorded their due importance. It is practices that actors encounter, but those practices have to be set in the context of the institutional logics that they make manifest. The concept of any particular society as comprising a bundle of institutional orders is compatible with the morphogenetic framework that Archer (1995) outlines. There may be relations of either complementarity or contradiction between these orders. It is open to social actors to seize hold of such relationships either to bolster their social position or to seek to change it. What the account provided here has pointed to is that, as well as inter-institutional relationships, we need to be attuned to the existence of intra-institutional difference. That is, any concrete instantiation of an institution like religion or the law, with its concomitant primary substance of faith or justice, is interpreted in different ways by adherents. Concrete social analysis thus has to translate an abstract institutional logic into the specific and contending forms of, say Christianity, Judaism or Islam in religion, or common or civil law systems. Each instantiation has distinctive organisational forms and associated practices, forms that can for long periods be self-contained. However, changes in the broader social context may cause them to collide and offer possibilities for change. In particular, the forms of involvement in practices that these specific forms allow may generate implications for shifts in the accompanying logics.

A further consideration is how actors experience logics, raising the question of reflexivity. As we have seen, reflexivity is a prime concern of Archer's work. Logics may condition such reflexivity, by providing the conditions under which it is exercised and the categories that shape it. As we have seen, Archer's account of reflexivity tends to downplay the conditions that shape reflexivity, choosing instead to focus on the situational logics that offer opportunities for its exercise. The study of institutional logics in historical context can suggest how such logics provide the categories with which to think. In addition, the account presented here has suggested that adherence to logics is as much a matter of feelings and emotions as of cognition. This remains an area for further investigation.

How are logics to be investigated? As we have noted, there are challenges posed to the investigation of practices historically. These, however, are problems for historians to tackle. The implications to be discussed here are those for organisational scholars. One implication is to challenge the status of existing categorisations of institutional logics. In particular, we need to consider the basis on which candidates for the status of societal logics are proposed. Rather than working inductively from the published organisational literature, I have suggested a deductive approach based on the properties of embodied human beings and their engagement with each other and the natural world. The candidate institutional logics that I have suggested are open to contest; like all concepts of social theory, they are provisional and corrigible, subject to revision through empirical application or conceptual debate. However, I would suggest that they provide the opportunity for a turning out of organisational institutionalism, where our starting point is the social ontology of the particular slice of social life that we are examining. In this endeavour, I suggest that we need both abstraction and concrete application. That is, while concrete social and organisational analysis needs to place logics in specific conjunctures of time and place, it also needs the abstract categories as a starting point for concrete analysis. One argument is that, if pitched at an appropriate level of analysis, the logics proposed here are capable of application across time and place. That is, what the precise composition of institutional orders is at any specific time and which have explanatory priority in conditioning social action is a matter of empirical investigation. What is being resisted here, however, is the generalising as if they are of universal and timeless application of ideas drawn from a particular time and place. I have argued, and this is mirrored in many of the sources that I have used, that attempts to treat phenomena to be found in the United States of America in the early twenty-first century as of universal applicability is a mistake. Of course, the sheer weight of any particular country both economically and culturally in an integrated world system is bound to have considerable impact, but that impact needs to be empirically investigated, not imposed as a matter of theoretical fiat.

Calls for a 'historic turn' in organisation studies have often rested at the level of conceptual discussion. I hope that the material presented in this book shows the value of history in particular and the humanities in general in opening up new lines of inquiry and challenging existing perspectives. Historical work offers more than just a quarry of interesting examples. It provides the opportunity to contextualise studies in the conditions developed over time and provides the conditions of possibility for change.

References

Allison, L. (2001) *Amateurism in Sport: An Analysis and a Defence*, Abingdon: Routledge.

Archer, M. (1995) *Realist Social Theory: The Morphogenetic Approach*, Cambridge: Cambridge University Press.

Archer, M. (1996) *Culture and Agency: The Place of Culture in Social Theory*,- Cambridge: Cambridge University Press.

Archer, M. (2007) *Making Our Way Through the World: Human Reflexivity and Social Mobility,* Cambridge: Cambridge University Press.

Berry, C. (2013) *The Idea of Commercial Society in the Scottish Enlightenment,* Edinburgh: Edinburgh University Press.

Billig, M. (1995) *Banal Nationalism,* London: Sage.

Bourdieu, P. and Passeron, J-C. (1977) *Reproduction in Education, Society and Culture,* London: Sage.

Ferguson, A. (1767) *An Essay on the History of Civil Society,*Cambridge: Cambridge University Press.

Fine, C. (2017) *Testosterone Rex: Unmaking the Myths of Our Gendered Minds,* London: Icon.

Fourcade, M. (2011) 'Cents and sensibility: economic valuation and the nature of "nature"', *American Journal of Sociology,* 116(6), 1721–1777.

Freil, D. (2005) 'Transferring a lean production concept from Germany to the United States: the impact of labor laws and training systems', *Academy of Management Executive,* 19(2), 50–58.

Friedland, R. andAlford, R. (1991) 'Bringing society back in: symbols, practices, and institutional contradictions',in Powell W. and DiMaggio P. (eds.),*The New Institutionalism in Organizational Analysis,* Chicago: University of Chicago Press, 1991, 232–266.

Friedland, R. (2009) 'Institution, practice and ontology: towards a religious sociology', *Research in the Sociology of Organizations,* 27, 45–83.

Friedson, E. (2001) *Professionalism: The Third Logic,*Cambridge:Polity.

Ganter, H. and Walgenbach, P. (2002) 'Middle managers: differences between Britain and Germany', in Geppert, M., Matten D. and Williams K. (eds.), *Challenges for European management in a Global Context,* Basingstoke: Palgrave Macmillan 165–188.

Hall, P. (1992) *Inventing the Nonprofit Sector and Other Essays on Philanthropy, Voluntarism and Nonprofit Organizations,* Baltimore, MD: Johns Hopkins University Press.

Johnson, V. (2007) 'What is organizational imprinting? Cultural entrepreneurship in the founding of the Paris opera',*American Journal of Sociology,* 113, 97–127.

Lehrer, M. (2001) 'Macro-varieties of capitalism and micro-varieties of strategic management in European Airlines',in Hall P. and Soskice D. (eds.), *Varieties of Capitalism,* Oxford:Oxford University Press, 2001, 361–386.

Markovits, A. and Hellerman, S. (2001) *Offside: Soccer and American Exceptionalism,* Princeton, NJ:Princeton University Press.

McLeod, K. (2016) *We Are the Champions: The Politics of Sports and Popular Music,* London: Routledge.

Moore, R. (1974) *Effects of Methodism in a Durham Mining Community : Pitmen, Preachers and Politics,* Cambridge: Cambridge University Press.

Neocleous, M. (2013) "O Effeminacy! Effeminacy!' War, masculinity and the myth of liberal peace', *European Journal of International Relations,* 19(1), 93–113.

New, C. (2005) 'Sex and gender: a critical realist approach', *New Formations,* 56, 54–70.

Panofsky, E. (1957) *Gothic Architecture and Scholasticism,* Cleveland: Meridian.

Pierson, P. (2004) *Politics in Time: History, Institutions, and Social Analysis*, Princeton: Princeton University Press.

Scotland, N. (1981) *Methodism and the Revolt of the Field: A Study of the Methodist Contribution to Agricultural Trade Unionism in East Anglia, 1872–1896*, Gloucester: Alan Sutton.

Scott, S. and Orlikowski, W. (2012) 'Great expectations: the materiality of commensurability in social media', in Leonardi, P., Nardi, B. and Kallinikos, J. (eds.), *Materiality and Organizing: Social Interaction in a Technological World*, Oxford: Oxford University Press, 2012, 113–133.

Sewell, W. (2005) *Logics of History: Social Theory and Social Transformation*, Chicago: University of Chicago Press.

Smith, C. (2010) *What Is a Person? : Rethinking Humanity, Social Life, and the Moral Good from the Person Up*, Chicago, IL:University of Chicago Press.

Thompson, E. (1968) *The Making of the English Working Class*, Harmondsworth: Penguin.

Thornton, P., Occasio, W. and Lounsbury, M. (2012) *The Institutional Logics Perspective: A New Approach to Culture, Structure, and Process*, Oxford: Oxford University Press.

Whittington, R. and Mayer, M. (2000) *The European Corporation: Strategy, Structure and Social Science*,Oxford: Oxford University Press.

Index